English-Farsi-English

Word to Word® Bilingual Dictionary

Compiled by:
C. Sesma, M.A.

Translated by:
Farsi Translation Services, Inc.

Bilingual Dictionaries, Inc.

Farsi Word to Word® Bilingual Dictionary
1st Edition © Copyright 2011

Published in the United States by:

Bilingual Dictionaries, Inc.
PO Box 1154
Murrieta, CA 92562
T: (951) 461-6893 • F: (951) 461-3092
www.BilingualDictionaries.com

ISBN13: 978-0-933146-33-4
ISBN: 0-933146-33-7
Printed in India

Preface

Bilingual Dictionaries, Inc. is committed to providing schools, libraries and educators with a great selection of bilingual materials for students. Along with bilingual dictionaries we also provide ESL materials, children's bilingual stories and children's bilingual picture dictionaries.

Sesma's Farsi Word to Word® Bilingual Dictionary was created specifically with students in mind to be used for reference and testing. This dictionary contains approximately 18,500 entries targeting common words used in the English language.

List of Irregular Verbs

present - past - past participle

arise - arose - arisen
awake - awoke - awoken, awaked
be - was - been
bear - bore - borne
beat - beat - beaten
become - became - become
begin - began - begun
behold - beheld - beheld
bend - bent - bent
beseech - besought - besought
bet - bet - betted
bid - bade (bid) - bidden (bid)
bind - bound - bound
bite - bit - bitten
bleed - bled - bled
blow - blew - blown
break - broke - broken
breed - bred - bred
bring - brought - brought
build - built - built
burn - burnt - burnt *
burst - burst - burst
buy - bought - bought
cast - cast - cast
catch - caught - caught
choose - chose - chosen
cling - clung - clung
come - came - come
cost - cost - cost
creep - crept - crept
cut - cut - cut
deal - dealt - dealt

dig - dug - dug
do - did - done
draw - drew - drawn
dream - dreamt - dreamed
drink - drank - drunk
drive - drove - driven
dwell - dwelt - dwelt
eat - ate - eaten
fall - fell - fallen
feed - fed - fed
feel - felt - felt
fight - fought - fought
find - found - found
flee - fled - fled
fling - flung - flung
fly - flew - flown
forebear - forbore - forborne
forbid - forbade - forbidden
forecast - forecast - forecast
forget - forgot - forgotten
forgive - forgave - forgiven
forego - forewent - foregone
foresee - foresaw - foreseen
foretell - foretold - foretold
forget - forgot - forgotten
forsake - forsook - forsaken
freeze - froze - frozen
get - got - gotten
give - gave - given
go - went - gone
grind - ground - ground
grow - grew - grown
hang - hung * - hung *
have - had - had

hear - heard - heard
hide - hid - hidden
hit - hit - hit
hold - held - held
hurt - hurt - hurt
hit - hit - hit
hold - held - held
keep - kept - kept
kneel - knelt * - knelt *
know - knew - known
lay - laid - laid
lead - led - led
lean - leant * - leant *
leap - lept * - lept *
learn - learnt * - learnt *
leave - left - left
lend - lent - lent
let - let - let
lie - lay - lain
light - lit * - lit *
lose - lost - lost
make - made - made
mean - meant - meant
meet - met - met
mistake - mistook - mistaken
must - had to - had to
pay - paid - paid
plead - pleaded - pled
prove - proved - proven
put - put - put
quit - quit * - quit *
read - read - read
rid - rid - rid
ride - rode - ridden

ring - rang - rung
rise - rose - risen
run - ran - run
saw - sawed - sawn
say - said - said
see - saw - seen
seek - sought - sought
sell - sold - sold
send - sent - sent
set - set - set
sew - sewed - sewn
shake - shook - shaken
shear - sheared - shorn
shed - shed - shed
shine - shone - shone
shoot - shot - shot
show - showed - shown
shrink - shrank - shrunk
shut - shut - shut
sing - sang - sung
sink - sank - sunk
sit - sat - sat
slay - slew - slain
sleep - sleep - slept
slide - slid - slid
sling - slung - slung
smell - smelt * - smelt *
sow - sowed - sown *
speak - spoke - spoken
speed - sped * - sped *
spell - spelt * - spelt *
spend - spent - spent
spill - spilt * - spilt *
spin - spun - spun

spit - spat - spat
split - split - split
spread - spread - spread
spring - sprang - sprung
stand - stood - stood
steal - stole - stolen
stick - stuck - stuck
sting - stung - stung
stink - stank - stunk
stride - strode - stridden
strike - struck - struck (stricken)
strive - strove - striven
swear - swore - sworn
sweep - swept - swept
swell - swelled - swollen *
swim - swam - swum
take - took - taken
teach - taught - taught
tear - tore - torn

tell - told - told
think - thought - thought
throw - threw - thrown
thrust - thrust - thrust
tread - trod - trodden
wake - woke - woken
wear - wore - worn
weave - wove * - woven *
wed - wed * - wed *
weep - wept - wept
win - won - won
wind - wound - wound
wring - wrung - wrung
write - wrote - written

Those tenses with an * also have regular forms.

English-Farsi

Bilingual Dictionaries, Inc.

Abbreviations

a - article
n - noun
e - exclamation
pro - pronoun
adj - adjective
adv - adverb
v - verb
iv - irregular verb
pre - preposition
c - conjunction

a _a_ یک

abandon _v_ ترک کردن

abandonment _n_ ترك

abbey _n_ صومعه

abbot _n_ راهب بزرگ

abbreviate _v_ مختصر کردن

abbreviation _n_ اختصار

abdicate _v_ واگذار کردن

abdication _n_ کناره گیری

abdomen _n_ شکم

abduct _v_ ربودن

abduction _n_ آدم ربایی

aberration _n_ انحراف

abhor _v_ تنفر داشتن

abide by _v_ پیروی کردن از

ability _n_ توانایی

ablaze _adj_ سوزان

able _adj_ توانا

abnormal _adj_ غیرعادی

abnormality _n_ ناهنجاری

aboard _adv_ داخل

abolish _v_ از میان بردن

abort _v_ سقط کردن

abortion _n_ سقطجنین

abound _v_ فراوان بودن

about _pre_ درباره

about _adv_ درباره

above _pre_ بالا

abreast _adv_ آگاه

abridge _v_ کوتاه کردن

abroad _adv_ خارج ازکشور

abrogate _v_ از میان بردن

abruptly _adv_ ناگهانی

absence _n_ غیبت

absent _adj_ غایب

absolute _adj_ مطلق

absolution _n_ عفو

absolve _v_ بخشیدن

absorb _v_ جذب کردن

absorbent _adj_ جاذب

abstain _v_ پرهیز کردن

abstinence _n_ کف نفس

abstract _adj_ خلاصه

absurd _adj_ پوچ

abundance _n_ فراوانی

abundant _adj_ فراوان

abuse _n_ سوء استفاده

abusive _adj_ ناسزاوار

abysmal _adj_ ژرف

abyss _n_ ورطه

academic _adj_ آکادمیک

academy _n_ دانشگاه

accelerate _v_ تند کردن

accelerator _n_ شتاب دهنده

accent _n_ لهجه

accept _v_ پذیرفتن

acceptable _adj_ قابل پذیرش

acceptance _n_ پذیرش

access _n_ دستیابی

accessible _adj_ در دسترس

accident _n_ حادثه

accidental *adj* تصادفی	acquire *v* به دست آوردن
acclaim *v* تحسین	acquisition *n* اکتساب
acclimatize *v* خو دادن	acquit *v* تبرئه کردن
accommodate *v* همساز کردن	acquittal *n* تبرئه
accompany *v* همراهی کردن	acre *n* جریب
accomplice *n* شریک جرم	acrobat *n* بندباز
accomplish *v* انجام دادن	across *pre* در عرض
accomplishment *n* پیشرفت	act *v* عمل
accord *n* تطبیق	action *n* عمل
according to *pre* طبق	activate *v* عمل کردن
accordion *n* آکاردئون	activation *n* فعال سازی
account *n* حساب؛ سبب	active *adj* فعال
account for *v* اقامه کردن دلیل	activity *n* فعالیت
accountable *adj* مسئول	actor *n* هنرپیشه
accountant *n* حسابدار	actress *n* هنرپیشه زن
accumulate *v* انباشتن	actual *adj* واقعی
accuracy *n* دقت	actually *adv* واقعاً
accurate *adj* درست	acute *adj* تیزرو؛ بحرانی
accusation *n* اتهام	adamant *adj* مقاوم
accuse *v* متهم کردن	adapt *v* وفق دادن
accustom *v* عادت دادن	adaptable *adj* سازگار
ace *n* تکخال	adaptation *n* انطباق
ache *n* درد	adapter *n* تنظیم کننده
achieve *v* دست یافتن	add *v* اضافه کردن
achievement *n* موفقیت	addicted *adj* خو گرفته
acid *n* اسید	addiction *n* اعتیاد
acidity *n* درجه ترشی	addictive *adj* معتاد کننده
acknowledge *v* قدردانی کردن	addition *n* جمع
acorn *n* بلوط	additional *adj* اضافی
acoustic *adj* صوتی	address *n* نشانی
acquaint *v* اشنا کردن	address *v* درست کردن
acquaintance *n* آشنایی	addressee *n* گیرنده

adequate *adj* کافی	adrift *adv* دستخوش حوادث
adhere *v* توافق داشتن	adulation *n* تملق
adhesive *adj* چسبنده	adult *n* بزرگسال
adjacent *adj* مجاور	adulterate *v* چیز تقلبی ساختن
adjective *n* صفت	adultery *n* زنا
adjoin *v* پیوستن	advance *v* پیشرفت کردن
adjoining *adj* مجاور	advance *n* پیشرفته
adjourn *v* به تعویق انداختن	advantage *n* مزیت
adjust *v* مطابق کردن	adventure *n* ماجرا
adjustable *adj* تعدیل پذیر	adverb *n* قید
adjustment *n* تنظیم	adversary *n* دشمن
administer *v* اداره کردن	adverse *adj* مخالف
admirable *adj* پسندیده	adversity *n* سختی
admiral *n* دریاسالار	advertise *v* آگهی دادن
admiration *n* تحسین	advertising *n* تبلیغ
admire *v* پسند کردن	advice *n* مشورت
admirer *n* دلباخته	advisable *adj* مقتضی
admissible *adj* پذیرفتنی	advise *v* نصیحت کردن
admission *n* پذیرش؛ مکش	adviser *n* مشاور
admit *v* پذیرفتن	advocate *v* دفاع کردن
admittance *n* اجازه ورود	aeroplane *n* هواپیما
admonish *v* نصیحت کردن	aesthetic *adj* ظریف طبع
admonition *n* تذکر	afar *adv* دور
adolescence *n* نوجوانی	affable *adj* مهربان
adolescent *n* نوجوان	affair *n* واقعه؛ کاروبار
adopt *v* قبول کردن	affect *v* اثر کردن
adoption *n* پذیرش	affection *n* محبت
adoptive *adj* انتخابی	affectionate *adj* بامحبت
adorable *adj* قابل ستایش	affiliate *v* مربوط ساختن
adoration *n* پرستش	affiliation *n* وابستگی
adore *v* پرستیدن	affinity *n* شباهت
adorn *v* زیبا کردن	affirm *v* اظهار کردن

affirmative adj مثبت	**agnostic** n لاادری
affix v پیوستن	**agonize** v عذاب دادن
afflict v آزردن	**agonizing** adj دردناك
affliction n مصیبت	**agony** n عذاب
affluence n ثروت	**agree** v خوشنود کردن
affluent adj ثروتمند	**agreeable** adj ملایم
afford v استطاعت داشتن	**agreement** n موافقتنامه
affordable adj قابل انجام	**agricultural** adj زراعتی
affront v توهین کردن	**agriculture** n کشاورزی
affront n توهین	**ahead** pre پیش
afloat adv شناور	**aid** n کمك
afraid adj ترسان	**aid** v کمک کردن
afresh adv دوباره	**aide** n دستیار
after pre بعداز	**ailing** adj بیمار
afternoon n بعدازظهر	**ailment** n بیماری
afterwards adv بعد از آن	**aim** v نشانه گرفتن
again adv دوباره	**aimless** adj بی هدف
against pre علیه	**air** n هوا
age n سن	**air** v بادخور کردن
agency n نمایندگی	**aircraft** n هواپیما
agenda n دستورکار	**airfield** n فرودگاه نظامی
agent n نماینده	**airline** n هواپیمایی
agglomerate v جمع کردن	**airmail** n پست هوایی
aggravate v خشمگین کردن	**airplane** n هواپیما
aggravation n تشدید	**airport** n فرودگاه
aggregate v متراکم کردن	**airspace** n فضای هوایی
aggression n پرخاشگری	**airstrip** n باند موقت
aggressive adj تهاجمی	**airtight** adj هوابندی شده
aggressor n متجاوز	**aisle** n راهرو
aghast adj بهت زده	**ajar** adj نیمه باز
agile adj سریع الانتقال	**akin** adj خویشاوند
agitator n محرك	**alarm** n هشدار

ساعت زنگ دار *n* **alarm clock**	وسوسه *n* **allure**
نگران کننده *adj* **alarming**	جذاب *adj* **alluring**
الكلى *adj* **alcoholic**	اشاره *n* **allusion**
الكليسم *n* **alcoholism**	متحد *n* **ally**
هشدار *n* **alert**	متحد کردن *v* **ally**
هشدار دادن *v* **alert**	تقویم نجومی *n* **almanac**
جبر *n* **algebra**	قدرتمند *adj* **almighty**
بیگانه *n* **alien**	بادام *n* **almond**
شعله ور *adv* **alight**	تقریباً *adv* **almost**
ردیف کردن *v* **align**	صدقه *n* **alms**
خط *n* **alignment**	تنها *adj* **alone**
شبیه *adj* **alike**	درطول *pre* **along**
زنده *adj* **alive**	درکنار *pre* **alongside**
تمام *adj* **all**	دور *adj* **aloof**
ادعا *n* **allegation**	بلند *adv* **aloud**
اقامه کردن *v* **allege**	الفبا *n* **alphabet**
ظاهراً *adv* **allegedly**	قبلاً *adv* **already**
وفاداری *n* **allegiance**	قابل قبول *adv* **alright**
تمثیل *n* **allegory**	هم *adv* **also**
آلرژی *adj* **allergic**	محراب *n* **altar**
آلرژی *n* **allergy**	تغییر دادن *v* **alter**
سبک کردن *v* **alleviate**	تغییر *n* **alteration**
کوچه *n* **alley**	ستیزه *n* **altercation**
اتحاد *n* **alliance**	متناوب کردن *v* **alternate**
متحد *adj* **allied**	جایگزین *adj* **alternate**
تمساح *n* **alligator**	جایگزین *n* **alternative**
اختصاص دادن *v* **allocate**	اگرچه *c* **although**
تخصیص دادن *v* **allot**	ارتفاع *n* **altitude**
تخصیص *n* **allotment**	رویهم رفته *adj* **altogether**
اجازه دادن *v* **allow**	آلومینیوم *n* **aluminum**
مقرری *n* **allowance**	همیشه *adv* **always**
آلیاژ *n* **alloy**	متراکم کردن *v* **amass**

amateur adj غیرحرفه ای	amplify v تقویت کردن
amaze v مبهوت کردن	amputate v جدا کردن
amazement n شگفتی	amputation n قطع
amazing adj حیرت انگیز	amuse v سرگرم کردن
ambassador n سفیر	amusement n سرگرمی
ambiguous adj مبهم	amusing adj خنده دار
ambition n جاه طلبی	an a یک
ambitious adj جاه طلب	analogy n شباهت
ambivalent adj مردد	analysis n تحلیل
ambulance n آمبولانس	analyze v تحلیل کردن
ambush v کمین کردن	anarchist n دولت ستیز
amenable adj حاضر	anarchy n بی دولتی
amend v اصلاح کردن	anatomy n کالبدشناسی
amendment n اصلاح	ancestor n جد
amenities n وسایل آسایش	ancestry n تبار
American adj آمریکایی	anchor n لنگر
amiable adj خوش خلق	anchovy n ماهی کولی
amicable adj دوستانه	ancient adj قدیمی
amid pre درمیان	and c و
ammonia n آمونیاك	anecdote n حکایت
ammunition n مهمات	anemia n کم خونی
amnesia n یادزدودگی	anemic adj کم خون
amnesty n عفو	anesthesia n بیهوشی
among pre بین	anew adv دوباره
amorphous adj بی شکل	angel n فرشته
amortize v بی حس کردن	angelic adj فرشته وار
amount n مقدار	anger v خشمگین کردن
amount to v بالغ شدن بر	anger n عصبانیت
amphibious adj دوزیست	angina n آنژین
amphitheater n آمفی تئاتر	angle n زاویه
ample adj فراوان	angry adj خشمگین
amplifier n تقویت کننده	anguish n اضطراب

animal *n* حیوان	antibiotic *n* پادزیست
animate *v* تحریک کردن	anticipate *v* پیش بینی کردن
animation *n* انیمیشن	anticipation *n* انتظار
animosity *n* دشمنی	antidote *n* پادزهر
ankle *n* قوزك	antipathy *n* تنفر
annex *n* ضمیمه	antiquated *adj* کهنه
annexation *n* انضمام	antiquity *n* قدمت
annihilate *v* نابود کردن	anvil *n* سندان
annihilation *n* انهدام	anxiety *n* اضطراب
anniversary *n* سالگرد	anxious *adj* نگران
annotate *v* یادداشت نوشتن	any *adj* چیزی
announce *v* اگهی دادن	anybody *pro* هر کسی
announcement *n* اعلان	anyhow *pro* به هرحال
announcer *n* گوینده	anyone *pro* هر کس
annoy *v* دلخورکردن	anything *pro* هر چیز
annoying *adj* ناراحت کننده	apart *adv* جدا از هم
annual *adj* سالانه	apartment *n* آپارتمان
annul *v* لغو کردن	apathy *n* بی تفاوتی
annulment *n* الغاء	ape *n* میمون
anoint *v* تدهین کردن	aperitif *n* اشتها آور
anonymity *n* گمنام ماندن	apex *n* راس
anonymous *adj* گمنام	apiece *adv* هریك
another *adj* دیگری	apocalypse *n* آخر زمان
answer *v* پاسخ دادن	apologize *v* عذر خواهی کردن
answer *n* جواب	apology *n* پوزش
ant *n* مورچه	apostle *n* حواری
antagonize *v* دشمن کردن	apostolic *adj* حواریون
antecedent *n* مرجع	apostrophe *n* آپوستروف
antecedents *n* پیشینیان	appall *v* ترساندن
antelope *n* بز کوهی	appalling *adj* وحشتناك
antenna *n* شاخك	apparel *n* جامه
anthem *n* سرود	apparent *adj* آشکار

apparently *adv* ظاهراً	approval *n* تائید
apparition *n* شبح	approve *v* تصدیق کردن
appeal *n* درخواست؛ جاذبه	approximate *adj* تقریبی
appeal *v* درخواست کردن	apricot *n* زردآلو
appealing *adj* خوش آیند	April *n* آوریل
appear *v* ظاهر شدن	apron *n* پیش بند
appearance *n* ظاهر	aptitude *n* استعداد
appease *v* ساکت کردن	aquarium *n* آکواریوم
appeasement *n* تسلی	aqueduct *n* آباره
appendix *n* پیوست	Arabic *adj* عربی
appetite *n* اشتها	arbiter *n* حکم
appetizer *n* اشتها آور	arbitrary *adj* اختیاری
applaud *v* تحسین کردن	arbitrate *v* داوری کردن
applause *n* تشویق	arbitration *n* حکمیت
apple *n* سیب	arc *n* قوس؛ کمان
appliance *n* اسباب	archbishop *n* اسقف اعظم
applicable *adj* قابل اجرا	architect *n* معمار
applicant *n* متقاضی	architecture *n* معماری
application *n* درخواست نامه	archive *n* آرشیو
apply *v* اجرا کردن	arctic *adj* بسیار سرد
apply for *v* اقدام کردن برای	ardor *n* حرارت
appoint *v* مامور کردن	arduous *adj* سخت
appointment *n* قرار ملاقات	area *n* منطقه
appraisal *n* ارزیابی	arena *n* عرصه؛ میدان
appraise *v* ارزیابی کردن	argue *v* بحث کردن
appreciate *v* قدردانی کردن	argument *n* مباحثه
appreciation *n* قدردانی	arise *iv* اتفاق بیافت
apprehend *v* دستگیر کردن	aristocracy *n* اشراف سالاری
apprentice *n* کارآموز	aristocrat *n* اشراف زاده
approach *v* رسیدن	arithmetic *n* حساب
approach *n* رهیافت	ark *n* کشتی نوح
approbation *n* قبولی	arm *n* بازو

arm v مسلح کردن	**artist** n هنرمند
armaments n تسلیحات	**artistic** adj هنری
armchair n مبل	**artwork** n کار هنری
armed adj مسلح	**as** c چنانچه
armistice n آتش بس موقت	**as** adv چنانچه
armor n حفاظت شده	**ascend** v صعود کردن
armpit n زیر بغل	**ascendancy** n تفوق
army n ارتش	**ascertain** v معلوم کردن
around pre اطراف	**ash** n خاکستر
arouse v بیدار کردن	**ashamed** adj شرمنده
arrange v مرتب کردن	**ashore** adv به ساحل
arrangement n ترتیب	**ashtray** n زیرسیگاری
array n آرایه	**aside** adv کنار
arrest v توقیف کردن	**aside from** adv کنار از
arrest n دستگیر	**ask** v پرسیدن
arrival n ورود	**asparagus** n مارچوبه
arrive v رسیدن	**aspect** n جنبه
arrogance n تکبر	**asphalt** n آسفالت
arrogant adj گستاخ	**asphyxiate** v خفه کردن
arrow n تیر	**asphyxiation** n خفگی
arsenal n تسلیحات	**aspiration** n آرزو
arsenic n آرسنیک	**aspire** v آرزو کردن
arson n ایجادحریق	**aspirin** n آسپیرین
arsonist n ایجادحریق عمدی	**assail** v حمله کردن
art n هنر	**assailant** n مهاجم
artery n شریان	**assassin** n تروریست
arthritis n التهاب مفصل	**assassinate** v به قتل رساندن
artichoke n آرتیشو	**assassination** n ترور
article n بند	**assault** n حمله
articulation n بیان	**assault** v حمله کردن
artillery n توپخانه	**assemble** v سوار کردن
artisan n صنعتگر	**assembly** n مونتاژ؛ مجمع

assent v موافقت کردن	astronomic adj نجومی
assert v حمایت کردن	astronomy n اخترشناسی
assertion n تاکید	astute adj زرنگ
assess v تشخیص دادن	asunder adv جدا
assessment n ارزیابی	asylum n پناهندگی
asset n دارایی	at pre در
assets n دارائی ها	atheism n الحاد
assign v واگذار کردن	atheist n ملحد
assignment n واگذاری	athlete n ورزشکار
assimilate v یکسان کردن	athletic adj ورزشی
assimilation n جذب	atmosphere n جو
assist v یاری کردن	atmospheric adj جوی
assistance n کمک	atom n اتم
associate v مربوط ساختن	atomic adj اتمی
association n انجمن	atone v جبران کردن
assorted adj مخلوط	atonement n جبران
assortment n مجموعه	atrocious adj بی رحم
assume v فرض کردن	atrocity n ظلم
assumption n فرض	atrophy v لاغر کردن
assurance n اطمینان	attach v پیوست کردن
assure v اطمینان دادن	attached adj ضمیمه
asterisk n ستاره	attachment n ضمیمه؛ توقیف
asteroid n سیارک	attack n حمله
asthma n آسم	attack v حمله کردن
astonish v متحیر کردن	attacker n مهاجم
astonishing adj حیرت انگیز	attain v دست یافتن
astound v مبهوت کردن	attainable adj دست یافتنی
astray v گمراه کردن	attainment n دستیابی
astrologer n طالع بین	attempt v تلاش کردن
astrology n طالع بینی	attempt n بکوشید
astronaut n فضانورد	attend v توجه کردن
astronomer n اخترشناس	attendance n حضور

attendant n شرکت کننده	**authorization** n اجازه
attention n توجه	**authorize** v اجازه دادن
attentive adj دقیق	**auto** n اتومبیل
attenuate v رقیق کردن	**autograph** n دست نویس
attest v شهادت دادن	**automatic** adj خودکار
attitude n نگرش	**automobile** n اتومبیل
attorney n وکیل دادگستری	**autonomous** adj مستقل
attract v جذب کردن	**autonomy** n خودمختاری
attraction n جذبه	**autopsy** n کالبدگشایی
attractive adj جذاب	**autumn** n پاییز
attribute v نسبت دادن	**auxiliary** adj نیروی امدادی
auction n مزایده	**avail** v سودمند بودن
auction v حراج کردن	**available** adj در دسترس
auctioneer n متصدی مزایده	**avalanche** n بهمن
audacious adj جسور	**avarice** n حرص
audacity n جسارت	**avaricious** adj حریص
audible adj قابل شنیدن	**avenge** v تلافی کردن
audience n شنوندگان	**avenue** n خیابان اصلی
audit v رسیدگی کردن	**average** n میانگین
auditorium n تالار	**averse** adj مخالف
augment v تکمیل کردن	**aversion** n بیزاری
August n اوت	**avert** v برگرداندن
aunt n خاله	**aviation** n هوانوردی
auspicious adj فرخنده	**aviator** n خلبان
austere adj سخت	**avid** adj مشتاق
austerity n سختی	**avoid** v دوری کردن از
authentic adj اصل	**avoidable** adj اجتناب پذیر
authenticate v اعتبار دادن	**avoidance** n اجتناب
authenticity n صحت	**avowed** adj اعتراف شده
author n نویسنده	**await** v منتظر بودن
authoritarian adj اقتدارطلب	**awake** iv بیدار شو
authority n قدرت	**awake** adj بیدار

awakening n بیداری

award v اعطا کردن

award n پاداش

aware adj آگاه

awareness n آگاهی

away adv خارج

awe n بهت زده

awesome adj شکوهمند

awful adj وحشتناک

awkward adj ناجور

awning n سایبان

ax n تبر

axiom n اصل متعارف

axis n محور

axle n محور

B

babble v یاوه گفتن

baby n بچه

babysitter n پرستار بچه

bachelor n مجرد

back n عقب

back adv عقب

back v پشتیبانی کردن

back up v پشتیبانی کردن

backbone n ستون مهره ها

backdoor n پنهانی

backfire v پس زدن شعله

background n زمینه

backing n حمایت

backlash n واکنش

backlog n کار عقب افتاده

backpack n کوله پشتی

backup n پشتیبان

backward adj به عقب

backwards adv به پشت

backyard n حیاط خلوت

bacon n ژامبون

bacteria n باکتری

bad adj بد

badge n آرم

badly adv بدجور

baffle v گمراه کردن

bag n کیف

baggage n بار

baggy adj بادکرده

baguette n باگت

bail n وجه الضمان

bail out v پریدن در آب

bailiff n مباشر

bait n طعمه

bake v طبخ کردن

baker n نانوا

bakery n نانوایی

balance v متعادل کردن

balance n تعادل؛ موجودی

balcony n بالکن

bald adj طاس

bale n عدل

ball n توپ؛ ساچمه

balloon n بادكنك	**bare** adj لخت
ballot n قرعه كشى	**barefoot** adj باپاى برهنه
ballroom n سالن رقص	**barely** adv به ندرت
balm n بلسان	**bargain** n مذاكره
balmy adj ملايم	**bargain** v چانه زدن
bamboo n نى	**bargaining** n چانه زدن
ban n حكم توقيف	**barge** n قايق بارى
ban v تحريم كردن	**bark** v پوست كندن
banality n ابتذال	**bark** n عوعو؛ پوست درخت
banana n موز	**barley** n جو
band n بند	**barmaid** n خادم ميخانه
bandage n باند	**barman** n خدمتكار
bandage v با نوار بستن	**barn** n انبار
bandit n راهزن	**barometer** n جوسنج
bang v بستن	**barracks** n پادگان
banish v تبعيد كردن	**barrage** n سد
banishment n تبعيد	**barrel** n بشكه
bank n بانك	**barren** adj بى ثمر
bankrupt v ورشكست شدن	**barricade** n مهار هواپيما
bankrupt adj ورشكسته	**barrier** n سد
bankruptcy n ورشكستگى	**barring** pre مگر اينكه
banner n نشان	**bartender** n ميخانه چى
banquet n ضيافت	**base** n پايه
baptism n غسل تعميد	**base** v تاسيس كردن
baptize v تعميد دادن	**baseball** n بيسبال
bar n ميله؛ نوار	**baseless** adj بى اساس
bar v قفل كردن	**basement** n زيرزمين
barbarian n وحشى	**bashful** adj كم رو
barbaric adj وحشى	**basic** adj اساسى
barbarism n وحشيگرى	**basics** n اصول
barbecue n منقل كباب	**basin** n لگن؛ تشتك
barber n آرايشگر	**basis** n اساس

bask v آفتاب خوردن	**bearded** adj ریشدار
basket n سبد	**bearer** n حامل
basketball n بسکتبال	**beast** n حیوان
bastard n حرامزاده	**beat** iv بزن؛ تپش کن
bat n خفاش؛ چماق	**beat** n ضربان؛ خسته
batch n یك دست؛ گروه	**beaten** adj زده شده
bath n حمام	**beating** n زدن
bathe v ستحمام کردن	**beautiful** adj زیبا
bathrobe n حوله حمام	**beautify** v زیبا کردن
bathroom n حمام	**beauty** n زیبایی
bathtub n وان	**beaver** n خرس آبی
baton n باتوم	**because** c زیرا
battalion n گردان	**because of** pre بخاطر
batter v خردکردن	**beckon** v اشاره کردن
battery n باتری	**become** iv بشو
battle n نبرد	**bed** n تختخواب؛ بستر
battle v نبرد کردن	**bedding** n روانداز
battleship n ناو جنگی	**bedroom** n اتاق خواب
bay n بخش	**bedspread** n روتختی
bayonet n سرنیزه	**bee** n زنبور عسل
bazaar n بازار	**beef** n گوشت گاو
be iv باش؛ بمان	**beehive** n کندو
be born v متولد شدن	**beer** n آبجو
beach n ساحل	**beet** n چغندر
beacon n فانوس دریایی	**beetle** n سوسك
beak n نوك	**before** adv قبلاً
beam n لبخند	**before** pre قبلاً
bean n دانه	**beforehand** adv قبلاً
bear n خرس	**beg** v خواهش کردن
bear iv تحمل کن؛ بزا	**beggar** n گدا
bearable adj تحمل پذیر	**begin** iv شروع ش
beard n ریش	**beginner** n مبتدی

B

beginning *n* شروع	bend *iv* خم شو
beguile *v* فریب دادن	bend down *v* خم کردن
behalf (on) *adv* از طرف	beneath *pre* کمتر از
behave *v* رفتارکردن	benediction *n* دعای خیر
behavior *n* رفتار	benefactor *n* آدم نیکوکار
behead *v* گردن زدن	beneficial *adj* سودمند
behind *pre* پشت	beneficiary *n* ذینفع
behold *iv* بنگر	benefit *n* سود
being *n* بودن	benefit *v* سود بردن
belated *adj* ازموقع گذشته	benevolence *n* خیرخواهی
belch *v* آروغ زدن	benevolent *adj* خیرخواه
belch *n* آروغ	benign *adj* مهربان
belfry *n* برج ناقوس	bequeath *v* وصیت کردن
Belgian *adj* بلژیکی	bereaved *adj* داغدار
Belgium *n* بلژیك	bereavement *n* مصیبت
belief *n* عقیده	beret *n* کلاه بره
believable *adj* قابل قبول	berserk *adv* عصبانی
believe *v* باور کردن	berth *n* لنگر
believer *n* مومن	beseech *iv* استدعا کن
belittle *v* تحقیر نمودن	beset *iv* احاطه کن
bell *n* زنگ؛ صدای زنگ	beside *pre* درکنار
bell pepper *n* فلفل زنگ	besides *pre* علاوه بر
belligerent *adj* ستیزه جو	besiege *iv* محاصره کن
belly *n* شکم	best *adj* بهترین
belly button *n* ناف	best man *n* ساقدوش
belong *v* تعلق داشتن	bestial *adj* جانوری
belongings *n* اسباب اثاثیه	bestiality *n* حیوانیت
beloved *adj* محبوب	bestow *v* بخشیدن
below *adv* زیر	bet *iv* شرطبندی کن
below *pre* زیر	bet *n* شرطبندی
belt *n* نوار	betray *v* لو دادن
bench *n* نیمکت	betrayal *n* خیانت

B

better *adj* بهتر

between *pre* مابین

beverage *n* آشامیدنی

beware *v* حذر کردن

bewilder *v* گیج کردن

bewitch *v* افسون کردن

beyond *adv* آنسوی

bias *n* باياس

bible *n* کتاب مقدس

bibliography *n* کتاب شناسی

bicycle *n* دوچرخه

bid *n* پیشنهادقیمت

bid *iv* پیشنهاد قیمت بده

big *adj* بزرگ

bigamy *n* دوزنی

bigot *adj* آدم متعصب

bigotry *n* تعصب

bike *n* دوچرخه

bile *n* صفرا

bilingual *adj* دوزبانه

bill *n* صورتحساب

billiards *n* بیلیارد

billion *n* بیلیون

billionaire *n* بیلیونر

bimonthly *adj* دو ماهانه

bin *n* مخزن

bind *iv* مقید کن

binding *adj* جلد

binoculars *n* دوربین دوچشمی

biography *n* زندگینامه

biological *adj* زیست شناختی

biology *n* زیست شناسی

bird *n* پرنده

birth *n* تولد

birthday *n* روز تولد

biscuit *n* بیسکویت

bishop *n* اسقف

bison *n* گاومیش

bit *n* ذره

bite *iv* گاز بگیر ؛ نیش بزن

bite *n* گاز

bitter *adj* تلخی

bitterly *adv* سخت

bitterness *n* تلخی

bizarre *adj* عجیب و غریب

black *adj* سیاه

blackberry *n* تمشك سياه

blackboard *n* تخته سیاه

blackmail *n* حق السکوت

blackmail *v* تهدید کردن

blackness *n* تاریکی

blackout *n* تاریك

blacksmith *n* آهنگر

bladder *n* مثانه

blade *n* تیغه

blame *n* سرزنش

blame *v* سرزنش کردن

blameless *adj* بی گناه

bland *adj* آرام

blank *adj* خالی

blanket *n* پتو

blaspheme *v* کفرگویی کردن

blasphemy *n* کفر

blast *n* دم

blaze *v* درخشیدن	**blond** *adj* سفیدرو
bleach *v* نفوذ کردن	**blood** *n* خون
bleach *n* سفید کننده	**bloodthirsty** *adj* سفاك
bleak *adj* ناامیدکننده	**bloody** *adj* خونین
bleed *iv* خونریزی کن	**bloom** *v* شکوفه کردن
bleeding *n* خونریزی	**blossom** *v* گل دادن
blemish *n* معیوب	**blot** *n* لکه
blemish *v* بدنام کردن	**blot** *v* لکه دار کردن
blend *n* مخلوط	**blouse** *n* بلوز
blend *v* ترکیب کردن	**blow** *n* بوزید
blender *n* مخلوط کن	**blow** *iv* بوز؛ بِدم
bless *v* تقدیس کردن	**blow out** *iv* فوران کن
blessed *adj* مقدس	**blow up** *iv* منفجر شو
blessing *n* رحمت	**blowout** *n* ترکیدن تایر
blind *v* اغفال کردن	**bludgeon** *v* مجبور کردن
blind *adj* کور	**blue** *adj* آبی
blindfold *n* چشم بند	**blueprint** *n* نقشه
blindfold *v* چشم بستن	**bluff** *v* توپ زدن
blindly *adv* کورکورانه	**blunder** *n* اشتباه بزرگ
blindness *n* کوری	**blunt** *adj* بی نوک؛ بی پرده
blink *v* چشمک زدن	**bluntness** *n* باکندی
bliss *n* لذت	**blur** *v* تیره کردن
blissful *adj* لذت بخش	**blurred** *adj* تیره وتارشده
blister *n* تاول	**blush** *v* شرمنده شدن
blizzard *n* بوران	**blush** *n* سرخی صورت
bloat *v* باد کردن	**boar** *n* گراز نر
bloated *adj* بادکرده	**board** *n* تخته؛ هیئت
block *n* بلوک؛ مانع	**board** *v* جا دادن
block *v* مسدود کردن	**boast** *v* خودستایی کردن
blockade *v* سدراه کردن	**boat** *n* قایق
blockade *n* راه بند	**bodily** *adj* بدنی
blockage *n* گرفتگی	**body** *n* بدن؛ متن

bog *n* باتلاق

bog down *v* گیر کردن

boil *v* جوشاندن

boil over *v* سرریز شدن

boiler *n* دیگ بخار

boisterous *adj* شدید

bold *adj* جسور؛ بی باک

boldness *n* جسارت

bolster *v* پشتیبانی کردن

bolt *n* پیچ، چفت

bolt *v* پیچ کردن

bomb *n* بمب

bomb *v* بمباران کردن

bombing *n* بمباران

bombshell *n* خبر غیرمترقبه

bond *n* پیوند؛ تعهد

bondage *n* بردگی

bone *n* استخوان

bone marrow *n* مغز استخوان

bonfire *n* آتش

bonus *n* جایزه

book *n* کتاب

bookcase *n* جاکتابی

bookkeeper *n* کتابدار

bookkeeping *n* کتابداری

booklet *n* کتابچه

bookseller *n* کتاب فروش

bookstore *n* کتاب فروشی

boom *n* جهش اقتصادی

boom *v* ترقی کردن

boost *v* ترقی دادن

boost *n* ترقی

boot *n* چکمه

booth *n* جای ویژه

booty *n* غنائم جنگی

booze *n* مشروب

border *n* مرز؛ زه

border on *v* حاشیه دار کردن

borderline *adj* مرز

bore *v* سوراخ کردن

bored *adj* خسته

boredom *n* بی حوصلگی

boring *adj* حفر

born *adj* زاده شده

borough *n* منطقه

borrow *v* قرض کردن

bosom *n* سینه

boss *n* رئیس

bossy *adj* رئیسی

botany *n* گیاه شناسی

botch *v* خراب کردن

both *adj* هردو

bother *v* زحمت دادن

bothersome *adj* مزاحم

bottle *n* بطری

bottle *v* دربطری ریختن

bottleneck *n* گلوگاه

bottom *n* پایین

bottomless *adj* عمیق

bough *n* شاخه

boulder *n* سنگ

boulevard *n* بلوار

bounce *v* پریدن

bounce *n* پرش

bound adj عازم	**brandy** n كنياك
bound for adj عازم باشید	**brat** n توله
boundary n مرز	**brave** adj شجاع
boundless adj بی حدوحصر	**bravely** adv شجاعانه
bounty n جایزه	**bravery** n شجاعت
bourgeois adj بورژوا	**brawl** n دعوا
bow n قوس؛ تعظیم	**breach** n نقض؛ قانون شکنی
bow v تعظیم کردن	**bread** n نان
bow out v عقب نشستن	**breadth** n عرض
bowels n روده	**break** n شکستگی؛ شکاف
bowl n کاسه؛ بولینگ	**break** iv بشکن
box n جعبه	**break away** v فرار کردن
box office n گیشه	**break down** v شکستن
boxer n مشت زن	**break free** v فرار کردن
boxing n مشت زنی	**break off** v قطع کردن
boy n پسر	**break out** v شیوع یافتن
boycott v تحریم کردن	**break up** v تفکیک کردن
boyfriend n دوست پسر	**breakable** adj شکستنی
boyhood n کودکی	**breakdown** n خرابی
bra n سینه بند	**breakfast** n صبحانه
bracelet n بازوبند	**breakthrough** n رخنه
bracket n کروشه	**breast** n سینه
brag v لاف زدن	**breath** n نفس
braid n گیس	**breathe** v نفس کشیدن
brain n مغز	**breathing** n تنفس
brake n ترمز	**breathtaking** adj خیره کننده
brake v ترمز کردن	**breed** iv پرورش بده؛ بزا
branch n شعبه	**breed** n نسل
branch office n دفتر انشعابی	**breeze** n نسیم
branch out v بسط دادن	**brethren** n برادران
brand n علامت	**brevity** n کوتاهی
brand-new adj نوع جدید	**brew** v دم کردن

B

brewery *n* آبجوسازی	**broad** *adj* وسیع
bribe *v* رشوه دادن	**broadcast** *v* منتشر کردن
bribe *n* رشوه	**broadcast** *n* پخش
bribery *n* رشوه دهی	**broadcaster** *n* گوینده
brick *n* آجر	**broaden** *v* پهن کردن
bricklayer *n* بنا	**broadly** *adv* به طور کلی
bridal *adj* عروسی	**broadminded** *adj* روشن فکر
bride *n* عروس	**brochure** *n* بروشور
bridegroom *n* داماد	**broil** *v* سرخ کردن
bridesmaid *n* ساقدوش	**broiler** *n* کباب پز
bridge *n* پل	**broke** *adj* شکسته
bridle *n* افسار	**broken** *adj* شکسته
brief *adj* خلاصه	**bronchitis** *n* برونشیت
brief *v* خلاصه کردن	**bronze** *n* برنز
briefcase *n* کیف دستی	**broom** *n* جارو
briefing *n* خلاصه	**broth** *n* سوپ
briefly *adv* بطور خلاصه	**brothel** *n* فاحشه خانه
briefs *n* خلاصه ها	**brother** *n* برادر
brigade *n* تیپ	**brotherhood** *n* برادری
bright *adj* روشن	**brother-in-law** *n* برادر زن
brighten *v* روشن کردن	**brotherly** *adj* برادرانه
brightness *n* روشنی	**brow** *n* پیشانی
brilliant *adj* درخشان	**brown** *adj* قهوه ای
brim *n* لبه	**browse** *v* مرور کردن
bring *iv* بیاور	**browser** *n* مرورگر
bring back *v* برگرداندن	**bruise** *n* خون مردگی
bring up *v* پرورش دادن	**bruise** *v* کوبیدن
brink *n* لبه	**brunch** *n* ناهار - صبحانه
brisk *adj* چابك	**brunette** *adj* زن سبزه
Britain *n* بریتانیا	**brush** *n* برس
British *adj* بریتانیایی	**brush** *v* مسواک زدن
brittle *adj* شکننده	**brush aside** *v* رفع کردن مانع

brush up v تجدید خاطره کردن	**bullet** n گلوله
brusque adj عجول	**bulletin** n مجله
brutal adj وحشی	**bully** adj قلدر
brutality n بیرحمی	**bulwark** n خاکریز
brutalize v وحشی شدن	**bum** n مزخرف
brute adj احمق	**bump** n دست انداز جاده؛
bubble n حباب	**bump into** v برخورد کردن با
bubble gum n آدامس بادکنکی	**bumper** n سپر
buck n گوزن نر	**bumpy** adj ناهموار
bucket n سطل	**bun** n کیک
buckle n قلاب	**bunch** n خوشه
buckle up v بستن کمربند	**bundle** n دسته
bud n جوانه	**bundle** v دسته کردن
buddy n رفیق	**bunker** n پناهگاه
budge v تکان دادن	**buoy** n بویه
budget n بودجه	**burden** n تحمیل
buffalo n گاومیش	**burden** v تحمیل کردن
bug n ساس	**burdensome** adj خطیر
bug v آزار دادن	**bureau** n اداره
build iv بساز	**bureaucracy** n دیوان سالاری
builder n سازنده	**bureaucrat** n دیوان سالار
building n ساختمان	**burger** n همبرگر
buildup n ساخته شده	**burglar** n دزد
built-in adj داخلی	**burglarize** v شبانه دزدیدن
bulb n لامپ	**burglary** n سرقت
bulge n برآمدگی	**burial** n تدفین
bulk n توده؛ حجم	**burly** adj قوی هیکل
bulky adj حجیم	**burn** iv بسوزان
bull n گاو نر	**burn** n سوختگی سطحی
bull fight n جنگ گاو نر	**burp** v آروغ زدن
bull fighter n جنگنده گاو نر	**burp** n آروغ
bulldoze v تهدید کردن	**burrow** n پناهگاه

B
C

burst *iv* بِترک

burst into *v* شروع کردن به

bury *v* دفن کردن

bus *n* اتوبوس

bus *v* با اتوبوس رفتن

bush *n* بوته

busily *adv* مشغولانه

business *n* حرفه

businessman *n* بازرگان

bust *n* سینه

bustling *adj* شلوغ

busy *adj* سرگرم؛ مشغول

but *c* اما

butcher *n* قصاب

butchery *n* قصابی

butler *n* ناظر؛ ابادارچی

butt *n* نوک؛ لولا

butter *n* کره

butterfly *n* پروانه

button *n* دکمه

buttonhole *n* جادکمه

buy *iv* بخر

buy off *v* تطمیع کردن

buyer *n* خریدار

buzz *n* همهمه کنید

buzzard *n* باز

buzzer *n* زنگ

by *pre* بوسیله

bye *e* خداحافظ

bypass *n* کنارگذر

bypass *v* کنار گذاشتن

by-product *n* محصول فرعی

bystander *n* تماشاچی

C

cab *n* تاکسی

cabbage *n* کلم

cabin *n* کابین

cabinet *n* قفسه؛ کابینه

cable *n* کابل

cafeteria *n* سلف سرویس

caffeine *n* کافئین

cage *n* قفس

cake *n* کیک

calamity *n* مصیبت

calculate *v* حساب کردن

calculation *n* محاسبه

calculator *n* ماشین حساب

calendar *n* تقویم

calf *n* ماهیچه ساق پا

caliber *n* کالیبر

calibrate *v* کالیبره کردن

call *n* تماس؛ فریاد

call *v* صدا کردن

call off *v* صرفنظر کردن

call on *v* مطالبه کردن

call out *v* اعلام خطر کردن

calling *n* پیشه

callous *adj* پینه بسته

calm *adj* آرام

C

calm *n* آرام	canned *adj* کنسرو شده
calm down *v* آرام شدن	cannibal *n* آدمخوار
calorie *n* کالری	cannon *n* توپ
calumny *n* افترا	canoe *n* قایق باریک
camel *n* شتر	canonize *v* شرعی کردن
camera *n* دوربین	cantaloupe *n* گرمک؛ طالبی
camouflage *v* مخفی کردن	canteen *n* غذاخوری
camouflage *n* استتار	canvas *n* کرباس
camp *n* اردو	canvas *v* بررسی کردن
camp *v* اردو زدن	canyon *n* دره باریک وتنگ
campaign *v* نبرد کردن	cap *n* کلاه؛ چاشنی
campaign *n* مبارزه	capability *n* قابلیت
campfire *n* آتش بازی	capable *adj* لایق
can *iv* بتوان	capacity *n* ظرفیت
can *v* قادر بودن	cape *n* دماغه؛ شنل
can *n* قوطی حلبی	capital *n* پایتخت
can opener *n* دربازکن قوطی	capital letter *n* نامه سرمایه
canal *n* کانال	capitalism *n* سرمایه داری
canary *n* قناری	capitulate *v* تسلیم شدن
cancel *v* لغو کردن	capsize *v* واژگون شدن
cancellation *n* ابطال	capsule *n* کپسول
cancer *n* سرطان	captain *n* کاپیتان
cancerous *adj* سرطانی	captivate *v* اسیر کردن
candid *adj* رک وراست	captive *n* اسیر
candidacy *n* نامزدی	captivity *n* اسارت
candidate *n* نامزد	capture *v* دستگیر کردن
candle *n* شمع	capture *n* بگیرید
candlestick *n* شمعدان	car *n* اتومبیل
candor *n* سفیدی	carat *n* عیار
candy *n* آب نبات	caravan *n* کاروان
cane *n* نی؛ نیشکر	carburetor *n* کاربوراتور
canister *n* قوطی	carcass *n* لاشه

C

card n کارت؛ برگ	**cart** n ارابه
cardboard n مقوا	**cart** v با گاری بردن
cardiac adj قلبی	**cartoon** n کاریکاتور
cardiac arrest n ایست قلبی	**cartridge** n فشنگ
cardiology n قلب شناسی	**carve** v حک کردن؛ بریدن
care n مراقبت	**cascade** n شرشره
care v محافظت کردن	**case** n مورد؛ پرونده
care about v دوست داشتن	**cash** n نقد
care for v دوست داشتن	**cashier** n صندوقدار
career n حرفه	**casino** n کازینو
carefree adj بی غم	**casket** n جعبه
careful adj بااحتیاط	**casserole** n پیرکس
careless adj بی دقت	**cassock** n قبای کشیشان
carelessness n بابی دقتی	**cast** iv بیانداز؛ جاری کن
caress n نوازش	**castaway** n عمق یابی
caress v دراغوش کشیدن	**caste** n کاست
caretaker n سرایدار	**castle** n قلعه
cargo n بار	**casual** adj اتفاقی
caricature n کاریکاتور	**casualty** n مجروح
caring adj بااهمیت دادن	**cat** n گربه
carnage n قتل عام	**cataclysm** n مصیبت
carnal adj شهوانی	**catacomb** n دخمه محل قبور
carnation n میخك	**catalog** n کاتالوگ
carol n سرود کریسمس	**cataract** n آبشار بزرگ
carpenter n درودگر	**catastrophe** n فاجعه
carpentry n نجاری	**catch** iv بگیر
carpet n فرش	**catch up** v رسیدن به
carriage n درشکه	**catching** adj واگیردار
carrot n هویج	**catchword** n شعار
carry v حمل کردن	**catechism** n اصول دین
carry on v ادامه دادن	**category** n طبقه
carry out v اجرا کردن	**cater to** v متنعم کردن

کرم حشره n caterpillar
کلیسای جامع n cathedral
جامع adj catholic
گله n cattle
گل کلم n cauliflower
باعث؛ سبب n cause
سبب شدن v cause
اخطار n caution
محتاط adj cautious
سواره نظام n cavalry
غار n cave
غار n cavern
حفره n cavity
ایستادن v cease
آتش بس n cease-fire
دائم adv ceaselessly
سقف n ceiling
جشن گرفتن v celebrate
جشن n celebration
آدم مشهور n celebrity
کرفس n celery
آسمانی adj celestial
تجرد n celibacy
مجرد adj celibate
زیرزمین n cellar
موبایل n cellphone
سیمان n cement
گورستان n cemetery
سانسور n censorship
سرزنش کردن v censure
سرشماری n census
سنت n cent

صدمین سالگرد n centenary
مرکز n center
متمرکز کردن v center
سانتی متر n centimeter
مرکزی adj central
متمرکز کردن v centralize
قرن n century
سرامیک n ceramic
غله n cereal
مغزی adj cerebral
تشریفات n ceremony
خاص adi certain
اطمینان n certainty
گواهی n certificate
تصدیق کردن v certify
یاس؛ غم و غصه n chagrin
زنجیر n chain
زنجیر کردن v chain
اره برقی n chainsaw
صندلی n chair
برصندلی نشاندن v chair
رئیس n chairman
کلبه کوهستانی n chalet
جام شراب n chalice
گچ n chalk
تخته سیاه n chalkboard
رقابت کردن v challenge
مبارزه n challenge
سخت adj challenging
محفظه n chamber
قهرمان n champ
قهرمان n champion

C

champion v پشتیبانی کردن	chase away v تعقیب کردن
chance n احتمال؛ فرصت	chasm n شکاف
chancellor n رئیس دانشگاه	chaste adj عفیف
chandelier n چلچراغ	chastise v تنبیه کردن
change v عوض کردن	chastisement n تنبیه
change n تغییر	chastity n عفت
channel n کانال	chat v گپ زدن
chant n سرود	chauffeur n راننده
chaos n اغتشاش	cheap adj ارزان
chaotic adj آشفته	cheat v فریب دادن
chapel n نمازخانه	cheater n فریبکار
chaplain n کشیش	check n وارسی؛ چک
chapter n فصل	check v مقابله کردن
char v برگشتن	check in v وارد شدن
character n مشخصه	check up n معاینه؛ چک آپ
characteristic adj ویژگی	checkbook n دسته چك
charade n ادا	cheek n فك
charcoal n زغال چوب	cheekbone n استخوان گونه
charge v شارژ کردن	cheeky adj پررو
charge n هزینه؛ شارژ؛ بار	cheer v تشویق کردن
charisma n جذبه جادویی	cheer up v روحیه دادن
charismatic adj فرهمند	cheerful adj خوش
charitable adj مهربان	cheers n به سلامتی
charity n محبت	cheese n پنیر
charm v افسون کردن	chef n سرآشپز
charm n افسون؛ طلسم	chemical adj ماده شیمیایی
charming adj دوست داشتنی	chemist n شیمی دان
chart n نمودار، نقشه	chemistry n شیمی
charter n قرارداد؛ اجاره نامه	cherish v گرامی داشتن
charter v پروانه دادن	cherry n گیلاس
chase n تعقیب	chess n شطرنج
chase v تعقیب کردن	chest n بدنه؛ سینه

C

chestnut *n* شاه بلوط	chopper *n* ساطور
chew *v* جویدن	chore *n* خرده کاری
chick *n* جوجه؛ نوزاد	chorus *n* هم سرایان
chicken *n* جوجه	christen *v* نام گذاری کردن
chicken out *v* تسلیم شدن	christening *n* مراسم تعمید
chicken pox *n* آبله جوجه	christian *adj* مسیحی
chide *v* سرزنش کردن	Christianity *n* مسیحیت
chief *n* رئیس	Christmas *n* کریسمس
chiefly *adv* بیشتر	chronic *adj* مزمن
child *n* بچه	chronicle *n* رویدادشمار
childhood *n* بچگی	chronology *n* ترتیب زمانی
childish *adj* بچگانه	chubby *adj* تپل
childless *adj* بی فرزند	chuckle *v* پیش خود خندیدن
children *n* بچه ها	chunk *n* تکه
chill *n* سرد؛ سرما	church *n* کلیسا
chill *v* سرد کردن	chute *n* سرسره
chilly *adj* سرد	cider *n* شراب سیب
chimney *n* دودکش	cigar *n* سیگار برگ
chimpanzee *n* شمپانزه	cigarette *n* سیگار
chin *n* چانه	cinder *n* چوب نیمسوز
chip *n* تراشه؛ خرده چوب	cinema *n* سینما
chisel *n* اسکنه	cinnamon *n* دارچین
chocolate *n* شکلات	circle *n* دایره
choice *n* انتخاب	circle *v* احاطه کردن
choir *n* همسرایان	circuit *n* مدار
choke *v* خفه کردن	circular *adj* بخشنامه
cholera *n* وبا	circulate *v* گردش کردن
cholesterol *n* کلسترول	circulation *n* جریان
choose *iv* انتخاب کن	circumcise *v* ختنه کردن
choosy *adj* مشکل پسند	circumcision *n* ختنه
chop *v* ریز ریز کردن	circumstance *n* وضعیت
chop *n* خرد؛ ضربه پیچشی	circumstancial *adj* رویدادی

C

circus *n* سیرك	claw *v* چنگ زدن
cistern *n* مبنع آب	clay *n* خاك رس
citizen *n* شهروند	clean *adj* تمیز
citizenship *n* تابعیت	clean *v* تمیز کردن
city *n* شهر	cleaner *n* تمیز کننده
city hall *n* سالن شهر	cleanliness *n* تمیزی
civic *adj* شهری	cleanse *v* پاک کردن
civil *adj* مدنی	clear *adj* صاف؛ شفاف
civilization *n* تمدن	clear *v* پاک کردن
civilize *v* متمدن کردن	clearance *n* پاکسازی
claim *v* ادعا کردن	clear-cut *adj* روشن؛ صریح
claim *n* ادعا؛ دادخواست	clearly *adv* به وضوح
clam *n* ساکت	clearness *n* روشنی
clamor *v* فریادکشیدن	cleft *n* شكاف
clamp *n* گیره	clemency *n* عفو
clan *n* طایفه	clench *v* پرچ کردن
clandestine *adj* پنهانی	clergy *n* روحانیون
clap *v* کف زدن	clergyman *n* روحانی
clarification *n* توضیح	clerical *adj* دفتری
clarify *v* واضح کردن	clerk *n* منشی
clarinet *n* قره نی	clever *adj* باهوش
clarity *n* وضوح	click *v* صدا کردن
clash *v* برخورد کردن	client *n* مشتری
clash *n* برخورد	clientele *n* مشتریان
class *n* کلاس؛ رده	cliff *n* صخره
classic *adj* کلاسیك	climate *n* آب و هوا
classify *v* دسته بندی کردن	climatic *adj* آب وهوا
classmate *n* هم کلاسی	climax *n* اوج، قله
classroom *n* کلاس درس	climb *v* صعود کردن
classy *adj* کلاسی	climbing *n* صعود
clause *n* شرط	clinch *v* محکم کردن
claw *n* پنجه	cling *iv* بچسب

clinic n درمانگاه	clutch n چنگ
clip v کوتاه کردن	coach v معلمی کردن
clipping n چیدن	coach n مربی
cloak n ردا	coaching n مربیگری
clock n ساعت	coagulate v بستن
clog v مسدود کردن	coagulation n انعقاد
cloister n منزوی	coal n زغال سنگ
clone v تولید مثل کردن	coalition n ائتلاف
cloning n همنوع سازی	coarse adj زمخت؛ بی ادب
close v بستن	coast n ساحل
close adj نزدیک	coastal adj ساحلی
close to pre نزدیك به	coastline n خط ساحلی
closed adj بسته	coat n آستر؛ پوشش
closely adv نزدیك	coax v نوازش کردن
closet n کمد	cob n قوی نر
closure n تکمیل	cobblestone n قلوه سنگ
clot n لخته بشوید	cobweb n تار عنکبوت
cloth n پارچه	cocaine n کوکائین
clothe v پوشاندن	cock n پرنده نر
clothes n لباس	cockpit n کابین خلبان
clothing n پوشاك	cockroach n سوسك
cloud n ابر	cocktail n کوکتل
cloudless adj بدون ابر	cocky adj صددرصدمطمئن
cloudy adj ابری	cocoa n کاکائو
clown n دلقك	coconut n نارگیل
club n باشگاه؛ چماق	cod n ماهی روغن
club v چماق زدن	code n رمز؛ كد
clue n راهنمایی	codify v قانون وضع کردن
clumsiness n با ناآزمودگی	coefficient n ضریب؛ ثابت
clumsy adj ناآزموده	coerce v ناگزیر کردن
cluster n خوشه	coercion n اجبار
cluster v دسته کردن	coexist v با هم زیستن

C

coffee *n* قهوه	colony *n* مستعمره
coffin *n* تابوت	color *n* رنگ
cohabit *v* با هم زندگی کردن	color *v* تغییر رنگ دادن
coherent *adj* منسجم	colorful *adj* رنگارنگ
cohesion *n* انسجام	colossal *adj* عظیم
coin *n* سکه	colt *n* کره اسب
coincide *v* همزمان بودن	column *n* ستون
coincidence *n* تصادف	coma *n* اغما
coincidental *adj* اتفاقی	comb *n* شانه
cold *adj* سرد	comb *v* شانه کردن
coldness *n* سردی	combat *n* رزمی
colic *n* قولنج	combat *v* مبارزه کردن
collaborate *v* با هم کار کردن	combatant *n* رزمنده
collaboration *n* همکاری	combination *n* ترکیب
collaborator *n* همکار	combine *v* ملحق شدن
collapse *v* فرو ریختن	combustible *n* موادسوختنی
collapse *n* سقوط	combustion *n* اشتعال
collar *n* یقه	come *iv* بیا
collarbone *n* استخوان ترقوه	come about *v* اتفاق افتادن
collateral *adj* متوازی	come across *v* برخورد کردن به
colleague *n* همکار	come apart *v* سقوط کردن
collect *v* جمع آوری کردن	come back *v* برگشتن
collection *n* جمع آوری	come down *v* پائین آمدن
collector *n* گردآوری کننده	come from *v* آمدن از
college *n* دانشکده	come in *v* وارد شدن
collide *v* تصادف کردن	come out *v* بیرون آمدن
collision *n* تصادف	come over *v* مسلط شدن بر
cologne *n* عطر؛ ادکلن	come up *v* پیش آمدن
colon *n* نشان دو نقطه	comeback *n* بازگشت
colonel *n* سرهنگ	comedian *n* کمدین
colonial *adj* مهاجرنشین	comedy *n* کمدی
colonize *v* ساکن شدن در	comet *n* ستاره دنباله دار

comfort *n* آسایش

comfortable *adj* راحت

comforter *n* راحتی بخش

comical *adj* مضحک

coming *n* باآمدن

coming *adj* باآمدن

comma *n* ویرگول

command *v* فرمان دادن

commander *n* فرمانده

commandment *n* فرمان

commence *v* شروع کردن

commend *v* ستایش کردن

commendation *n* تحسین

comment *v* تفسیر نوشتن

comment *n* اظهاریه

commerce *n* بازرگانی

commercial *adj* بازرگانی

commission *n* ماموریت

commit *v* سپردن

commitment *n* تعهد

committed *adj* متعهد

committee *n* کمیته

common *adj* عادی

commotion *n* هیاهو

communicate *v* گفتگو کردن

communication *n* ارتباط

communion *n* ارتباط

communism *n* کمونیسم

communist *adj* کمونیست

community *n* اجتماع

commute *v* تبدیل کردن

compact *adj* فشرده

compact *v* فشرده کردن

companion *n* معاشر

companionship *n* مجالست

company *n* شرکت

comparable *adj* قابل مقایسه

comparative *adj* مقایسه ای

compare *v* مقایسه کردن

comparison *n* مقایسه

compartment *n* قسمت

compass *n* قطب نما

compassion *n* مهربانی

compassionate *adj* مهربان

compatibility *n* سازگاری

compatible *adj* سازگار

compatriot *n* هم میهن

compel *v* مجبور کردن

compelling *adj* محکم

compendium *n* خلاصه

compensate *v* تاوان دادن

compensation *n* جبران

compete *v* رقابت کردن

competence *n* کفایت

competent *adj* صالح

competition *n* رقابت

competitive *adj* رقابتی

competitor *n* رقیب

compile *v* گردآوردن

complain *v* شکایت کردن

complaint *n* شکایت

complement *n* مکمل

complete *adj* کامل

complete *v* انجام دادن

C

completely *adv* کاملا	**compute** *v* محاسبه کردن
completion *n* تکمیل	**computer** *n* رایانه
complex *adj* مجموعه	**comrade** *n* دوست
complexion *n* رنگ و رو	**con man** *n* متقلب
complexity *n* پیچیدگی	**conceal** *v* پنهان کردن
compliance *n* اطاعت	**concede** *v* واگذار کردن
compliant *adj* مطیع	**conceited** *adj* مغرور
complicate *v* پیچیده کردن	**conceive** *v* تصور کردن
complication *n* پیچیدگی	**concentrate** *v* متمرکز کردن
complicity *n* شرکت درجرم	**concentration** *n* تمرکز
compliment *n* تعریف	**concentric** *adj* هم مرکز
complimentary *adj* تحسین آمیز	**concept** *n* مفهوم
comply *v* موافقت کردن	**conception** *n* تصور
component *n* مولفه	**concern** *v* مربوط بودن
compose *v* سرودن	**concern** *n* شرکت؛ نگرانی
composed *adj* ترکیب شده	**concerning** *pre* درباره
composer *n* آهنگ ساز	**concert** *n* کنسرت
composition *n* ترکیب	**concession** *n* اعطا
compost *n* کود	**conciliate** *v* ساکت کردن
composure *n* آرامش	**conciliatory** *adj* آشتی جویانه
compound *n* مرکب	**conciousness** *n* هوشیاری
compound *v* ترکیب کردن	**concise** *adj* موجز
comprehend *v* درک کردن	**conclude** *v* به پایان رساندن
comprehensive *adj* کامل	**conclusion** *n* نتیجه؛ عقد
compress *v* متراکم کردن	**conclusive** *adj* قاطع
compression *n* بهم فشردگی	**concoct** *v* درست کردن
comprise *v* شامل بودن	**concoction** *n* معجون؛ ترکیب
compromise *n* بینابین	**concrete** *n* بتون
compromise *v* تسویه کردن	**concrete** *adj* بتون
compulsion *n* زور	**concur** *v* موافقت کردن
compulsive *adj* وسواسی	**concurrent** *adj* هم زمان
compulsory *adj* اجباری	**concussion** *n* ضربه مغزی

condemn v محکوم کردن	confiscation n مصادره
condemnation n محکومیت	conflict n تضاد
condensation n تراکم	conflict v مبارزه کردن
condense v ذخیره کردن	conflicting adj متضاد
condescend v فروتنی کردن	conform v همنوایی کردن
condiment n چاشنی	confound v پریشان کردن
condition n شرط	confront v روبرو شدن
conditional adj جمله شرطی	confrontation n مواجهه
conditioner n نرم کننده	confuse v گیج کردن
condo n مالکیت مشترک	confusing adj گیج کننده
condolences n تسلیت	confusion n آشفتگی
condone v چشم پوشی کردن	congenial adj مطلوب
conducive adj موجب	congested adj شلوغ
conduct n رفتار	congestion n تراکم
conduct v هدایت کردن	congratulate v تبریک گفتن
conductor n رسانا	congratulations n تبریك
cone n مخروط	congregate v جمع شدن
confer v؛ مشورت کردن	congress n کنگره
conference n جلسه	conjecture n تخمین
confess v اعتراف کردن	conjugal adj زناشویی
confession n اعتراف	conjugate v صرف کردن
confessional n اعتراف گاه	conjunction n تلفیق
confidant n محرم	conjure up v احضار کردن
confide v اطمینان کردن	connect v وصل کردن
confidence n اعتماد	connection n اتصال
confident adj مطمئن	connive v چشم پوشی کردن
confidential adj محرمانه	connote v دلالت ضمنی کردن
confine v محدود کردن	conquer v فتح کردن
confinement n زندان	conqueror n فاتح
confirm v تایید کردن	conquest n فتح
confirmation n تایید	conscience n وجدان
confiscate v توقیف کردن	conscious adj هوشیار

C

تقدیس کردن v **consecrate**	یبوست دادن v **constipate**
تقدیس n **consecration**	یبس adj **constipated**
متوالی adj **consecutive**	یبوست n **constipation**
توافق n **consensus**	تشکیل دادن v **constitute**
رضایت دادن v **consent**	قانون اساسی n **constitution**
رضایت n **consent**	تحمیل کردن v **constrain**
نتیجه n **consequence**	الزام؛ محدودیت n **constraint**
نتیجه adj **consequent**	ساختن v **construct**
حفاظت n **conservation**	ساختن n **construction**
محافظه کار adj **conservative**	سازنده adj **constructive**
نگهداری کردن v **conserve**	کنسول n **consul**
حفظ n **conserve**	کنسولگری n **consulate**
رسیدگی کردن v **consider**	همفکری کردن v **consult**
قابل توجه adj **considerable**	مشورت n **consultation**
باملاحظه adj **considerate**	مصرف کردن v **consume**
توجه n **consideration**	مصرف کننده n **consumer**
محموله n **consignment**	مصرف n **consumption**
شامل بودن v **consist**	تماس گرفتن v **contact**
سازگاری n **consistency**	تماس n **contact**
سازگار؛ استوار adj **consistent**	واگیردار adj **contagious**
دلداری n **consolation**	دارا بودن v **contain**
دلداری دادن v **console**	ظرف n **container**
محکم کردن v **consolidate**	آلوده کردن v **contaminate**
صامت n **consonant**	آلودگی n **contamination**
شناخته شده adj **conspicuous**	تفکر کردن v **contemplate**
توطئه n **conspiracy**	هم عصر adj **contemporary**
توطئه گر n **conspirator**	تحقیر n **contempt**
توطئه چیدن v **conspire**	ستیزه کردن v **contend**
پایداری n **constancy**	حریف n **contender**
ثابت adj **constant**	محتوا adj **content**
صورت فلکی n **constellation**	راضی کردن v **content**
بهت n **consternation**	ستیزه جو adj **contentious**

C

contents n محتویات	**convenience** n سهولت
contest n منازعه؛ مسابقه	**convenient** adj مناسب
contestant n شرکت کننده	**convent** n صومعه
context n بافت	**convention** n مجمع
continent n قاره	**conventional** adj مرسوم
continental adj قاره ای	**converge** v همگرا بودن
contingency n احتمال	**conversation** n گفتگو
contingent adj اتفاق	**converse** v صحبت کردن
continuation n ادامه	**conversely** adv بر عکس
continue v ادامه دادن	**conversion** n تبدیل
continuity n تداوم	**convert** v وارونه کردن
continuous adj پیوسته	**convert** n تبدیل
contour n طرح	**convey** v رساندن
contraband n قاچاق	**convict** v محکوم کردن
contract v پیمان بستن	**conviction** n محکومیت
contract n قرارداد	**convince** v متقاعد کردن
contraction n انقباض	**convincing** adj قانع کننده
contradict v رد کردن	**convoluted** adj پرچین وشکنج
contradiction n تناقض	**convoy** n اسکورت
contrary adj مقابل	**convulse** v تکان دادن
contrast v برابر کردن	**convulsion** n تشنج
contrast n تضاد	**cook** v پختن
contribute v اعانه دادن	**cook** n بپزید
contribution n کمک؛ همکاری	**cookie** n شیرینی
contributor n کمک کننده	**cooking** n پختن
contrition n پشیمانی	**cool** adj خنك؛ باحال
control n کنترل	**cool** v خنک کردن
control v کنترل کردن	**cool down** v آرام شدن
controversial adj بحث انگیز	**cooling** adj خنك کننده
controversy n جدال	**coolness** n خنکی
convalescent adj بهگرا	**cooperate** v همیاری کردن
convene v گرد آمدن	**cooperation** n همکاری

C

cooperative *adj* تعاونی

coordinate *v* هماهنگ کردن

coordination *n* هماهنگی

coordinator *n* هم آهنگ کننده

cop *n* تو هچل بیافتید

cope *v* حریف شدن

copier *n* کپی کننده

copper *n* مس

copy *v* کپی کردن

copy *n* رونوشت

copyright *n* حق تالیف

cord *n* ریسمان؛ کابل

cordial *adj* شربت

cordless *adj* بی ریسمان

cordon *n* صف پلیس

cordon off *v* بریدن

core *n* هسته

cork *n* چوب پنبه

corn *n* ذرت

corner *n* گوشه

cornerstone *n* اساس

cornet *n* کورنت

corollary *n* نتیجه

coronary *adj* سکته قلبی

coronation *n* تاجگذاری

corporal *adj* سرجوخه

corporal *n* سرجوخه

corporation *n* شرکت

corpse *n* جسد

corpulent *adj* چاق

corpuscle *n* گلبول

correct *v* تصحیح کردن

correct *adj* صحیح

correction *n* تصحیح

correspond *v* برابر بودن

correspondent *n* خبرنگار

corresponding *adj* قرینه

corridor *n* راهرو

corroborate *v* تائید کردن

corrode *v* زنگ زدن

corrupt *v* فاسد کردن

corrupt *adj* فاسد؛ خراب

corruption *n* فساد

cosmetic *n* ظاهری

cosmic *adj* کیهانی

cosmonaut *n* فضانورد

cost *iv* قیمت بدار

cost *n* قیمت

costly *adj* گران

costume *n* طرزلباس

cottage *n* کلبه

cotton *n* پنبه

couch *n* تخت

cough *n* سرفه

cough *v* سرفه کردن

council *n* شورا

counsel *v* توصیه کردن

counsel *n* مشورت؛ مجمع

counselor *n* مشاور

count *v* شمردن

count *n* شمار؛ حساب

countenance *n* سیما

counter *n* پیشخوان

counter *v* مقابله کردن

counteract v بی اثر کردن	cow n گاو
counterfeit v جعل کردن	coward n آدم ترسو
counterfeit adj جعلی	cowardice n بزدلی
counterpart n همتا	cowardly adv ترسو
countess n کنتس	cowboy n کابوی
countless adj بی شمار	cozy adj دنج؛ راحت
country n کشور	crab n غریزنید
countryman n روستایی	crack n ماهر
countryside n نواحی روستایی	crack v ترک خوردن
county n استان	cradle n گهواره
coup n ضربه کاری	craft n صنعت
couple n دو تا؛ جفت	craftsman n صنعتگر
coupon n کوپن	cram v پر کردن
courage n جرات	cramp n چنگه
courageous adj شجاع	cramped adj تنگ
courier n پیک	crane n درنا
course n دوره؛ خط سیر	crank n چرخاننده
court n دادگاه	cranky adj عجیب و غریب
court v اظهار عشق کردن	crap n گندم سیاه
courteous adj مودب	crash n تصادف
courtesy n ادب	crash v خرد کردن
courthouse n دادگاه	crass adj کامل
courtship n عشقبازی	crave v آرزو کردن
courtyard n حیاط	craving n اشتیاق
cousin n عموزاده	crawl v خزیدن
cove n خلیج کوچك	crayon n مدادشمعی
covenant n قرارداد	craziness n دیوانگی
cover n پوشش؛ روکش	crazy adj شوریده
cover v پوشاندن	creak v شکایت کردن
coverage n پوشش	creak n غژغژ
covert adj پناهگاه	cream n کرم
coverup n پنهانکاری	creamy adj خامه ای

crease n چروك؛ چین	criticize v نقد ادبی کردن
crease v چروک شدن	critique n نقد
create v خلق شدن	crockery n ظروف سفالی
creation n آفرینش	crocodile n تمساح
creative adj خلاق	crony n دوست صمیمی
creativity n آفرینندگی	crook n کج
creator n آفریننده	crooked adj کج؛ نادرست
creature n موجود	crop n محصول
credibility n قابلیت قبول	cross n متقاطع
credible adj باورکردنی	cross adj متقاطع
credit n اعتبار	cross v روبرو شدن
creditor n طلبکار	cross out v خط زدن
creed n کیش	crossing n مسافرت
creek n خور	crossroads n تقاطع
creep v خزیدن	crosswalk n گذرگاه عابرپیاده
creepy adj ترس آور	crouch v قوز کردن
cremate v خاکستر کردن	crow n بانگ خروس
crest n کاکل	crow v بانگ زدن
crevice n شکاف	crowbar n دیلم
crew n خدمه	crowd n ازدحام
crib n سرقت ادبی	crowd v ازدحام کردن
cricket n کریکت؛ جیرجیرک	crowded adj پرجمعیت
crime n جرم	crown n تاج
criminal adj جنایی	crown v تاج گذاری کردن
cripple adj ناقص	crowning n بهترین
cripple v لنگ کردن	crucial adj بسیار مهم
crisis n بحران	crucifix n صلیب
crisp adj ترد	crucifixion n تصلیب
crispy adj برشته	crucify v به دار آویختن
criterion n ملاک	crude adj خام؛ زمخت
critical adj حساس	cruel adj بی رحم
criticism n نقد	cruelty n بیرحمی

cruise v گشت زدن	cumbersome adj دست وپاگیر
crumb n خرده نان	cunning adj مکر
crumble v خرد شدن	cup n فنجان
crunchy adj ترد	cupboard n قفسه
crusade n جهاد	curable adj قابل علاج
crusader n مجاهد	curator n متصدی
crush v مچاله کردن	curb v بازداشت کردن
crushing adj خردکننده	curb n زنجیر
crust n رویه؛ ادم جسور	curdle v بستن
crusty adj برشته	cure v بهبودی دادن
crutch n چوب زیربغل	cure n درمان
cry n گریه	curfew n منع رفت و آمد
cry v فریاد زدن	curiosity n کنجکاوی
cry out v فریاد کشیدن	curious adj کنجکاو
crying n گریان	curl v حلقه کردن
crystal n بلور	curl n پیچ
cub n توله	curly adj حلقه حلقه
cube n مکعب	currency n ارز
cubic adj مکعب	current adj جاری
cubicle n رخت کن	currently adv هم اکنون
cucumber n خیار	curse v نفرین کردن
cuddle v درآغوش گرفتن	curtail v کوتاه کردن
cuff n مچ؛ سرآستین	curtain n پرده
cuisine n آشپزی	curve n پیچ
culminate v به اوج رسیدن	curve v خمیدن
culpability n تقصیر	cushion n کوسن
culprit n مقصر	cushion v مستهلک شدن
cult n فرقه	cuss v فحش دادن
cultivate v کشت کردن	custard n فرنی
cultivation n کشت	custodian n سرپرست
cultural adj فرهنگی	custody n سرپرستی
culture n فرهنگ	custom n رسم

C
D

customary adj مرسوم
customer n مشتری
custom-made adj عرفی
customs n آداب ورسوم
cut n برید
cut iv ببر
cut back v تقلیل دادن
cut down v خرد کردن
cut off v بریدن
cut out v قطع کردن
cute adj بانمك
cutlery n قاشق وچنگال
cutter n برش کار
cyanide n سیانور
cycle n چرخه
cyclist n دوچرخه سوار
cyclone n گردباد
cylinder n استوانه
cynic adj بدبین
cynicism n بدبینی
cypress n سرو
cyst n کیست
czar n تزار

dad n بابا
dagger n خنجر
daily adv روزانه
daisy n مینا
dam n سد
damage n آسیب
damage v زیان زدن
damaging adj آسیب رساننده
damn v لعنت کردن
damnation n لعنت
damp adj نم دار
dampen v مرطوب کردن
dance n رقص
dance v رقصیدن
dancing n رقص
dandruff n شوره سر
danger n خطر
dangerous adj خطرناك
dangle v آویزان کردن
dare v یارا بودن
dare n جرات
daring adj جسور
dark adj تاریك
darken v تاریک کردن
darkness n تاریکی
darling adj محبوب
darn v رفو کردن
dart n دارت
dash v بسرعت رفتن

D

پرجنب وجوش *adj* **dashing**	مدیرداخلی *n* **dean**
داده ها *n* **data**	عزیز *adj* **dear**
پایگاه داده *n* **database**	بسیار *adv* **dearly**
تاریخ؛ خرما *n* **date**	مرگ *n* **death**
تاریخ گذاشتن *v* **date**	قتلگاه *n* **death trap**
دختر *n* **daughter**	بستر مرگ *n* **deathbed**
عروس *n* **daughter-in-law**	پست کردن *v* **debase**
رام کردن *v* **daunt**	قابل بحث *adj* **debatable**
دلهره آور *adj* **daunting**	مناظره کردن *v* **debate**
سپیده بزنید *n* **dawn**	بحث *n* **debate**
روز *n* **day**	بدهی *n* **debit**
خیال باطل کردن *v* **daydream**	پرسش کردن *v* **debrief**
گیج کردن *v* **daze**	بازمانده ها *n* **debris**
گیج *adj* **dazed**	بدهی *n* **debt**
خیره کردن *v* **dazzle**	بدهکار *n* **debtor**
خیره کننده *adj* **dazzling**	کم ارزش کردن *v* **debunk**
لوکس *adj* **de luxe**	اولین اجرا *n* **debut**
خادم کلیسا *n* **deacon**	دهه *n* **decade**
مرده *adj* **dead**	سقوط *n* **decadence**
بن بست *n* **dead end**	گردن زدن *v* **decapitate**
خرف کردن *v* **deaden**	از بین رفتن *v* **decay**
موعد *n* **deadline**	خراب؛ فاسد *n* **decay**
بن بست *adj* **deadlock**	مرحوم *adj* **deceased**
مهلك *adj* **deadly**	فریبکاری *n* **deceit**
کر *adj* **deaf**	فریبکار *adj* **deceitful**
کر کردن *v* **deafen**	فریب دادن *v* **deceive**
گوش خراش *adj* **deafening**	دسامبر *n* **December**
کری *n* **deafness**	شایستگی *n* **decency**
از عهده بربیا *iv* **deal**	شایسته *adj* **decent**
معامله *n* **deal**	فریبکاری *n* **deception**
فروشنده *n* **dealer**	فریبنده *adj* **deceptive**
معامله *n* **dealings**	تصمیم گرفتن *v* **decide**

D

deciding *adj* تصمیم گیرنده	deface *v* بدشکل کردن
decimal *adj* اعشاری	defame *v* بدنام کردن
decipher *v* کشف کردن	defeat *v* شکست دادن
decision *n* تصمیم	defeat *n* شکست
decisive *adj* سرنوشت ساز	defect *n* عیب
deck *n* عرشه	defect *v* ترک کردن
declaration *n* اعلام	defection *n* ترک
declare *v* اظهار داشتن	defective *adj* ناقص
declension *n* صرف	defend *v* حمایت کردن
decline *v* رد کردن	defendant *n* متهم
decline *n* کاهش	defender *n* مدافع
decompose *v* تجزیه شدن	defense *n* دفاع
décor *n* دکور	defenseless *adj* بی دفاع
decorate *v* آذین کردن	defer *v* عقب انداختن
decorative *adj* تزیینی	defiance *n* نافرمانی
decorum *n* ادب	defiant *adj* نافرمان
decrease *v* نزول کردن	deficiency *n* کمبود
decrease *n* کاهش	deficient *adj* کم
decree *n* حکم	deficit *n* کسری
decree *v* حکم کردن	defile *v* آلوده کردن
decrepit *adj* فرتوت	define *v* مشخص کردن
dedicate *v* اهدا کردن	definite *adj* صریح
dedication *n* اهدا	definition *n* تعریف
deduce *v* استنباط کردن	definitive *adj* قطعی
deduct *v* کم کردن	deform *v* زشت کردن
deductible *adj* کسرپذیر	defray *v* پرداختن
deduction *n* کاهش	defrost *v* آب کردن یخ
deed *n* سند مالکیت	deft *adj* ماهر
deem *v* پنداشتن	defuse *v* بی اثر کردن
deep *adj* عمیق	defy *v* به مبارزه طلبیدن
deepen *v* گود کردن	degenerate *v* فاسد شدن
deer *n* گوزن	degenerate *adj* تنزل کنید

degeneration *n* فساد	demanding *adj* پرزحمت
degradation *n* کاهش	demean *v* پست کردن
degrade *v* تنزل کردن	demeaning *adj* تحقیرآمیز
degrading *adj* تحقیرآمیز	demeanor *n* رفتار
degree *n* درجه	demented *adj* دیوانه
dehydrate *v* بی آب کردن	demise *n* فوت
deign *v* تمکین کردن	democracy *n* دموکراسی
deity *n* الوهیت	democratic *adj* دموکراتیك
dejected *adj* غمگین	demolish *v* ویران کردن
delay *v* تاخیر کردن	demolition *n* تخریب
delay *n* تاخیر	demon *n* ابلیس
delegate *v* وکالت دادن	demonstrate *v* اثبات کردن
delegate *n* نمایندگی	demonstrative *adj* برون گرا
delegation *n* نمایندگی	demote *v* تنزل رتبه دادن
delete *v* حذف کردن	den *n* غار
deliberate *v* تعمد کردن	denial *n* انکار
deliberate *adj* عمدی	denigrate *v* لکه دار کردن
delicacy *n* ظرافت	Denmak *n* دانمارک
delicate *adj* مطبوع	denominator *n* مخرج کسر
delicious *adj* خوشمزه	denote *v* مشخص کردن
delight *n* لذت	denounce *v* متهم کردن
delight *v* دلشاد کردن	dense *adj* غلیظ؛ چگال
delightful *adj* خوشایند	density *n* فشردگی
delinquency *n* بزهکاری	dent *v* دندانه کردن
delinquent *adj* بزهکارانه	dent *n* گودی
deliver *v* آزاد کردن	dental *adj* صامت دندانی
delivery *n* تحویل؛ پرتاب توپ	dentist *n* دندانپزشك
delude *v* فریب دادن	dentures *n* دندان مصنوعی
deluge *n* سیل	deny *v* انکار کردن
delusion *n* وهم	deodorant *n* ضدبو
demand *v* تقاضا کردن	depart *v* حرکت کردن
demand *n* تقاضا	department *n* قسمت

D

D

departure n عزیمت	**derive** v نتیجه گرفتن
depend v وابسته بودن	**derogatory** adj توهین آمیز
dependable adj مطمئن	**descend** v پایین آمدن
dependence n وابستگی	**descendant** n زاده
dependent adj وابسته	**descent** n فرود؛ توارث؛ نژاد
depict v نمایش دادن	**describe** v شرح دادن
deplete v تهی کردن	**description** n توصیف
deplorable adj تاسف آور	**descriptive** adj توصیفی
deplore v دلسوزی کردن	**desecrate** v بی حرمت کردن
deploy v گسترش یافتن	**desegregate** v لغو کردن
deployment n استقرار	**desert** n بیابان
deport v تبعید کردن	**desert** v ترک کردن؛ گریختن
deportation n تبعید	**deserted** adj خلوت
depose v معزول کردن	**deserter** n فراری
deposit n بگذارید	**deserve** v سزاوار بودن
depot n انبار؛ بارانداز	**deserving** adj شایسته
deprave adj منحرف	**design** n طراحی؛ طرح
depravity n انحطاط	**designate** v نامزد کردن
depreciate v کم بها کردن	**desirable** adj مطلوب
depreciation n کاهش	**desire** n تمایل
depress v دلتنگ کردن	**desire** v میل داشتن
depressing adj غم انگیز	**desist** v دست کشیدن
depression n افسردگی	**desk** n میز؛ میز تحریر
deprivation n محرومیت	**desolate** adj ویران
deprive v بی بهره کردن	**desolation** n ویرانی
deprived adj محروم	**despair** n ناامید
depth n عمق	**desperate** adj مستاصل
derail v از خط خارج کردن	**despicable** adj نفرت انگیز
deranged adj آشفته	**despise** v خوار شمردن
derelict adj متروک	**despite** c با وجود اینکه
deride v تمسخر کردن	**despondent** adj نومید
derivative adj مشتق	**despot** n فرمانروای مستبد

despotic *adj* مستبد	**devaluation** *n* کاهش نرخ
dessert *n* دسر	**devalue** *v* تنزل قیمت دادن
destination *n* مقصد	**devastate** *v* ویران کردن
destiny *n* تقدیر	**devastating** *adj* ویران شده
destitute *adj* فقیر	**devastation** *n* ویرانی
destroy *v* تخریب کردن	**develop** *v* توسعه دادن
destroyer *n* ناوشکن	**development** *n* توسعه
destruction *n* خرابی	**deviation** *n* انحراف
destructive *adj* مخرب	**device** *n* وسیله
detach *v* تفکیک کردن	**devil** *n* شیطان
detachable *adj* جداشدنی	**devious** *adj* پرپیچ وخم
detail *n* جزئی	**devise** *v* تدبیر کردن
detain *v* حبس کردن	**devoid** *adj* عاری از
detect *v* پیدا کردن	**devote** *v* وقف کردن
detective *n* کارآگاه	**devotion** *n* صرف
detector *n* حس کننده	**devour** *v* بلعیدن
detention *n* بازداشت	**devout** *adj* مومن
deter *v* بازداشتن	**dew** *n* شبنم
detergent *n* ماده پاک کننده	**diabetes** *n* بیماری قند
deteriorate *v* وخیم شدن	**diabolical** *adj* شیطانی
deterioration *n* وخامت	**diagnose** *v* تشخیص دادن
determination *n* تعیین	**diagnosis** *n* تشخیص
determine *v* تصمیم گرفتن	**diagonal** *adj* قطری
deterrence *n* بازداشت	**diagram** *n* نمودار
detest *v* تنفر داشتن از	**dial** *n* شماره گیری
detestable *adj* نفرت انگیز	**dial** *v* شماره گرفتن
detonate *v* منفجر شدن	**dial tone** *n* صدای تلفن
detonation *n* انفجار	**dialect** *n* لهجه
detonator *n* چاشنی	**dialogue** *n* گفتگو
detour *n* راه فرعی	**diameter** *n* قطر
detriment *n* ضرر	**diamond** *n* الماس
detrimental *adj* زیان بخش	**diaper** *n* کهنه بچه

diarrhea n اسهال	**dim** v تیره کردن
diary n دفتر یادداشت	**dimension** n بعد
dice n تاس	**diminish** v کم شدن
dictate v دستور دادن	**dine** v شام خوردن
dictator n دیکتاتور	**diner** n واگن رستوران
dictatorial adj استبدادی	**dining room** n اتاق ناهارخوری
dictatorship n استبداد	**dinner** n شام
dictionary n واژه نامه	**dinosaur** n داینا‌سور
die v فوت کردن	**diocese** n قلمرو اسقف
die out v محو شدن	**diphthong** n مصوت مرکب
diet n رژیم	**diploma** n دیپلم
differ v فرق داشتن	**diplomacy** n دیپلماسی
difference n تفاوت	**diplomat** n نماینده سیاسی
different adj متفاوت	**diplomatic** adj دیپلماتیک
difficult adj مشکل	**dire** adj وحشتناک
difficulty n مشکل	**direct** adj مستقیم
diffuse v پخش شدن	**direct** v دستور دادن
dig iv بِکَن	**direction** n جهت
digest v هضم کردن	**director** n مدیر
digestion n هضم	**directory** n دفتر راهنما
digestive adj گوارشی	**dirt** n کثافت
digit n رقم	**dirty** adj کثیف
dignify v تکریم کردن	**disability** n معلولیت
dignitary n مقام عالی رتبه	**disabled** adj معلول
dignity n ارزش	**disadvantage** n عیب
digress v منحرف شدن	**disagree** v موافق نبودن
dilapidated adj ویران	**disagreeable** adj بداخم
dilemma n دوراهی	**disagreement** n اختلاف
diligence n جدیت	**disappear** v ناپدید شدن
diligent adj سخت کوش	**disappearance** n ناپدیدشدگی
dilute v رقیق کردن	**disappoint** v مایوس کردن
dim adj تیره	**disappointing** adj یاس آور

disappointment *n* دلسردی	discreet *adj* محتاط
disapproval *n* عدم رضایت	discrepancy *n* تفاوت
disapprove *v* ناپسند شمردن	discretion *n* احتیاط
disarm *v* خلع سلاح کردن	discrimination *n* تبعیض
disarmament *n* خلع سلاح	discuss *v* بحث کردن
disaster *n* فاجعه	discussion *n* بحث
disastrous *adj* فاجعه آمیز	disdain *n* تحقیر
disband *v* بر هم زدن	disease *n* بیماری
disbelief *n* ناباوری	disembark *v* پیاده کردن
disburse *v* پرداختن	disenchanted *adj* سرخورده
discard *v* دور انداختن	disentangle *v* رها کردن
discern *v* تشخیص دادن	disfigure *v* بد شکل کردن
discharge *v* خالی کردن	disgrace *n* بی آبرو
discharge *n* دشارژ؛ تأدیه	disgrace *v* خفت آوردن بر
disciple *n* مرید	disgraceful *adj* زشت
discipline *n* انظباط	disgruntled *adj* ناراضی
disclaim *v* رد کردن	disguise *v* تغییر قیافه دادن
disclose *v* فاش کردن	disguise *n* مبدل
discomfort *n* ناراحتی	disgust *n* متنفر
disconnect *v* منفصل کردن	disgusting *adj* نفرت انگیز
discontent *adj* ناراضایی	dish *n* ظرف
discontinue *v* ادامه ندادن	dishearten *v* دلسرد کردن
discord *n* اختلاف	dishonest *adj* نادرست
discordant *adj* متضاد	dishonesty *n* نادرستی
discount *n* تخفیف	dishonor *n* ننگ
discount *v* تخفیف دادن	dishonorable *adj* پست؛ بی آبرو
discourage *v* دلسرد کردن	disillusion *n* سرخوردگی
discouragement *n* دلسردی	disinfect *v* ضد عفونی کردن
discouraging *adj* دلسردکننده	disinfectant *n* ماده ضدعفونی
discourtesy *n* بی ادبی	disinherit *v* عاق کردن
discover *v* پی بردن	disintegrate *v* متلاشی شدن
discovery *n* کشف	disintegration *n* تجزیه

D

D

disinterested *adj* بی طرف	**displease** *v* خوش آیند نبودن
disk *n* دیسك	**displeasing** *adj* ناخوشایند
dislike *v* دوست نداشتن	**displeasure** *n* رنجش
dislike *n* بیزاری	**disposable** *adj* یك بار مصرف
dislocate *v* جابجا كردن	**disposal** *n* دسترس
dislodge *v* راندن	**dispose** *v* مرتب كردن
disloyal *adj* خائن	**disprove** *v* رد كردن
disloyalty *n* خیانت	**dispute** *n* بحث
dismal *adj* غمگین	**dispute** *v* جدال كردن
dismantle *v* بی مصرف كردن	**disregard** *v* نادیده گرفتن
dismay *n* بترسانید	**disrepair** *n* خراب
dismay *v* ترسانیدن	**disrespect** *n* بی احترامی
dismiss *v* مرخص كردن	**disrespectful** *adj* بی ادب
dismissal *n* اخراج	**disrupt** *v* منقطع كردن
dismount *v* پیاده كردن	**disruption** *n* اختلال
disobedience *n* نافرمانی	**dissatisfied** *adj* ناراضی
disobedient *adj* سركش	**disseminate** *v* منتشر كردن
disobey *v* نافرمانی كردن	**dissent** *v* جداشدن
disorder *n* بی نظمی	**dissident** *adj* مخالف
disorganized *adj* آشفته	**dissimilar** *adj* متفاوت
disoriented *adj* گیج شده	**dissipate** *v* پراكندگی كردن
disown *v* عاق كردن	**dissolute** *adj* هرزه؛ بد اخلاق
disparity *n* تفاوت	**dissolution** *n* تجزیه
dispatch *v* ارسال كردن	**dissolve** *v* آب كردن
dispel *v* برطرف كردن	**dissonant** *adj* ناموزون
dispensation *n* پخش	**dissuade** *v* منصرف كردن
dispense *v* توزیع كردن	**distance** *n* مسافت
dispersal *n* پخش	**distant** *adj* فاصله دار
disperse *v* پراكنده شدن	**distaste** *n* بی میلی
displace *v* جابجا كردن	**distasteful** *adj* بابی میلی
display *n* صفحه نمایش	**distill** *v* تقطیر شدن
display *v* نمایش دادن	**distinct** *adj* واضح

distinction *n* تمایز	**diving** *n* غواصی
distinctive *adj* متمایز	**divinity** *n* الوهیت
distinguish *v* تشخیص دادن	**divisible** *adj* قابل قسمت
distort *v* کج کردن	**division** *n* بخش
distortion *n* تغییر شکل	**divorce** *n* طلاق
distraction *n* حواس پرتی	**divorce** *v* طلاق دادن
distraught *adj* پریشان	**divorcee** *n* زن بیوه
distress *n* اندوه؛ تنگدستی	**divulge** *v* فاش کردن
distress *v* مضطرب کردن	**dizziness** *n* سرگیجه
distressing *adj* غم انگیز	**dizzy** *adj* گیج
distribute *v* توزیع کردن	**do** *iv* انجام بده
distribution *n* توزیع	**docile** *adj* سر به راه
district *n* منطقه	**docility** *n* سر به راهی
distrust *n* بدگمانی	**dock** *n* جایگاه
distrust *v* عتماد نداشتن	**dock** *v* بریدن
distrustful *adj* بدگمان	**doctor** *n* دکتر
disturb *v* مختل کردن	**doctrine** *n* نظریه
disturbance *n* شورش	**document** *n* مدرک
disturbing *adj* نگران کننده	**documentary** *n* مستند
disunity *n* عدم اتحاد	**dodge** *v* جاخالی دادن
disuse *n* عدم استعمال	**dog** *n* سگ
ditch *n* چاله	**dogmatic** *adj* جزمی
dive *v* شیرجه رفتن	**dole out** *v* قسمت کردن
diver *n* غواص	**doll** *n* عروسک
diverse *adj* گوناگون	**dollar** *n* دلار
diversify *v* متنوع کردن	**dolphin** *n* دلفین
diversion *n* تغییر مسیر	**dome** *n* گنبد
diversity *n* گوناگون	**domestic** *adj* بومی؛ خانگی
divert *v* منحرف کردن	**domesticate** *v* اهلی کردن
divide *v* تقسیم کردن	**dominate** *v* تسلط داشتن
dividend *n* سود سهام	**domination** *n* سلطه
divine *adj* خدایی	**domineering** *adj* سلطه جو

D

dominion n حاکمیت

donate v بخشیدن

donation n اهدا

donkey n الاغ

donor n اهداکننده

doom n حکم مجازات

doomed adj محکوم

door n درب

doorbell n زنگ در

doorstep n پله در

doorway n در

dope n دوپینگ

dope v پیش بینی کردن

dormitory n خوابگاه

dosage n مقدار خوراک

dossier n پرونده

dot n نقطه

double adj دوبرابرشوید

double v دوبرابر کردن

double-cross v خیانت کردن

doubt n شک

doubt v تردید کردن

doubtful adj مردد

dough n خمیر

dove n کبوتر

down adv پائین

down payment n پیش قسط

downcast adj افسرده

downfall n سقوط

downhill adv سرازیری

downpour n رگبار

downsize v اندازه را کم کردن

downstairs adv طبقه پایین

down-to-earth adj عملی

downtown n مرکز شهر

downtrodden adj ستمدیده

downturn n رکود

dowry n جهیزیه

doze n دوز

doze v چرت زدن

dozen n دوجین

draft n پیش نویس

draft v پیش نویس کردن

draftsman n تنظیم کننده

drag v کشیده شدن

dragon n اژدها

drain v خالی کردن آب

drainage n زهکشی

dramatic adj تاثرانگیز

drape n بیاویزید

drastic adj بنیادی

draw n نقاشی

draw iv بیرون بکش

drawback n برگشت

drawer n نقاش

drawing n ترسیم

dread v ترسیدن

dreaded adj وحشتناک

dreadful adj وحشتناک

dream iv خواب ببین

dream n رویایی

dress n لباسی

dress v لباس پوشیدن

dresser n میز آرایش

dressing n لباس؛ مرهم	**drunkenness** n باده گساری
dried adj خشك	**dry** v خشك کردن
drift v جمع شدن	**dry** adj خشك
drifter n جسم شناور	**dual** adj دوگانه
drill v سوراخ کردن	**dubious** adj مشکوك
drill n مته؛ مشق نظامی	**duchess** n دوشس
drink iv بنوش	**duck** n اردک
drink n بنوشید	**duck** v زیر آب رفتن
drinkable adj قابل شرب	**duct** n مجرا
drinker n مشروب خور	**due** adj حق
drip v چکیدن	**duel** n دوئل
drip n چکه	**dues** n حق عضویت
drive n دنده، گرداننده	**duke** n دوك
drive iv بران	**dull** adj کدر
drive at v قصد کردن	**duly** adv به موقع
driver n راننده	**dumb** adj لال؛ بی معنی
driveway n جاده	**dummy** n ساختگی
drizzle v ریز باریدن	**dummy** adj ساختگی
drizzle n نم نم باران	**dump** v انباشتن
drop n قطره	**dump** n رونوشت؛ انباشت
drop v انداختن	**dung** n تپاله
drop in v انداختن در	**dungeon** n سیاه چال
drop off v به خواب رفتن	**dupe** v گول زدن
drop out v حذف کردن	**duplicate** v دو نسخه کردن
drought n خشکسالی	**duplication** n رونوشت
drown v غرق کردن	**durable** adj بادوام
drowsy adj خواب آور	**duration** n مدت
drug n دارو	**during** pre در طی
drug v دوا زدن	**dusk** n غروب
drugstore n داروخانه	**dust** n گرد و خاك
drum n طبل؛ غلطک	**dusty** adj پرازگردوخاك
drunk adj آدم مست	**Dutch** adj هلندی

duty *n* وظیفه
dwarf *n* کوتوله
dwell *iv* سکنی بگزین
dwelling *n* محل اقامت
dye *v* رنگ کردن
dye *n* رنگ
dying *adj* درحال مرگ
dynamic *adj* پویا
dynamite *n* دینامیت
dynasty *n* سلسله

E

each *adj* هر
each other *adj* یکدیگر
eager *adj* مشتاق
eagerness *n* اشتیاق
eagle *n* عقاب
ear *n* گوش؛ گوشواره
earache *n* گوش درد
eardrum *n* پرده گوش
early *adv* فوری
earmark *v* نشان کردن
earn *v* تحصیل کردن
earnestly *adv* به طور جدی
earnings *n* درآمد
earphones *n* گوشی ها
earring *n* گوشواره
earth *n* زمین

earthquake *n* زمین لرزه
earwax *n* چرک گوش
ease *v* راحت کردن
ease *n* آسانی
easily *adv* به آسانی
east *n* شرق
eastbound *adj* عازم شرق
Easter *n* عید پاك
eastern *adj* شرقی
easterner *n* شرقی تر
eastward *adv* به سوی شرق
easy *adj* آسان
eat *iv* بخور
eat away *v* اذیت کردن
ebb *v* فروکش کردن
eccentric *adj* آدم غیر عادی
echo *n* طنین
eclipse *n* گرفتگی
ecology *n* بوم شناسی
economical *adj* اقتصادی
economy *n* اقتصاد
ecstasy *n* وجد
ecstatic *adj* وجد
edge *n* حاشیه بدهید
edgy *adj* عصبی
edible *adj* خوراکی
edifice *n* بنا
edit *v* تصحیح کردن
edition *n* چاپ
educate *v* تربیت کردن
educational *adj* آموزشی
eerie *adj* خوف انگیز

effect *n* اثر	elegance *n* وقار
effective *adj* موثر	elegant *adj* برازنده
effectiveness *n* تاثیر	element *n* عنصر
efficiency *n* کارآئی	elementary *adj* مقدماتی
efficient *adj* کارآمد	elephant *n* فیل
effigy *n* نقش برجسته	elevate *v* بلند کردن
effort *n* سعی	elevation *n* ارتقا
effusive *adj* احساساتی	elevator *n* آسانسور
egg *n* تخم	eleven *adj* یازده
egoism *n* خودخواهی	eleventh *adj* یازدهم
egoist *n* خودخواه	eligible *adj* قابل قبول
eight *adj* هشت	eliminate *v* رفع کردن
eighteen *adj* هیجده	elm *n* درخت نارون
eighth *adj* هشتم	eloquence *n* فصاحت
eighty *adj* هشتاد	else *adv* آنگاه
either *adj* هم	elsewhere *adv* جای دیگری
either *adv* هم	elude *v* اجتناب کردن از
eject *v* بیرون کردن	elusive *adj* گریزپا
elapse *v* گذشتن	emaciated *adj* لاغر
elastic *adj* کش	emanate *v* ناشی شدن
elated *adj* شاد	emancipate *v* از قید رها کردن
elbow *n* آرنج	embalm *v* مومیایی کردن
elder *n* بزرگ	embark *v* سوار کردن
elderly *adj* مسن	embarrass *v* خجالت دادن
elect *v* انتخاب کردن	embassy *n* سفارت
election *n* انتخابات	embellish *v* آرایش کردن
electric *adj* الکتریکی	embers *n* بقایای آتش
electrician *n* برقکار	embezzle *v* دزدیدن
electricity *n* برق	embitter *v* ناگوار کردن
electrify *v* الکتریکی کردن	emblem *n* آرم
electrocute *v* با برق کشتن	embody *v* مجسم کردن
electronic *adj* الکترونیکی	emboss *v* پوشاندن

embrace v	در آغوش گرفتن
embrace n	آغوش
embroider v	گلدوزی کردن
embroidery n	گلدوزی
embroil v	به نزاع انداختن
embryo n	رویان
emerald n	زمرد
emerge v	پدیدار شدن
emergency n	وضع اضطراری
emigrant n	مهاجر
emigrate v	مهاجرت کردن
emission n	صدور
emit v	خارج کردن
emotion n	عاطفه
emotional adj	عاطفی
emperor n	امپراتور
emphasis n	تاکید
emphasize v	تایید کردن
empire n	امپراتوری
employ v	مشغول کردن
employee n	کارمند
employer n	کارفرما
employment n	اشتغال
empress n	ملکه
emptiness n	خلاء
empty adj	خالی
empty v	خالی کردن
enable v	قادر ساختن
enchant v	افسون کردن
enchanting adj	افسونگر
encircle v	احاطه کردن
enclave n	سرزمین محصور

enclose v	در میان گذاشتن
enclosure n	پیوست
encompass v	احاطه کردن
encounter v	روبرو شدن
encounter n	مواجه
encourage v	تشویق کردن
encyclopedia n	دانشنامه
end n	آخرین
end v	تمام کردن
end up v	پایان دادن
endanger v	به مخاطره انداختن
endeavor v	تلاش کردن
endeavor n	سعی
ending n	پایان
endless adj	بی پایان
endorse v	پشت نویس کرد
endorsement n	پشت نویسی
endure v	تحمل کردن
enemy n	دشمن
energetic adj	فعال
energy n	انرژی
enforce v	اجرا کردن
engage v	استخدام کردن
engaged adj	مشغول
engagement n	نامزدی؛ اشتغال
engine n	موتور
engineer n	مهندس
England n	انگلستان
English adj	انگلیسی
engrave v	قلم زدن
engraving n	حکاکی
engrossed adj	مجذوب

engulf v غرق کردن در	entreat v درخواست کردن
enhance v بالا بردن	entree n ورود
enjoy v لذت بردن	entrepreneur n کارآفرین
enjoyable adj لذت بخش	entrust v سپردن
enjoyment n لذت	entry n ورود
enlarge v بزرگ کردن	enumerate v شمردن
enlargement n توسعه	envelop v احاطه کردن
enlighten v تعلیم دادن	envelope n پاکت
enlist v نام نویسی کردن	envious adj حسود
enormous adj بزرگ	environment n محیط
enough adv به حدکافی	envisage v روبرو شدن
enrage v عصبانی کردن	envoy n فرستاده
enrich v غنی کردن	envy n حسادت
enroll v ثبت نام کردن	envy v حسد بردن
enrollment n ثبت نام	epidemic n بیماری همه گیر
ensure v متقاعد کردن	epilepsy n صرع
entail v شامل بودن	episode n رویداد
entangle v گرفتار کردن	epistle n مکتوب
enter v وارد شدن	epitomize v خلاصه کردن
enterprise n شرکت	epoch n دوره
entertain v پذیرایی کردن	equal adj یکسان
entertaining adj پذیرا	equality n برابری
entertainment n سرگرمی	equate v برابر کردن
enthrall v بغلامی درآوردن	equation n معادله
enthralling adj جذاب	equator n خط استوا
enthusiasm n اشتیاق	equilibrium n تعادل
entice v فریفتن	equip v آراستن
enticement n اغوا	equipment n تجهیزات
enticing adj وسوسه انگیز	equivalent adj برابر
entire adj تمام	era n عصر
entirely adv کاملاً	eradicate v از ریشه کندن
entrance n ورودی	erase v پاک کردن

E

eraser n مداد پاك كن	**Europe** n اروپا
erect v برپا كردن	**European** adj اروپایی
erect adj برپا	**evacuate** v خالی كردن
err v خطا كردن	**evade** v گریز زدن از
errand n دستور	**evaluate** v ارزیابی كردن
erroneous adj غلط	**evaporate** v تبخیر كردن
error n اشتباه	**evasion** n گریز
erupt v جوانه زدن	**evasive** adj طفره آمیز
eruption n فوران؛ جوش	**eve** n حوا
escalate v ترقی دادن	**even** adj حتی
escalator n پله برقی	**even if** c حتی اگر
escapade n ماجرا	**even more** c حتی بیشتر
escape v فرار كردن	**evening** n عصر
escort n محافظت	**event** n رویداد
esophagus n مری	**eventuality** n اتفاق
especially adv به خصوص	**eventually** adv سرانجام
espionage n جاسوسی	**ever** adv تابه حال
essay n مقاله	**everlasting** adj ابدی
essence n وجود	**every** adj هر
essential adj ضروری	**everybody** pro همه
establish v تاسیس كردن	**everyday** adj هر روز
estate n ملك	**everyone** pro هركس
esteem v لایق دانستن	**everything** pro هرچیز
estimate v تخمین زدن	**evict** v فیصله دادن
estimation n نظر	**evidence** n مدرك
estranged adj جدا شده	**evil** n شرارت
estuary n مصب	**evil** adj شرور
eternity n ابدیت وازلیت	**evoke** v احضار كردن
ethical adj اخلاقی	**evolution** n تكامل
ethics n اخلاق	**evolve** v باز كردن
etiquette n آداب معاشرت	**exact** adj دقیق
euphoria n سرخوشی	**exaggerate** v اغراق آمیز كردن

exalt v بلند کردن	**exemption** n معافیت
examination n آزمایش	**exercise** n تمرین؛ ورزش
examine v امتحان کردن	**exercise** v استعمال کردن
example n مثال؛	**exert** v اعمال کردن
exasperate v خشمگین کردن	**exertion** n تلاش؛ فشار
excavate v کاویدن	**exhaust** v تهی کردن
exceed v تجاوز کردن	**exhausting** adj خسته کننده
exceedingly adv فوق العاده	**exhaustion** n خستگی
excel v برتری داشتن بر	**exhibit** v نمایش دادن
excellence n ممتازی	**exhibition** n نمایشگاه
excellent adj عالی	**exhilarating** adj وجدآور
except pre بجز	**exhort** v نصحیت کردن
exception n استثناء	**exile** v تبعید کردن
exceptional adj استثنایی	**exile** n تبعیدی
excerpt n قطعه	**exist** v زیستن
excess n مازاد	**existence** n وجود
excessive adj بیش ازحد	**exit** n محل خروج
exchange v مبادله کردن	**exodus** n خروج جمعی
excite v برآشفتن	**exonerate** v تبرئه کردن
excitement n هیجان	**exorbitant** adj گزاف
exciting adj هیجان انگیز	**exorcist** n جن گیر
exclaim v اعلام کردن	**exotic** adj غیربومی
exclude v محروم کردن	**expand** v بسط دادن
excruciating adj شدید	**expansion** n گسترش
excursion n گردش	**expect** v انتظار داشتن
excuse v معذور داشتن	**expectancy** n انتظار
excuse n بهانه	**expectation** n انتظار
execute v اجرا کردن	**expediency** n مصلحت
executive n مدیر	**expedient** adj تدبیر
exemplary adj نمونه	**expedition** n اردو
exemplify v بامثال فهمانیدن	**expel** v بیرون انداختن
exempt adj معاف	**expenditure** n صرف

E

expense *n* هزینه

expensive *adj* گران

experience *n* تجربه

experiment *n* آزمایش

expert *adj* کارشناس

expiate *v* کفاره دادن

expiation *n* کفاره

expiration *n* انقضا

expire *v* سپری شدن

explain *v* توضیح دادن

explicit *adj* صریح

explode *v* منفجر شدن

exploit *v* به کار انداختن

exploit *n* بهره برداری

explore *v* کاوش کردن

explorer *n* جهانگرد

explosion *n* انفجار

explosive *adj* انفجار

exploitation *n* بهره برداری

export *v* صادر کردن

expose *v* بی حفاظ گذاردن

exposed *adj* بی حفاظ

express *adj* صریح؛ سریع

express *v* بیان کردن

expression *n* بیان

expressly *adv* با صراحت

expulsion *n* اخراج

exquisite *adj* عالی

extend *v* توسعه دادن

extension *n* بسط

extent *n* وسعت

extenuating *adj* تخفیف دهنده

exterior *adj* بیرون

exterminate *v* برانداختن

external *adj* خارجی

extinct *adj* خاموش

extinguish *v* خاموش کردن

extort *v* به زور گرفتن

extortion *n* اخاذی

extra *adv* فوق العاده

extract *v* استخراج کردن

extradition *n* استرداد مجرم

extraneous *adj* نامربوط

extravagance *n* زیاده روی

extravagant *adj* ولخرج

extreme *adj* نهایت

extremist *adj* آدم افراطی

extremities *n* خشونت

extricate *v* رها کردن

extroverted *adj* برون گرا

exude *v* تراوش کردن

exult *v* شادی کردن

eye *n* چشم

eyebrow *n* ابرو

eye-catching *adj* جذاب

eyeglasses *n* عینک

eyelash *n* مژه

eyelid *n* پلک

eyesight *n* بینایی

eyewitness *n* شاهدعینی

fable *n* افسانه

fabric *n* ساختار

fabricate *v* ساختن

fabulous *adj* شگفت آور

face *n* صورت

face up to *v* پذیرفتن

facet *n* تراش

facilitate *v* آسان کردن

facing *pre* در مواجه با

fact *n* حقیقت

factor *n* عامل

factory *n* کارخانه

factual *adj* واقعی

faculty *n* استعداد

fad *n* گرایش

fade *v* محو کردن

faded *adj* رنگ رفته

fail *v* شکست خوردن

failure *n* شکست

faint *v* ضعف کردن

faint *n* ضعیف

faint *adj* ضعیف

fair *n* نمایشگاه

fair *adj* عادلانه؛ زیبا

fairness *n* انصاف

fairy *n* پری

faith *n* ایمان؛ دین

faithful *adj* باوفا

fake *v* وانمود کردن

fake *adj* تقلبی

fall *n* پائیز؛ آبشار

fall *iv* بیافت

fall behind *v* عقب افتادن

fall down *v* افتادن

fall through *v* به نتیجه نرسیدن

fallacy *n* سفسطه

fallout *n* بارش رادیواکتیو

falsehood *n* دروغ

falsify *v* تحریف کردن

falter *v* گیر کردن

fame *n* شهرت

familiar *adj* آشنا

family *n* خانواده

famine *n* قحطی

famous *adj* مشهور

fan *n* پنکه؛ هوادار

fanatic *adj* متعصب

fancy *adj* تخیلی

fang *n* دندان نیش

fantastic *adj* خارق العاده

fantasy *n* خیال پردازی

far *adv* دور

faraway *adj* دور

farce *n* نمایش کمدی

fare *n* کرایه

farewell *n* خداحافظی

farm *n* کشاورزی

farmer *n* کشاورز

farming *n* کشاورزی

farmyard *n* حیاط مزرعه

farther *adv* دورتر

fascinate v مجذوب کردن

fashion n شیوه

fashionable adj مد

fast adj سریع

fasten v بستن

fat n چربی

fat adj چربی

fatal adj مهلك

fate n تقدیر

fateful adj تعیین کننده

father n پدر

fatherhood n پدری

father-in-law n پدرزن

fatherly adj پدرانه

fatigue n خستگی

fatten v فربه کردن

fatty adj چرب

faucet n شیر

fault n عیب

faulty adj معیوب

favor n لطف؛ توجه

favorable adj مطلوب

favorite adj برگزیده

fear n ترس

fearful adj هولناك

feasible adj عملی

feast n جشن

feat n کار عظیم

feather n پر

feature n مشخصه

February n فوریه

fed up adj خسته

federal adj فدرال

fee n اجرت

feeble adj ضعیف

feed iv تغذیه کن

feedback n بازتاب

feel iv احساس کن

feeling n احساس

feelings n احساسات

feet n پا

feign v وانمود کردن

fellow n همکار

fellowship n رفاقت

felon n جنایت کار

felony n جنایت

female n زن؛ مونث

feminine adj صورت مونث

fence n حصار

fencing n شمشیر بازی

fend v دفع کردن

fend off v دور کردن

fender n حفاظ

ferment v ترش شدن

ferment n مخمر؛ اضطراب

ferocious adj وحشی

ferocity n وحشیگری

ferry n گذرگاه

fertile adj بارور

fertility n باروری

fertilize v بارور کردن

fervent adj مشتاق

fester v چرک کردن

festive adj جشنی

festivity *n* جشن	film *n* فیلم
fetid *adj* بدبو	filter *n* تصفیه؛ فیلتر
fetus *n* جنین	filter *v* تصفیه کردن
feud *n* دعوا	filth *n* کثافت
fever *n* تب	filthy *adj* کثیف
feverish *adj* تب دار	fin *n* باله
few *adj* خیلی کم	final *adj* نهایی
fewer *adj* کمتر	finalize *v* به پایان رساندن
fiancé *n* نامزد	finance *v* پول تهیه کردن
fiber *n* تار	financial *adj* مالی
fickle *adj* متغیر	find *iv* بیاب
fiction *n* داستان	find out *v* پی بردن
fictitious *adj* مجازی	fine *n* خوب
fiddle *n* کمانچه	fine *v* جریمه کردن
fidelity *n* وفاداری	fine *adv* خوب
field *n* زمینه	fine *adj* خوب
fierce *adj* خشن	fine print *n* حروف ریز
fiery *adj* مشتعل	finger *n* انگشت
fifteen *adj* پانزده	fingernail *n* ناخن
fifth *adj* پنجم	fingerprint *n* اثر انگشت
fifty *adj* پنجاه	fingertip *n* سر انگشت
fifty-fifty *adv* پنجاه‌پنجاه	finish *v* تمام کردن
fig *n* شکل	Finland *n* فنلاند
fight *iv* جنگ کن	Finnish *adj* فنلاندی
fight *n* جنگ	fire *v* آتش زدن
fighter *n* جنگنده	fire *n* آتش
figure *n* رقم	firearm *n* اسلحه گرم
figure out *v* کشف کردن	firecracker *n* ترقه
file *v* اصلاح کردن	firefighter *n* آتش نشان
file *n* بایگانی؛ فایل	fireplace *n* بخاری دیواری
fill *v* پر کردن	firewood *n* هیزم
filling *n* لفاف؛ پر کننده	fireworks *n* آتش بازی

firm *adj* محکم	**flavor** *n* مزه
firm *n* محکم	**flaw** *n* عیب
firmness *n* سفتی	**flawless** *adj* بی نقص
first *adj* اول	**flea** *n* کک
fish *n* ماهی	**flee** *iv* بگریز
fisherman *n* ماهیگیر	**fleece** *n* پشم جانوران
fishy *adj* مشکوک	**fleet** *n* عبور سریع
fist *n* مشت	**fleeting** *adj* گذرا
fit *n* متناسب بنمایید	**flesh** *n* گوشت
fit *v* اندازه بودن	**flex** *v* خم کردن
fitness *n* مناسبت	**flexible** *adj* انعطاف پذیر
fitting *adj* پرو	**flicker** *v* لرزیدن
five *adj* پنج	**flier** *n* خلبان
fix *v* درست کردن	**flight** *n* پرواز؛ مهاجرت
fjord *n* آبدره	**flimsy** *adj* سست
flag *n* پرچم	**flirt** *v* لاس زدن
flagpole *n* میله پرچم	**float** *v* شناور شدن
flamboyant *adj* شعله دار	**flock** *n* مخملی
flame *n* شعله	**flog** *v* شلاق زدن
flammable *adj* قابل اشتعال	**flood** *v* غرق کردن
flank *n* دامنه	**floodgate** *n* آب بند
flare *n* مشعل	**flooding** *n* سیل
flare-up *v* منفجر شدن	**floodlight** *n* نور افکن
flash *n* درخشش	**floor** *n* کف
flashlight *n* فلاش	**flop** *n* تلپ
flashy *adj* پرزرق وبرق	**floss** *n* نخ
flat *n* آپارتمان	**flour** *n* آرد
flat *adj* صاف	**flourish** *v* رشد کردن
flatten *v* پهن کردن	**flow** *v* جاری بودن
flatter *v* چاپلوسی کردن	**flow** *n* جریان
flattery *n* تملق	**flower** *n* گل
flaunt *v* بالیدن	**flowerpot** *n* گلدان

F

flu n آنفلوآنزا	**foot** n پا
fluctuate v نوسان داشتن	**football** n فوتبال
fluently adv فصیحانه	**footnote** n زیرنویس
fluid n مایع	**footprint** n جای پا
flunk v شکست خوردن	**footstep** n قدم
flush v به هیجان آمدن	**footwear** n کفش
flute n فلوت	**for** pre برای
flutter v سراسیمه بودن	**forbid** iv ممنوع کن
fly iv پرواز کن	**force** n اجبار؛ نیرو
fly n پرواز؛ مگس	**forceful** adj محکم
foam n ابر	**forcibly** adv به زور
focus n تمرکز	**forecast** iv پیش بینی کن
focus on تمرکز کردن بر	**forefront** n صف مقدم
foe n دشمن	**foreground** n پیش زمینه
fog n مه	**forehead** n پیشانی
foggy adj مه آلود	**foreign** adj خارجی
foil v بی اثر کردن	**foreigner** n خارجی
fold v تا کردن	**foreman** n سرکارگر
folder n پوشه	**foremost** adj سرشناس ترین
folks n قوم وخویش	**foresee** iv پیش بینی کن
folksy adj بی ریا	**foreshadow** v از پیش خبر دادن
follow v پیروی کردن	**foresight** n آینده نگری
follower n پیرو	**forest** n جنگل
folly n حماقت	**foretaste** n مقدمه
fond adj علاقمند؛ شیفته	**foretell** v پیشگویی کردن
fondle v نوازش کردن	**forever** adv همیشه
fondness n علاقه	**foreword** n پیشگفتار
food n غذا	**forfeit** v جریمه کردن
foodstuff n ماده غذایی	**forge** v جعل کردن
fool v فریب دادن	**forgery** n جعل
fool adj احمق	**forget** v فراموش کردن
foolproof adj خطاناپذیر	**forgivable** adj بخشودنی

F

forgive v عفو کردن	**four** adj چهار
forgiveness n بخشایش	**fourteen** adj چهارده
fork n چنگال	**fourth** adj چهارم
form n تاسیس؛ شکل	**fox** n روباه
formal adj رسمی	**foxy** adj مکار
formality n رسمیت	**fraction** n بخش
formalize v رسمی کردن	**fracture** n ترک؛ شکاف
formally adv به طور رسمی	**fragile** adj شکستنی
format n شکل	**fragment** n خردبشوید
formation n شکل گیری	**fragrance** n عطر
former adj اولی	**fragrant** adj خوشبو
formerly adv قبلاً	**frail** adj ضعیف
formidable adj هولناک	**frailty** n ضعف
formula n فرمول	**frame** n قاب؛ کالبد
forsake iv ترک کن	**frame** v قاب کردن
fort n قلعه	**framework** n چارچوب؛ کالبد
forthcoming adj نزدیک؛ در شرف	**France** n فرانسه
forthright adj رک	**franchise** n امتیاز
fortify v مستحکم کردن	**frank** adj رک
fortitude n پایمردی	**frankly** adv بطور صریح
fortress n دژ	**frankness** n صراحت
fortunate adj خوش شانس	**frantic** adj سراسیمه
fortune n بخت	**fraternal** adj برادرانه
forty adj چهل	**fraternity** n برادری
forward adv جلویی	**fraud** n کلاه برداری
fossil n فسیل	**fraudulent** adj جعلی
foster v غذا دادن	**freckle** n لکه؛ لکه صورت
foul adj پلید	**freckled** adj خالدار
foundation n بنیاد؛ موسسه	**free** v آزاد کردن
founder n موسس	**free** adj آزاد؛ رایگان
foundry n ریخته گری	**freedom** n آزادی
fountain n فواره	**freeway** n آزادراه

freeze iv یخ ببند	**frontier** n مرز
freezer n فریزر	**frost** n ژاله؛ شبنم
freezing adj انجماد	**frostbite** n سرمازدگی
freight n حمل	**frostbitten** adj سرمازده
French adj فرانسوی	**frosty** adj بسیار سرد
frenetic adj داغ	**frown** v اخم کردن
frenzied adj هیجان زده	**frozen** adj یخ زده
frenzy n هیجان	**frugal** adj مقتصد
frequency n تعدد	**frugality** n قناعت
frequent adj متناوب	**fruit** n میوه
frequent v تکرار کردن	**fruitful** adj مفید
fresh adj تازه	**fruity** adj میوه ای
freshen v تازه کردن	**frustrate** v ناامید کردن
freshness n تازگی	**frustration** n شکست
friar n راهب صومعه	**fry** v سرخ کردن
friction n اصطکاك	**frying pan** n ماهی تابه
Friday n جمعه	**fuel** n سوخت
fried adj سرخ کرده	**fugitive** n فراری
friend n دوست	**fulfill** v انجام دادن
friendship n دوستی	**fulfillment** n تکمیل
frigate n ناو محافظ	**full** adj کامل
fright n ترس	**fully** adv کاملاً
frighten v ترساندن	**fumes** n دود
frightening adj ترس آور	**fumigate** v بخار دادن
frigid adj بسیار سرد	**fun** n تفریح
fringe n طوق؛ منگنه	**function** n عمل
frivolous adj بی خیال	**fund** n اعتبار؛ موجودی
frog n قورباغه	**fundamental** adj بنیادی
from pre از	**funds** n وجوه
front n جلو؛ جبهه	**funeral** n تدفین
front adj جلو	**fungus** n قارچ
frontage n ضلع	**funny** adj خنده دار

F

fur *n* جامعه خزدار

furious *adj* عصبانی

furiously *adv* باعصبانیت

furnace *n* کوره

furnish *v* مجهز کردن

furnishings *n* اسباب واثاثیه

furniture *n* اسباب واثاثیه

furor *n* دیوانگی

furrow *n* زمین شخم زده

furry *adj* پشمالو

further *adv* بیشتر

furthermore *adv* علاوه بر این

fury *n* عصبانیت

fuse *n* فیوز

fusion *n* ذوب

fuss *n* اذیت

fussy *adj* جنجالی

futile *adj* بیهوده

futility *n* بیهودگی

future *n* آینده

fuzzy *adj* پرزی

gadget *n* ابزار

gag *n* ساکت

gag *v* محدود کردن

gage *v* اندازه گرفتن

gain *v* به دست آوردن

gain *n* منفعت؛ بهره

gal *n* دختر

galaxy *n* کهکشان

gale *n* توفان

gall bladder *n* کیسه صفرا

gallant *adj* دلاور

gallery *n* نگارخانه

gallon *n* گالن

gallop *v* تازیدن

gallows *n* چوبه دار

galvanize *v* سفید کردن

gamble *v* قمار کردن

game *n* بازی

gang *n* باند

gangrene *n* قانقاریا

gangster *n* گانگستر

gap *n* شکاف؛ گاف

garage *n* گاراژ

garbage *n* آشغال

garden *n* باغ

gardener *n* باغبان

gargle *v* غرغره کردن

garland *n* حلقه گل

garlic *n* سیر

garment *n* لباس	genocide *n* نسل کشی
garnish *v* آرایش دادن	genteel *adj* مبادی آداب
garnish *n* پارچه سفید	gentle *adj* مهربان
garrison *n* پادگان	gentleman *n* آقای محترم
garrulous *adj* پرحرف	gentleness *n* مهربانی
garter *n* بندجوراب	genuflect *v* زانو خم کردن
gas *n* گاز	genuine *adj* اصل
gash *n* برید	geography *n* جغرافیا
gasoline *n* بنزین	geology *n* زمین شناسی
gasp *v* نفس نفس زدن	geometry *n* هندسه
gastric *adj* معده ای	germ *n* میکروب
gate *n* دریچه	German *adj* آلمانی
gather *v* گرد آوری کردن	Germany *n* آلمان
gathering *n* اجتماع	germinate *v* جوانه زدن
gauge *v* سنجیدن	gerund *n* اسم فعل
gauze *n* گاز	gestation *n* بارداری
gaze *v* خیره نگاه کردن	gesture *n* ایما و اشاره
gear *n* لوازم	get *iv* بگیر
geese *n* غازها	get along *v* بسر بردن
gem *n* جواهر	get away *v* فرار کردن
gender *n* جنس	get by *v* نگهداری کردن
gene *n* ژن	get down *v* پیاده شدن
general *n* عمومی	get down to *v* تمرکز کردن بر
generalize *v* عمومیت دادن	get in *v* جمع اوری کردن
generate *v* تولید کردن	get off *v* رهایی یافتن
generation *n* نسل	get out *v* بیرن رفتن
generator *n* مولد	get over *v* فایق آمدن بر
generic *adj* اسم عام	get together *v* فراهم آوردن
generosity *n* سخاوت	get up *v* بیدار شدن
genetic *adj* وراثت شناختی	geyser *n* آبفشان
genial *adj* خوش مشرب	ghastly *adj* رنگ پریده
genius *n* نابغه	ghost *n* شبه

G

giant *n* غول

gift *n* هدیه

gifted *adj* بااستعداد

gigantic *adj* غول پیکر

gimmick *n* ژست

ginger *n* زنجبیلی

gingerly *adv* بااحتیاط

giraffe *n* زرافه

girl *n* دختر

girlfriend *n* دوست دختر

give *iv* بده

give away *v* از دست دادن

give back *v* پس دادن

give in *v* تسلیم شدن

give out *v* بیرون دادن

give up *v* تسلیم شدن

glacier *n* یخچال

glad *adj* خوشحال

gladiator *n* گلادیاتور

glamorous *adj* دلربا

glance *v* برانداز کردن

glance *n* نگاه

gland *n* غده

glare *n* درخشش

glass *n* شیشه

glasses *n* عینك

glassware *n* ظروف بلوری

gleam *v* نور دادن

glide *v* سر خوردن

glimmer *n* سوسو

glimpse *n* نگاه آنی

glimpse *v* به یک نظر دیدن

glitter *v* درخشیدن

globe *n* کره زمین

globule *n* قطره

gloom *n* تاریکی

gloomy *adj* تیره

glorify *v* تجلیل کردن

glorious *adj* باشکوه

glory *n* افتخار

gloss *n* جلا

glossary *n* واژه نامه

glossy *adj* براق

glove *n* دستکش

glow *v* تابیدن

glucose *n* گلوکز

glue *n* چسب

glue *v* چسباندن

glut *n* اشباع

glutton *n* پرخور

gnaw *v* خاییدن

go *iv* برو

go ahead *v* ادامه دادن

go away *v* ترک کردن

go back *v* برگشتن

go down *v* پائین رفتن از

go in *v* داخل شدن در

go on *v* ادامه دادن

go out *v* بیرون رفتن

go over *v* مرور کردن

go through *v* مرور کردن

go under *v* شکست خوردن

go up *v* بالا رفتن

goad *v* تحریک کردن

goal *n* هدف	gracious *adj* خوشایند
goalkeeper *n* دروازه بان	grade *n* رتبه
goat *n* بز	gradual *adj* تدریجی
gobble *v* حریصانه خوردن	graduate *v* درجه گرفتن
God *n* خداوند	graduation *n* فارغ التحصیلی
goddess *n* الهه	graft *v* پیوند زدن
godless *adj* بی دین	graft *n* وصله
goggles *n* عینك ایمنی	grain *n* دانه
gold *n* طلا	gram *n* گرم
golden *adj* طلایی	grammar *n* دستور زبان
good *adj* خوب	grand *adj* بزرگ
good-looking *adj* خوش نما؛ زیبا	grandchild *n* نوه
goodness *n* خوبی	granddad *n* بابا بزرگ
goods *n* كالا	grandfather *n* پدربزرگ
goodwill *n* حسن نیت	grandmother *n* مادربزرگ
goof *v* اشتباه كردن	grandparents *n* جدها
goof *n* شخص احمق	grandson *n* نوه
goose *n* غاز	granite *n* سنگ خارا
gorge *n* حلق؛ گلوگاه	granny *n* مامان بزرگ
gorgeous *adj* عالی	grant *v* موافقت كردن
gorilla *n* گوریل	grant *n* اعطائیه
gory *adj* خونی	grape *n* انگور
gospel *n* تعالیم	grapefruit *n* دارابی
gossip *n* غیبت	grapevine *n* درخت مو
gout *n* نقرس	graphic *adj* گرافیك
govern *v* حكومت كردن	grasp *n* چنگ
government *n* دولت	grasp *v* به چنگ آوردن
governor *n* فرماندار	grass *n* چمن
gown *n* لباس بلند	grassroots *adj* عامه مردم
grab *v* ربودن	grateful *adj* سپاسگزار
grace *n* لطف	gratify *v* خشنود كردن
graceful *adj* جذاب	gratifying *adj* خوشحال كننده

G

gratitude *n* سپاس

gratuity *n* انعام

grave *adj* گور

grave *n* گور

gravel *n* شن

gravely *adv* موقرانه

gravestone *n* سنگ قبر

graveyard *n* گورستان

gravitate *v* سنگین کردن

gravity *n* گرانش

gravy *n* سس گوشت

gray *adj* خاکستری

grayish *adj* خاکستری گانه

graze *v* تغذیه کردن

graze *n* تیر تراش؛ خراش

grease *v* روغن زدن

grease *n* روغن

greasy *adj* چرب

great *adj* بزرگ

greatness *n* بزرگی

Greece *n* یونان

greed *n* طمع

greedy *adj* حریص

Greek *adj* یونانی

green *adj* سبز

green bean *n* دانه سبز

greenhouse *n* گلخانه

Greenland *n* گرینلند

greet *v* تبریک گفتن

greetings *n* تبریکات

gregarious *adj* جمعیت دوست

grenade *n* نارنجک

greyhound *n* سگ تازی

grief *n* غصه

grievance *n* نارضایی

grieve *v* غمگین کردن

grill *n* گوشت کباب کن

grill *n* گوشت کباب کن

grim *adj* عبوس

grimace *n* ادا و اصول

grime *n* چرک

grind *iv* آسیاب کن

grip *v* نیرو گرفتن

grip *n* برش

gripe *n* تسمه قایق

grisly *adj* مخوف

groan *v* ناله کردن

groan *n* ناله

groceries *n* خواربار

groin *n* کشاله ران

groom *n* تیمار

groove *n* شیار

gross *adj* ناخالص؛ وحشی

grossly *adv* فوق العاده

grotesque *adj* سبک گروتسک

grotto *n* غار

grouch *v* بد خلقی کردن

grouchy *adj* بدخلق

ground *n* زمینی

ground floor *n* طبقه هم کف

groundless *adj* بی اساس

group *n* گروه

grow *iv* رشد کن

grow up *v* بزرگ شدن

غرغر کردن *v* **growl**	ساده لوح *adj* **gullible**
بالغ *n* **grown-up**	قورت دادن *v* **gulp**
رشد *n* **growth**	جرعه *n* **gulp**
اکراه *n* **grudge**	بلعیدن *v* **gulp down**
با اکراه *adv* **grudgingly**	صمغ؛ آدامس *n* **gum**
سخت *adj* **gruelling**	سلاح *n* **gun**
وحشتناک *adj* **gruesome**	کشتن با تفنگ *v* **gun down**
گله کردن *v* **grumble**	شلیک *n* **gunfire**
بداخلاق *adj* **grumpy**	دزدمسلح *n* **gunman**
تعهد کردن *v* **guarantee**	باروت *n* **gunpowder**
ضمانت *n* **guarantee**	گلوله *n* **gunshot**
ضامن *n* **guarantor**	تندباد *n* **gust**
محافظت *n* **guard**	شور و شوق *n* **gusto**
سرپرست *n* **guardian**	توفانی *adj* **gusty**
چریک *n* **guerrilla**	روده *n* **gut**
حدس زدن *v* **guess**	روده *n* **guts**
حدس *n* **guess**	ناودان *n* **gutter**
مهمان *n* **guest**	(فرد (مذکر *n* **guy**
راهنمایی *n* **guidance**	بلعیدن *v* **guzzle**
راهنمایی کردن *v* **guide**	سالن ورزش *n* **gymnasium**
راهنمایی *n* **guide**	پزشکی زنان *n* **gynecology**
کتاب راهنما *n* **guidebook**	کولی *n* **gypsy**
رهنمود *n* **guidelines**	
صنف *n* **guild**	
نیرنگ *n* **guile**	
گیوتن *n* **guillotine**	
گناه *n* **guilt**	
مقصر *adj* **guilty**	
ظاهر *n* **guise**	
گیتار *n* **guitar**	
خلیج *n* **gulf**	
مرغ نوروزی *n* **gull**	

G

H

habit *n* عادت

habitable *adj* قابل سکونت

habitual *adj* عادی

hack *v* زخم زدن

haggle *v* چانه زدن

hail *n* تگرگ

hail *v* سلام کردن

hair *n* موی

hairbrush *n* برس مو

haircut *n* اصلاح

hairdo *n* آرایشگر زنانه

hairdresser *n* سلمانی

hairpiece *n* کاکل

hairy *adj* مودار

half *n* نیم

half *adj* نیم

hall *n* سالن

hallucinate *v* هذیانی شدن

hallway *n* تالار ورودی

halt *v* مکث کردن

halve *v* دونیم کردن

ham *n* ژامبون

hamburger *n* همبرگر

hamlet *n* هاملت

hammer *n* باچکش بزنید

hammock *n* تختخواب سفری

hand *n* دست

hand down *v* به ارث گذاشتن

hand out *v* پخش کردن

hand over *v* تحویل دادن

handbag *n* کیف زنانه

handbook *n* کتاب مبانی

handcuffs *n* دستبند

handful *n* یک مشت

handgun *n* تفنگ دستی

handicap *n* نقص

handkerchief *n* دستمال

handle *v* دست زدن به

handle *n* فرمان

handmade *adj* دست ساز

handout *n* صدقه

handrail *n* نرده

handshake *n* دست دادن

handsome *adj* زیبا

handwritting *n* دست نوشته

handy *adj* ماهر

hang *iv* آویزان کن

hang on *v* ادامه دادن

hang up *v* قطع کردن گوشی

hanger *n* آویزه

hangup *n* وسواس

happen *v* روی دادن

happening *n* رویداد

happiness *n* خوشحالی

happy *adj* خوشحال

harass *v* اذیت کردن

harassment *n* اذیت

harbor *n* لنگرگاه

hard *adj* سخت

harden *v* مشکل کردن

hardly *adv* بسختی

hardness n سختی	**haughty** adj متکبر
hardship n سختی	**haul** v کشیدن
hardware n سخت افزار	**haunt** v دیدار مکرر کردن
hardwood n چوب جنگلی	**have** iv داشته باش
hardy adj پرطاقت	**have to** v بایستن
hare n خرگوش	**haven** n پناهگاه
harm v صدمه زدن	**havoc** n خسارت
harm n آسیب	**hawk** n شاهین
harmful adj مضر	**hay** n علف خشك
harmless adj بی ضرر	**hazard** n خطر
harmonize v هم آهنگ کردن	**hazardous** adj پرخطر
harmony n هم آهنگی	**haze** n غبارآلود
harp n چنگ	**hazelnut** n فندق
harpoon n زوبین صید نهنگ	**hazy** adj مه آلود
harrowing adj دلخراش	**he** pro او
harsh adj خشن	**head** n سر
harshly adv با خشونت	**headache** n سردرد
harshness n زبری	**heading** n عنوان
harvest n محصول	**head-on** adv شاخ به شاخ
harvest v درو کردن	**headphones** n گوشی
hashish n حشیش	**headquarters** n ستاد
hassle v بحث کردن	**headway** n پیشروی
hassle n زجر	**heal** v شفا دادن
haste n شتاب	**healer** n شفابخش
hasten v شتاباندن	**health** n سلامت
hastily adv عجولانه	**healthy** adj سالم
hasty adj عجول	**heap** n کپه
hat n کلاه	**heap** v توده کردن
hatchet n تبر	**hear** iv بشنو
hate v نفرت داشتن از	**hearing** n شنیدن
hateful adj نفرت انگیز	**hearsay** n شایعه
hatred n تنفر	**hearse** n آمبولانس

H

heart *n* قلب

heartbeat *n* ضربان قلب

heartburn *n* ترش کردگی

hearten *v* جرات دادن

heartfelt *adj* صمیمانه

hearth *n* آتشدان

heartless *adj* سنگدل

hearty *adj* صمیمانه

heat *v* برانگیختن

heat *n* گرما

heater *n* بخاری

heathen *n* کافر

heating *n* گرمایش

heatstroke *n* گرمازدگی

heatwave *n* موج هوای گرم

heaven *n* بهشت

heavenly *adj* بهشتی

heaviness *n* سنگینی

heavy *adj* سنگین

heckle *v* شانه کردن

hectic *adj* پرتکاپو

heed *v* اعتنا کردن

heel *n* پاشنه پا

height *n* ارتفاع

heighten *v* بلند کردن

heinous *adj* فجیع

heir *n* وارث

heiress *n* وارث

heist *n* سرقت

helicopter *n* هلیکوپتر

hell *n* جهنم

hello *e* سلام

helm *n* سکان کشتی

helmet *n* کلاه ایمنی

help *v* کمک کردن

help *n* کمک

helper *n* یاور

helpful *adj* مفید

helpless *adj* ناتوان

hem *n* گوشه جامه

hemisphere *n* نیمکره

hemorrhage *n* خونریزی

hen *n* مرغ

hence *adv* به این دلیل

henchman *n* طرفدار

her *adj* به او

herald *v* اعلام کردن

herald *n* جارچی

herb *n* علف

here *adv* اینجا

hereafter *adv* آینده

hereby *adv* بدین وسیله

hereditary *adj* ارثی

heresy *n* ارتداد

heretic *adj* مرتد

heritage *n* میراث

hermetic *adj* کیپ

hermit *n* معتکف

hernia *n* فتق

hero *n* قهرمان

heroic *adj* قهرمانانه

heroin *n* هروئین

heroism *n* قهرمانی

hers *pro* مال او

herself pro خودش	**hint** n اشاره
hesitant adj مردد	**hint** v اشاره کردن
hesitate v تامل کردن	**hip** n کفل
hesitation n تردید	**hire** v کرایه کردن
heyday n اوج خوشبختی	**his** adj مال او
hiccup n سکسکه	**his** pro مال او
hidden adj نهان	**Hispanic** adj همسایگان
hide iv مخفی کن	**hiss** v هیس کردن
hideaway n مخفی گاه	**historian** n تاریخ نویس
hideous adj زشت	**history** n تاریخ
hierarchy n سلسله مراتب	**hit** n ضربه؛ موفقیت
high adj بالا	**hit** iv بزن
highlight n برجسته	**hitch** n بند؛ اتصال
highly adv بسیار	**hitchhike** n مسافرت مفتی
Highness n بلندی	**hitherto** adv تا کنون
highway n بزرگراه	**hive** n اندختن
hijack v راه دزدی	**hoard** v ذخیره کردن
hijack n برباید	**hoarse** adj خشن
hijacker n هواپیماربا	**hoax** n دست انداختن
hike v مبلغ را بالا بردن	**hobby** n سرگرمی
hike n پیاده روی	**hog** n گراز
hilarious adj مضحک	**hoist** v بالا بردن
hill n تپه	**hoist** n بالابر
hillside n دامنه تپه	**hold** iv نگه بدار
hilltop n سرتپه	**hold back** v مانع شدن
hilly adj تپه ماهور	**hold on to** v گرفتن
hilt n دسته	**hold out** v بسط یافتن
hinder v عقب انداختن	**hold up** v مانع شدن
hindrance n مزاحم	**holdup** n تاخیر
hindsight n واپس نگری	**hole** n سوراخ
hinge v لولا زدن	**holiday** n تعطیل
hinge n بستگی	**holiness** n تقدس

Holland n هلند

hollow adj حفره

holocaust n همه سوزی

holy adj مقدس

homage n ادای احترام

home n خانه

homeland n وطن

homeless adj بی خانمان

homely adj صمیمانه

homemade adj خانگی

homesick adj غربت زده

hometown n زادگاه

homework n تکلیف

homicide n قتل

homily n موعظه

honest adj صادق

honesty n صداقت

honey n عسل

honeymoon n ماه عسل

honk v بوق زدن

honor n احترام

hood n کلاهک

hoodlum n گانگستر

hoof n سم

hook n قلاب؛ ضربه

hooligan n لات

hop v پریدن

hope n امید

hopeful adj امید

hopefully adv امیدوارانه

hopeless adj ناامید

horizon n افق

horizontal adj افقی

hormone n هورمون

horn n شاخ

horrendous adj ترسناک

horrible adj مخوف

horrify v ترساندن

horror n وحشت

horse n اسب

hose n شیلنگ

hospital n بیمارستان

hospitality n مهمان نوازی

hospitalize v بستری کردن

host n میزبان

hostage n گروگان

hostess n میزبان

hostile adj دشمن

hostility n دشمنی

hot adj داغ

hotel n هتل

hound n سگ شکاری

hour n ساعت

hourly adv هر یک ساعت

house n خانه

household n خانواده

housekeeper n خدمتکار

housewife n خانم خانه

housework n کارخانه

hover v در تردید بودن

how adv چطور

however c بهرحال

howl v فریاد زدن

howl n زوزه

hub *n* توپی	**hurricane** *n* توفان
huddle *v* روی هم ریختن	**hurriedly** *adv* باشتاب
hug *v* درآغوش گرفتن	**hurry** *v* شتاب کردن
hug *n* بغل	**hurry up** *v* عجله کردن
huge *adj* بزرگ	**hurt** *iv* آسیب رساندن
hull *n* بدنه؛ جدار	**hurt** *adj* آسیب دیده
hum *v* همهمه کردن	**hurtful** *adj* مضر
human *adj* انسان	**husband** *n* شوهر
human being *n* انسان	**hush** *n* ساکت
humanities *n* علوم انسانی	**hush up** *v* سکوت کردن
humankind *n* بشریت	**husky** *adj* سگ قطبی
humble *adj* فروتن	**hustle** *n* عجله
humbly *adv* متواضعانه	**hut** *n* کلبه
humid *adj* مرطوب	**hydraulic** *adj* هیدرولیك
humidity *n* رطوبت	**hydrogen** *n* هیدروژن
humiliate *v* تحقیر کردن	**hyena** *n* کفتار
humility *n* تواضع	**hygiene** *n* بهداشت
humor *n* شوخی	**hymn** *n* سرود مذهبی
humorous *adj* خنده دار	**hyphen** *n* هایفن
hump *n* قلنبه	**hypnosis** *n* خواب مصنوعی
hunch *n* قوز	**hypocrisy** *n* ریا
hunchback *n* آدم قوزپشت	**hypocrite** *adj* ریاکار
hunched *adj* خم شده	**hypothesis** *n* فرضیه
hundred *adj* صد	**hysteria** *n* هیستری
hundredth *adj* صدم	**hysterical** *adj* هیستریایی
hunger *n* گرسنگی	
hungry *adj* گرسنه	
hunt *v* شکار کردن	
hunter *n* شکارچی	
hunting *n* شکار	
hurdle *n* پرش از روی مانع	
hurl *v* پرتاب کردن	

H

I

I *pro* من	
ice *n* یخ	
ice cream *n* بستنی	
ice cube *n* قالب یخ	
iceberg *n* کوه یخ	
icebox *n* یخدان	
ice-cold *adj* فوق العاده سرد	
icon *n* نشان	
icy *adj* بسیار سرد	
idea *n* ایده	
ideal *adj* کمال مطلوب	
identical *adj* همان	
identify *v* شناختن	
identity *n* هویت	
ideology *n* مرام	
idiom *n* اصطلاح	
idiot *n* احمق	
idiotic *adj* احمقانه	
idle *adj* بیکار	
idol *n* بت	
idolatry *n* بت پرستی	
if *c* اگر	
ignite *v* آتش زدن	
ignorance *n* بی خبری	
ignorant *adj* ناآگاه	
ignore *v* صرفنظر کردن	
ill *adj* ناخوش	
illegal *adj* غیرقانونی	
illegible *adj* ناخوانا	

illegitimate *adj* بچه حرام زاده
illicit *adj* غیرقانونی
illiterate *adj* بی سواد
illness *n* بیماری
illogical *adj* غیرمنطقی
illuminate *v* روشن کردن
illusion *n* تصور غلط
illustrate *v* توضیح دادن
illustration *n* توضیح
illustrious *adj* برجسته
image *n* تصویر
imagination *n* قدرت تخیل
imagine *v* تصور کردن
imbalance *n* عدم توازن
imitate *v* تقلید کردن
imitation *n* تقلید
immaculate *adj* پاک
immature *adj* نابالغ
immaturity *n* عدم بلوغ
immediately *adv* فوری
immense *adj* بسیار بزرگ
immensity *n* عظمت
immerse *v* فرو بردن
immersion *n* غوطه وری
immigrant *n* مهاجر
immigrate *v* مهاجرت کردن
immigration *n* مهاجرت
imminent *adj* نزدیک
immobile *adj* بی حرکت
immobilize *v* جمع کردن
immoral *adj* غیر اخلاقی
immorality *n* اخلاق ستیزی

immortal adj فناناپذیر	**impose** v تحمیل کردن
immortality n ابدیت	**imposing** adj باابهت
immune adj ایمن	**imposition** n وضع
immunity n مصونیت	**impossibility** n عدم امکان
immutable adj تغییر ناپذیر	**impossible** adj ناممکن
impact n برخورد	**impotent** adj ناتوان
impact v بهم فشردن	**impound** v توقیف کردن
impair v خراب کردن	**impoverished** adj فقیر
impartial adj بی طرف	**impractical** adj غیرقابل عمل
impatience n بی صبری	**imprecise** adj نادقیق
impatient adj بی صبر	**impressive** adj باعظمت
impeccable adj بی عیب	**imprison** v زندان کردن
impediment n مانع	**improbable** adj نامحتمل
impending adj نزدیک	**impromptu** adv فی البداهه
imperfection n عیب	**improper** adj نابجا
imperial adj باشکوه	**improve** v بهبودی دادن
imperialism n امپریالیسم	**improvement** n بهبود
impersonal adj غیرشخصی	**improvise** v بالبداهه ساختن
impertinence n گستاخی	**impulse** n تکان
impertinent adj گستاخ	**impulsive** adj تکانشی
impetuous adj عجول	**impunity** n بخشودگی
implacable adj سرسخت	**impure** adj آلوده
implant v کاشتن	**in** pre درون
implement v انجام دادن	**in depth** adv در عمق
implicate v دلالت کردن بر	**inability** n ناتوانی
implication n درگیری	**inaccessible** adj دورازدسترس
implicit adj ضمنی	**inaccurate** adj نادرست
imply v دلالت کردن	**inadequate** adj ناکافی
impolite adj بی ادب	**inadmissible** adj غیرقابل قبول
import v وارد کردن	**inappropriate** adj نامناسب
importance n اهمیت	**inasmuch as** c چون
importation n واردات	**inaugurate** v افتتاح کردن

incalculable *adj* بی شمار	increasing *adj* افزایش یابنده
incapable *adj* ناتوان	incredible *adj* باورنکردنی
incapacitate *v* ناقابل ساختن	increment *n* افزایش
incarcerate *v* زندانی کردن	incur *v* متحمل شدن
incense *n* خشم	incurable *adj* بیمار علاج ناپذیر
incentive *n* مشوق	indecency *n* زشتی
inception *n* شروع	indecision *n* بی تصمیمی
incessant *adj* بی وقفه	indecisive *adj* غیرقاطع
inch *n* اینچ	indeed *adv* در واقع
incident *n* حادثه	indefinite *adj* نامحدود
incidentally *adv* به طور اتفاقی	indemnify *v* تاوان دادن
incision *n* بریدگی	indemnity *n* تضمین
incite *v* تحریک کردن	independence *n* استقلال
incitement *n* تحریك	independent *adj* مستقل
inclination *n* گرایش	index *n* شاخص
incline *v* خم کردن	indicate *v* نشان دادن
include *v* در برداشتن	indication *n* نشان
inclusive *adv* شامل	indict *v* متهم کردن
incoherent *adj* فاقد انسجام	indifference *n* بی اعتنایی
income *n* درآمد	indifferent *adj* بی اعتنا
incoming *adj* درحال آمدن	indigent *adj* تهیدست
incompatible *adj* ناسازگار	indigestion *n* سوء هاضمه
incompetence *n* عدم صلاحیت	indirect *adj* غیرمستقیم
incompetent *adj* بدون صلاحیت	indiscreet *adj* بی احتیاط
incomplete *adj* ناتمام	indiscretion *n* بی احتیاطی
inconsistent *adj* ناسازگار	indispensable *adj* ضروری
inconvenient *adj* ناراحت کننده	indisposed *adj* ناخوش
incorporate *v* متحد کردن	indisputable *adj* غیرقابل بحث
incorrect *adj* غلط	indivisible *adj* تقسیم نشدنی
incorrigible *adj* اصلاح ناپذیر	indoctrinate *v* آموختن
increase *v* افزایش دادن	indoor *adv* داخلی
increase *n* افزایش	induce *v* فراهم کردن

indulge v مخالفت نکردن	inflation n تورم
indulgent adj آسان گیر	inflexible adj خشک
industrious adj سخت کوش	inflict v ضربت زدن
industry n صنعت	influence n نفوذ
ineffective adj بی نتیجه	influential adj بانفوذ
inefficient adj کم بازده	influenza n آنفلوآنزا
inept adj نابجا	influx n هجوم
inequality n نابرابری	inform v آگاهی دادن
inevitable adj اجتناب ناپذیر	informal adj غیر رسمی
inexcusable adj نابخشودنی	informant n آگاهی دهنده
inexpensive adj ارزان	information n اطلاعات
inexperienced adj بی تجربه	informer n جاسوس
inexplicable adj غیرقابل توضیح	infraction n نقش؛ تخلف
infallible adj بری از اشتباه	infrequent adj نادر
infamous adj بدنام	infuriate v آتشی کردن
infancy n کودکی	infusion n محلول خیسانده
infant n کودک	ingenuity n ابتکار
infantry n پیاده نظام	ingest v قورت دادن
infect v آلوده کردن	ingot n شمش
infection n ابتلا	ingrained adj ریشه دار
infectious adj مسری	ingratitude n ناسپاسی
infer v استنتاج کردن	ingredient n جزء
inferior adj زیردست	inhabit v ساکن شدن
infertile adj ناباور	inhabitable adj مسکونی
infested adj پربوده شده	inhabitant n ساکن
infidelity n کفر	inhale v تنفس کردن
infiltrate v نفوذ کردن	inherit v وارث شدن
infiltration n نفوذ	inheritance n میراث
infinite adj بی پایان	inhibit v منع کردن
infirmary n بیمارستان	inhuman adj ظالم
inflammation n التهاب	initial adj نخستین
inflate v متورم شدن	initially adv درآغاز

اصلی ها *n* **initials**	ناحساس *adj* **insensitive**
راه انداختن *v* **initiate**	جدا نشدنی *adj* **inseparable**
ابتکار *n* **initiative**	درج کردن *v* **insert**
تزریق کردن *v* **inject**	درج *n* **insertion**
تزریق *n* **injection**	درون *adj* **inside**
آسیب زدن *v* **injure**	داخل *pre* **inside**
زیانمند *adj* **injurious**	کاملاً *adv* **inside out**
آسیب *n* **injury**	کم اهمیت *adj* **insignificant**
بی عدالتی *n* **injustice**	ریاکار *adj* **insincere**
جوهر *n* **ink**	ریا *n* **insincerity**
اشاره *n* **inkling**	تلقین کردن *v* **insinuate**
مرصع *adj* **inlaid**	کنایه *n* **insinuation**
هم بند *n* **inmate**	بی مزه *adj* **insipid**
مسافرخانه *n* **inn**	اصرار ورزیدن *v* **insist**
ذاتی *adj* **innate**	پافشاری *n* **insistence**
داخلی *adj* **inner**	وقیح *adj* **insolent**
بی گناهی *n* **innocence**	حل نشدنی *adj* **insoluble**
آدم بی گناه *adj* **innocent**	بی خوابی *n* **insomnia**
نوآوری *n* **innovation**	بازرسی کردن *v* **inspect**
کنایه *n* **innuendo**	بازرسی *n* **inspection**
بی شمار *adj* **innumerable**	بازرس *n* **inspector**
ورودی *n* **input**	الهام *n* **inspiration**
تحقیق *n* **inquest**	استنشاق کردن *v* **inspire**
پرسش کردن *v* **inquire**	بی ثباتی *n* **instability**
درخواست *n* **inquiry**	کار گذاشتن *v* **install**
تحقیق *n* **inquisition**	نصب *n* **installation**
دیوانه *adj* **insane**	نصب *n* **installment**
دیوانگی *n* **insanity**	مورد *n* **instance**
سیری ناپذیر *adj* **insatiable**	لحظه *n* **instant**
نوشته *n* **inscription**	آناً *adv* **instantly**
حشره *n* **insect**	در عوض *adv* **instead**
ناامنی *n* **insecurity**	برانگیختن *v* **instigate**

instil v چکاندن	**interest** n علاقه
instinct n غریزه	**interested** adj علاقه مند
institute v بنیاد گذاشتن	**interesting** adj جالب
institution n نهاد	**interfere** v دخالت کردن
instruct v آموزاندن	**interference** n دخالت
instructor n معلم	**interior** adj داخل
insufficient adj ناکافی	**interlude** n فاصله
insulate v جدا کردن	**intermediary** n واسطه
insulation n عایق بندی	**intern** v داخل شدن در
insult v توهین کردن به	**interpret** v ترجمه کردن
insult n توهین	**interpretation** n تفسیر
insurance n بیمه	**interpreter** n مترجم
insure v بیمه کردن	**interrogate** v بازپرسی کردن
insurgency n تمرد؛ شورش	**interrupt** v گسیختن
insurrection n شورش	**interruption** n وقفه
intact adj دست نخورده	**intersect** v تقسیم کردن
intake n ورودی	**intertwine** v درهم پیچیدن
integrate v تمام کردن	**interval** n فاصله
integration n پیوستگی	**intervene** v در میان آمدن
integrity n تمامیت	**intervention** n مداخله
intelligent adj باهوش	**interview** n مصاحبه
intend v قصد داشتن	**intestine** n روده
intense adj شدید	**intimacy** n صمیمیت
intensify v سخت کردن	**intimate** adj صمیمی
intensity n شدت	**intimidate** v ترساندن
intensive adj فشرده	**intolerable** adj غیرقابل تحمل
intention n قصد	**intolerance** n فقدان رواداری
intercede v وساطت کردن	**intoxicated** adj مست
intercept v بریدن	**intravenous** adj داخل وریدی
intercession n شفاعت	**intrepid** adj نترس
interchange v مبادله کردن	**intricate** adj پیچیده
interchange n مبادله	**intrigue** n توطئه

intriguing adj فتنه جویانه	**involvement** n درگیری
intrinsic adj ذاتی	**inward** adj درونی
introduce v معرفی کردن	**inwards** adv به سمت داخل
introduction n معرفی	**iodine** n ید
introvert adj درون گرا	**irate** adj غضب آلود
intrude v سرزده آمدن	**Ireland** n ایرلند
intruder n مزاحم	**Irish** adj ایرلندی
intrusion n مزاحمت	**iron** n آهنی
intuition n شهود	**iron** v اتو کردن
inundate v سیل زده کردن	**ironic** adj طنزآمیز
invade v تهاجم کردن	**irony** n طنز
invader n مهاجم	**irrational** adj فاقدعقل
invalid n بی اعتبار	**irrefutable** adj انکارناپذیر
invalidate v ناتوان کردن	**irregular** adj نامنظم
invaluable adj ارزشمند	**irrelevant** adj نامربوط
invasion n تهاجم	**irreparable** adj جبران ناپذیر
invent v اختراع کردن	**irresistible** adj مقاومت ناپذیر
invention n اختراع	**irrespective** adj بی طرف
inventory n موجودی	**irreversible** adj غیرقابل تغییر
invest v گذاردن	**irrevocable** adj قطعی
investigate v رسیدگی کردن	**irrigate** v آبیاری کردن
investigation n تحقیق	**irrigation** n آبیاری
investment n سرمایه گذاری	**irritate** v عصبانی کردن
investor n سرمایه گذار	**irritating** adj باعصبانی کردن
invincible adj سرسخت	**Islamic** adj اسلامی
invisible adj نامرئی	**island** n جزیره
invitation n دعوت	**isle** n جزیره
invite v دعوت کردن	**isolate** v مجزا کردن
invoice n فاکتور	**isolation** n انزوا
invoke v طلب کردن	**issue** n صدور؛ مسأله
involve v گرفتار کردن	**Italian** adj ایتالیایی
involved v گرفتار کردن	**italics** adj حروف ایتالیک

Italy n ایتالیا	**jerk** n آدم احمق و نادان
itch v خاریدن	**jersey** n ژرسه
itchiness n احساس خارش	**Jew** n یهودی
item n قلم	**jewel** n جواهر
itemize v جزء به جزء نوشتن	**jeweler** n جواهرساز
itinerary n برنامه مسافرت	**Jewish** adj یهودی
ivory n عاج	**jigsaw** n اره مویی
	job n کار
	jobless adj بیکار
	join v ملحق کردن

J

	joint n مفصل؛ شرکت
	jointly adv مشترکاً
	joke n شوخی
jackal n شغال	**joke** v شوخی کردن
jacket n کت	**jokingly** adv به شوخی
jackpot n جایزه بزرگ	**jolly** adj خوشحال
jaguar n جگوار	**jolt** v تکان دادن
jail n زندان	**jolt** n تکان
jail v حبس کردن	**journal** n نشریه
jailer n زندانبان	**journalist** n روزنامه نگار
jam n فشردگی؛ مربا	**journey** n سفر
janitor n دربان	**jovial** adj شاد
January n ژانویه	**joy** n شادی
Japan n ژاپن	**joyful** adj شاد
Japanese adj ژاپنی	**joyfully** adv با شادی
jasmine n یاسمن	**jubilant** adj سرمست
jaw n آرواره	**Judaism** n یهودیت
jealous adj حسود	**judge** n قاضی
jealousy n حسادت	**judgment** n قضاوت
jeans n شلوارجین	**judicious** adj صاحب قوه تمیز
jeopardize v به خطر انداختن	**jug** n پارچ
jerk v تکان سریع دادن	**juggler** n تردست

juice *n* عصاره	key *n* کلید؛ راهنما
juicy *adj* آبدار	key ring *n* جاکلیدی
July *n* ژوئیه	keyboard *n* صفحه کلید
jump *v* جستن	kick *v* لگد زدن
jump *n* بپرید	kickback *n* لگد زدن
jumpy *adj* عصبی	kid *n* بچه
junction *n* اتصال	kidnap *v* آدم دزدی کردن
June *n* ژوئن	kidnapper *n* بچه دزد
jungle *n* جنگل	kidnapping *n* بچه دزدی
junior *adj* کوچک	kidney *n* کلیه
junk *n* آشغال	kidney bean *n* لوبیا سبز
jury *n* هیئت منصفه	kill *v* کشتن
just *adj* هم اکنون	killer *n* قاتل
justice *n* عدالت	killing *n* قتل
justify *v* توجیه کردن	kilogram *n* کیلوگرم
justly *adv* عادلانه	kilometer *n* کیلومتر
juvenile *n* نوجوان	kilowatt *n* کیلووات
juvenile *adj* نوجوان	kind *adj* نوع
	kindle *v* روشن شدن
	kindly *adv* صمیمانه
	kindness *n* مهربانی
	king *n* پادشاه
	kingdom *n* پادشاهی

J
K

kangaroo *n* کانگورو	kinship *n* خویشاوندی
karate *n* کاراته	kiosk *n* باجه
keep *iv* نگهداری کن	kiss *v* بوسیدن
keep on *v* ادامه دادن	kiss *n* بوسید
keep up *v* تحمل کردن	kitchen *n* آشپزخانه
keg *n* چلیک کوچک	kite *n* بادبادک
kennel *n* لانه سگ	kitten *n* بچه گربه
kettle *n* کتری	knee *n* زانو
	kneecap *n* کشکک زانو

kneel iv زانو بزن	**lake** n دریاچه
knife n کارد	**lamb** n بره
knight n شوالیه	**lame** adj لنگ؛ عاجز
knit v بافتن	**lament** v تاسف خوردن
knob n دستگیره	**lament** n سوگواری
knock n ضربه	**lamp** n چراغ
knock v کوبیدن	**lamppost** n تیر چراغ
knot n گره	**lampshade** n حباب
know iv بشناس	**land** n زمین
know-how n دانش فنی	**land** v پیاده شدن
knowingly adv عمدی	**landfill** n کپه آشغال
knowledge n دانش	**landing** n فرود
	landlady n صاحبخانه
	landlord n صاحبخانه
	landscape n منظره
	lane n راه
L	**language** n زبان
	languish v افسرده شدن
lab n آزمایشگاه	**lantern** n فانوس
label n برچسب	**lap** n یک دور
labor n کار	**lapse** n لغزش؛ انصراف
laborer n کارگر	**lapse** v سپری شدن
labyrinth n ماز	**larceny** n سرقت
lace n بند	**lard** n روغن خوک
lack v نداشتن	**large** adj زیاد
lack n عدم؛ فاقد	**larynx** n حنجره
lad n جوان	**laser** n لیزر
ladder n نردبان	**lash** n شلاق؛ تسمه
laden adj انباشته	**lash** v شلاق خوردن
lady n بانو	**lash out** v حمله زبانی کردن
ladylike adj مثل یک خانم	**last** v دوام داشتن
lagoon n مرداب	**last** adj گذشته

K
L

last name *n* نام خانوادگی	**lax** *adj* اهمال کار
last night *adv* شب گذشته	**laxative** *adj* ملین
lasting *adj* بادوام	**lay** *n* راه؛ طرح *h*
lastly *adv* در پایان	**lay** *iv* نصب کن؛ قرار بده
latch *n* چفت	**lay off** *v* متوقف ساختن
late *adv* دیر	**layer** *n* لایه
lately *adv* اخیراً	**layman** *n* آدم غیرحرفه ای
later *adv* بعداً	**lay-out** *n* صفحه آرایی
later *adj* آخرین	**laziness** *n* تنبلی
lateral *adj* جانبی	**lazy** *adj* تنبل
latest *adj* آخرین	**lead** *iv* هدایت کن
lather *n* کف	**lead** *n* هدایت؛ سرب
latitude *n* وسعت	**leaded** *adj* سرب گرفته
latter *adj* دومی	**leader** *n* رهبر
laugh *v* خندان بودن	**leadership** *n* رهبری
laugh *n* بخندید	**leading** *adj* پیشرو؛ عمده
laughable *adj* خنده دار	**leaf** *n* ورق
laughing stock *n* منفور	**leaflet** *n* نشریه
laughter *n* خنده	**league** *n* لیگ
launch *n* راه اندازی	**leak** *v* تراوش کردن
launch *v* شروع کردن	**leak** *n* نشت
laundry *n* شستشو	**leakage** *n* نشتی
lavatory *n* توالت	**lean** *adj* لاغر؛ اندک
lavish *adj* فراوان	**lean** *iv* خم شو
lavish *v* اسراف کردن	**lean back** *v* لم دادن
law *n* قانون	**lean on** *v* لم دادن
law-abiding *adj* مطابق با قانون	**leaning** *n* تمایل
lawful *adj* مجاز؛ قانونی	**leap** *iv* بپر
lawmaker *n* قانون گذار	**leap** *n* بپرید
lawn *n* چمن	**leap year** *n* سال کبیسه
lawsuit *n* دعوای حقوقی	**learn** *iv* یاد بگیر
lawyer *n* مشاور حقوقی	**learned** *adj* دانشمند

L

learner *n* یادگیرنده	lengthy *adj* مفصل
learning *n* یادگیری	leniency *n* نرمش
lease *v* اجاره دادن	lenient *adj* ملایم
lease *n* اجاره	lense *n* لنز
leash *n* مهار	Lent *n* قرض داده شده
least *adj* کمترین کار	lentil *n* عدس
leather *n* چرم	leopard *n* پلنگ
leave *iv* ترک کن	leper *n* بیمارجذامی
leave out *v* جا گذاشتن	leprosy *n* جذام
lectern *n* تریبون	less *adj* کمتری
lecture *n* سخنرانی	lessee *n* مستاجر
ledger *n* دفترحسابداری	lessen *v* تخفیف یافتن
leech *n* زالو	lesser *adj* کمتر
leftovers *n* پس ماندها	lesson *n* درس
leg *n* پا	lessor *n* موجر
legacy *n* میراث	let *iv* اجازه بده
legal *adj* قانونی	let down *v* مأیوس کردن
legality *n* تطابق باقانون	let go *v* رها کردن
legalize *v* قانونی کردن	let in *v* اجازه دخول دادن
legend *n* افسانه	let out *v* اجازه خروج دادن
legible *adj* خوانا	lethal *adj* مهلک
legion *n* سپاه	letter *n* نامه؛ حرف
legislate *v* قانون وضع کردن	lettuce *n* کاهو
legislation *n* قانون گذاری	leukemia *n* سرطان خون
legislature *n* هیئت مقننه	level *v* مسطح کردن
legitimate *adj* مجاز	level *n* سطح؛ تراز
leisure *n* فراغت	lever *n* اهرم
lemon *n* لیموترش	leverage *n* عمل اهرم
lemonade *n* لیموناد	levy *v* وضع کردن مالیات
lend *iv* قرض بده	lewd *adj* شهوت ران
length *n* طول	liability *n* مسئولیت
lengthen *v* دراز کردن	liable *adj* مسئول

L

liaison n ارتباط	**lightly** adv به نرمی
liar adj دروغگو	**lightning** n برق
libel n هجو	**lightweight** n سبك
liberate v آزاد کردن	**likable** adj دوست داشتنی
liberation n آزادسازی	**like** pre مانند
liberty n آزادی	**like** v دوست داشتن
librarian n کتابدار	**likelihood** n احتمال
library n کتابخانه	**likely** adv محتمل
lice n شپش ها	**likeness** n شباهت
licence n پروانه	**likewise** adv همانطور
license v مرخص کردن	**liking** n علاقه
lick v لیسیدن	**limb** n دست
lid n سرپوش	**lime** n لیموترش
lie iv قرار بگیر	**limestone** n سنگ آهك
lie v دروغ گفتن	**limit** n حد؛ حریم
lie n دروغ	**limit** v محدود کردن
lieu n به جای	**limitation** n محدودیت
lieutenant n ستوان	**limp** v لنگیدن
life n زندگی	**limp** n لنگ
lifeguard n نجات غریق	**linchpin** n میخ محور
lifeless adj بی جان	**line** n خط
lifestyle n شیوه زندگی	**line up** v به خط شدن
lifetime adj عمر	**linen** n کتان
lift v بلند کردن	**linger** v درنگ کردن
lift-off n بلند شدن	**lingerie** n لباس زیرزنانه
ligament n پیوند	**lingering** adj طولانی
light iv روشن کن	**lining** n آستر
light adj روشن	**link** v بهم پیوستن
light n روشن	**link** n پیوند
lighter n فندك	**lion** n شیر
lighthouse n فانوس دریایی	**lioness** n ماده شیر
lighting n نوررسانی	**lip** n لب

L

liqueur *n* ليکور	load *v* بار کردن
liquid *n* مايع	load *n* بار
liquidate *v* تسويه کردن	loaded *adj* بار شده؛ مست
liquidation *n* تصفيه	loaf *n* قرص نان
liquor *n* مشروب الکلی	loan *v* قرض دادن
list *v* فهرست کردن	loan *n* قرض
list *n* فهرست	loathe *v* نفرت داشتن از
listen *v* شنيدن	loathing *n* تنفر
listener *n* شنونده	lobby *n* تالار نشيمن
litany *n* مناجات	lobby *v* تحميل گری کردن
liter *n* ليتر	lobster *n* خرچنگ
literal *adj* اشتباه چاپی	local *adj* محلی
literally *adv* لفظ به لفظ	localize *v* متمرکز کردن
literate *adj* باسواد	locate *v* مکان يابی کردن
literature *n* ادبيات	located *adj* واقع
litigate *v* مرافعه کردن	location *n* محل
litigation *n* دادخواهی	lock *v* قفل کردن
litre *n* ليتر	lock *n* قفل
litter *n* ريخته وپاشيده	lock up *v* حبس کردن
little *adj* کم	locker room *n* رخت کن
little bit *n* خيلی کم	locksmith *n* قفل ساز
little by little *adv* کم کم	locust *n* ملخ
liturgy *n* آئين نماز	lodge *v* منزل کردن
live *adj* زنده؛ دایر	lodging *n* مسکن
live *v* زندگی کردن	lofty *adj* رفيع
livelihood *n* معاش	log *n* کنده؛ ثبت
lively *adj* زنده	log *v* ثبت کردن
liver *n* جگر	log off *v* خروج از سيستم
livestock *n* دام	logic *n* منطق
livid *adj* کبود	logical *adj* منطقی
living room *n* اتاق نشيمن	loin *n* کمر
lizard *n* مارمولك	loiter *v* تاخير کردن

L

loneliness *n* تنهایی	loss *n* زیان
lonely *adv* تنها	lot *adv* تمام
loner *n* تنهاتر	lotion *n* محلول
lonesome *adj* تك و تنها	lots *adj* زیاد
long *adj* بلند	lottery *n* بخت آزمایی
longing *n* آرزو	loud *adj* بلند
longitude *n* طول جغرافیایی	loudly *adv* بلند
long-standing *adj* پایا	loudspeaker *n* بلندگو
long-term *adj* بلندمدت	lounge *n* لم
look *n* نگاه؛ منظر	louse *n* شپش
look *v* نگاه کردن	lousy *adj* شپشو
look after *v* مراقب بودن	lovable *adj* دوست داشتنی
look at *v* نگاه کردن به	love *v* دوست داشتن
look down *v* با نگاه از رو بردن	love *n* عشق
look for *v* گشتن به دنبال	lovely *adj* دوست داشتنی
look into *v* رسیدگی کردن	lover *n* عاشق
look out *v* مراقبت کردن	loving *adj* دوست داشتنی
look over *v* معاینه کردن	low *adj* پائین
look through *v* به دقت دیدن	lower *adj* پایینی
looking glass *n* آیینه	lowly *adj* خوار؛ بی ادب
looks *n* نگاه ها	loyal *adj* وفادار
loom *n* هاله روشنائی	loyalty *n* وفاداری
loophole *n* تیرکش	lubricate *v* روغن زدن
loose *v* رها کردن	lubrication *n* روغن کاری
loose *adj* شل	lucid *adj* روشن
loosen *v* شل کردن	luck *n* موفقیت
loot *v* غارت کردن	lucky *adj* خوش بخت
loot *n* غنائم	lucrative *adj* سودآور
lord *n* فرمانروا	ludicrous *adj* مضحك
lordship *n* اربابی	luggage *n* چمدان
lose *iv* گم کن	lukewarm *adj* ولرم
loser *n* بازنده	lull *n* آرام

L

lumber n تلنبار	**madness** n دیوانگی
luminous adj درخشان	**magazine** n مجله
lump n یکجا؛ غلنبه	**magic** n سحر
lunacy n دیوانگی	**magical** adj سحرآمیز
lunatic adj بیمارروانی	**magician** n ساحر
lunch n ناهار	**magnet** n مغناطیس
lung n ریه	**magnetic** adj مغناطیسی
lure v فریفتن	**magnetism** n مغناطیس
lurid adj سرخ فام	**magnificent** adj عالی
lurk v کمین کردن	**magnify** v درشت کردن
lush adj پرپشت	**magnitude** n بزرگی
lust v شهوت داشتن	**maid** n خدمتکار
lust n شهوی	**maiden** n دوشیزه
lustful adj شهوی	**mail** v با پست فرستادن
luxurious adj مجلل	**mail** n نامه؛ میل
luxury n تجمل	**mailbox** n صندوق پست
lynch v زجر کشی کردن	**mailman** n پستچی
lynx n سیاه گوش	**main** adj اصلی
lyrics n غزلها	**mainland** n قطعه اصلی
	mainly adv بیشتر
	maintain v پشتیبانی کردن
	maintenance n نگهداری
	majestic adj باعظمت
	majesty n عظمت
	major n اصلی

machine n ماشین	**major** adj اصلی
machine gun n مسلسل	**major in** v تخصص یافتن در
mad adj دیوانه	**majority** n اکثریت
madam n خانم	**make** n بسازید
madden v دیوانه کردن	**make** iv بساز
madly adv دیوانه وار	**make up** v ساختن
madman n دیوانه	**make up for** v جبران کردن

L
M

maker n سازنده	**manner** n طرز
makeup n آرایش	**mannerism** n اداواصول
malaria n مالاریا	**manners** n طرزها
male n مرد	**manpower** n نیروی انسانی
malevolent adj بدخواه	**mansion** n خانه مجلل
malfunction v بدعمل کردن	**manslaughter** n قتل غیرعمد
malfunction n خرابی	**manual** n راهنما
malice n غرض	**manual** adj راهنما
malign v بدخواهی کردن	**manufacture** v درست کردن
malignancy n شرارت	**manure** n کود
malignant adj شرور	**manuscript** n دست نویس
mall n مرکزخرید	**many** adj خیلی
malnutrition n سوءتغذیه	**map** n نقشه
malpractice v سوء اداره کردن	**marble** n سنگ مرمر
mammal n پستاندار	**march** v راه پیمایی کردن
mammoth n ماموت	**march** n قدم رو
man n مرد	**March** n مارس
manage v اداره کردن	**mare** n کابوس
manageable adj کنترل پذیر	**margin** n حاشیه
management n مدیریت	**marginal** adj حاشیه ای
manager n مدیر	**marine** adj دریایی
mandate n وکالت نامه	**marital** adj زناشویی
mandatory adj قیم	**mark** n علامت
maneuver n مانور	**mark** v علامت گذاشتن
manger n آخور	**mark down** v پائین آوردن قیمت
mangle v له کردن	**marker** n علامت
manhandle v بد رفتاری کردن	**market** n بازار
maniac adj شیدا	**marksman** n تیرانداز ماهر
manifest v بازنمود کردن	**marmalade** n مربای پرتقال
mankind n بشر	**marriage** n ازدواج
manliness n مردانگی	**married** adj متاهل
manly adj مردانه	**marrow** n مغز استخوان

M

marry v	ازدواج کردن
Mars n	مریخ
marshal n	ارتشبد؛ مارشال
martyr n	شهید
martyrdom n	شهادت
marvel n	تعجب
marvelous adj	حیرت آور
marxist adj	مارکسیست
masculine adj	مذکر
mash v	نرم کردن
mask n	ماسک
masochism n	آزارطلبی
mason n	بنا
masquerade v	جعل هویت کردن
mass n	جمعی؛ جرم
massacre n	قتل عام
massage n	ماساژ
massage v	ماساژ دادن
masseur n	ماساژور
masseuse n	ماساژور
massive adj	بزرگ
mast n	دکل
master n	اصلی
master v	ماهر شدن
mastermind n	مغز متفکر
mastermind v	ابداع کردن
masterpiece n	شاهکار
mastery n	مهارت
mat n	مات
match n	سازگار؛ جفت
match v	وصلت دادن؛
mate n	جفت

material n	مواد؛ ماده
materialism n	ماده گرایی
maternal adj	مادری
maternity n	مادری
math n	ریاضی
matriculate v	نام نویسی کردن
matrimony n	زناشویی
matter n	موضوع؛ ماده
mattress n	تشک
mature adj	بالغ
maturity n	بلوغ
maul v	صدمه زدن
maxim n	مثل
maximum adj	حداکثر
May n	می
may iv	مجاز کن
may-be adv	شاید
mayhem n	جار و جنجال
mayor n	شهردار
maze n	مارپیچ
meadow n	علفزار
meager adj	لاغر
meal n	غذا
mean iv	منظور بدار
mean adj	میانگین
meaning n	معنی
meaningful adj	بامعنی
meaningless adj	بی معنی
meanness n	پستی
means n	وسیله
meantime adv	در ضمن
meanwhile adv	در ضمن

M

measles *n* سرخك	melt *v* آب شدن
measure *v* اندازه گرفتن	member *n* عضو
measurement *n* اندازه گیری	membership *n* عضویت
meat *n* گوشت	membrane *n* غشا
meatball *n* کوفته قلقلی	memento *n* یادگاری
mechanic *n* مکانیک	memo *n* یادداشت
mechanism *n* سازوکار	memoirs *n* خاطرات
mechanize *v* ماشینی کردن	memorize *v* بخاطر سپردن
medal *n* مدال	memory *n* حافظه
medallion *n* قاب بند تزیینی	men *n* مردها
meddle *v* فضولی کردن	menace *n* تهدید
mediate *v* وساطت کردن	mend *v* تعمیر کردن
mediator *n* میانجی	meningitis *n* مننژیت
medication *n* دارو	menopause *n* یائسگی
medicinal *adj* دارویی	menstruation *n* قاعدگی
medicine *n* پزشکی	mental *adj* ذهنی
medieval *adj* قرون وسطی	mentality *n* توانایی ذهنی
mediocre *adj* معمولی	mentally *adv* ازنظر روانی
mediocrity *n* کم هوشی	mention *v* اشاره کردن
meditate *v* تفکر کردن	mention *n* ذکر
meditation *n* تفکر	menu *n* فهرست
medium *adj* رسانه	merchandise *n* کالا
meek *adj* آرام	merchant *n* بازرگان
meekness *n* بردباری	merciful *adj* بخشنده
meet *iv* ملاقات کن	merciless *adj* بیرحم
meeting *n* ملاقات	mercury *n* جیوه
melancholy *n* مالیخولیا	mercy *n* بخشندگی
mellow *adj* برسید	merely *adv* صرفاً
mellow *v* نرم کردن	merge *v* یکی کردن
melodic *adj* آهنگین	merger *n* ادغام کننده
melody *n* نوا	merit *n* شایستگی
melon *n* خربزه	merit *v* شایسته بودن

M

mermaid *n* پری دریایی	midwife *n* ماما
merry *adj* شاد	mighty *adj* زورمند
mesh *n* صید	migraine *n* میگرن
mess *n* بهم ریختگی	migrant *n* مهاجر
mess around *v* درنگ کردن	migrate *v* مهاجرت کردن
mess up *v* ضایع کردن	mild *adj* آرام
message *n* پیام	mildew *n* کپك
messenger *n* قاصد	mile *n* مایل
Messiah *n* مسیح	mileage *n* مسافت پیموده
messy *adj* نامرتب	milestone *n* مسافت نما
metal *n* فلز	militant *adj* سختگیر
metallic *adj* فلزی	milk *n* شیر
metaphor *n* استعاره	milky *adj* شیری
meteor *n* شهاب	mill *n* آسیاب
meter *n* متر	millennium *n* هزاره
method *n* روش	milligram *n* میلی گرم
methodical *adj* منظم	millimeter *n* میلی متر
meticulous *adj* بسیار دقیق	million *n* میلیون
metric *adj* متری	millionaire *n* میلیونر
metropolis *n* کلان شهر	mime *v* تقلید در آوردن
Mexican *adj* مکزیکی	mince *v* ریز ریز کردن
mice *n* موش ها	mind *v* یادآوری کردن
microbe *n* میکروب	mind *n* ذهن
microphone *n* میکروفن	mind-boggling *adj* متحیر کننده
microscope *n* میکروسکپ	mindful *adj* متوجه
microwave *n* ریزموج	mindless *adj* بی توجه
midday *n* ظهر	mine *n* مال من
middle *n* وسط	mine *v* استخراج کردن
middleman *n* واسطه	mine *pro* مال من
midget *n* آدم کوتاه	minefield *n* میدان مین
midnight *n* نیمه شب	miner *n* کارگر معدن
midsummer *n* چله تابستان	mineral *n* کانی

M

mingle *v* آمیختن	misguided *adj* گمراه
miniature *n* مینیاتور	misjudge *v* بدقضاوت کردن
minimize *v* دست کم گرفتن	mislead *v* گمراه کردن
minimum *n* حداقل	misleading *adj* گمراه کننده
miniskirt *n* دامن کوتاه	mismanage *v* بد اداره کردن
minister *n* وزیر؛ کشیش	misprint *n* غلط‌چاپی
minister *v* کمک کردن	miss *v* از دست دادن
ministry *n* وزارت؛ وزارتخانه	miss *n* خطا
minor *adj* کوچکتر	missile *n* موشک
minority *n* اقلیت	missing *adj* گم شده
mint *n* نعنا	mission *n* ماموریت
mint *v* اختراع کردن	missionary *n* مبلغ مذهبی
minus *adj* منفی	mist *n* مه آلود
minute *n* دقیقه	mistake *iv* اشتباه کن
miracle *n* معجزه	mistake *n* اشتباه
miraculous *adj* معجزه آسا	mistaken *adj* اشتباه
mirage *n* سراب	mister *n* آقای
mirror *n* آینه	mistreat *v* بدرفتاری کردن
misbehave *v* بد رفتاری کردن	mistreatment *n* بد رفتاری
miscarriage *n* سقط	mistress *n* بانو
miscarry *v* نتیج ندادن	mistrust *n* بی اعتمادی
mischief *n* شیطنت	mistrust *v* اطمینان نکردن به
mischievous *adj* شیطان	misty *adj* مه آلود
misconduct *n* رابطه نامشروع	misuse *n* استفاده نابجا
misconstrue *v* بد تعبیر کردن	mitigate *v* سبک کردن
misdemeanor *n* خلاف؛ گناه	mix *v* مخلوط کردن
miser *n* پول دوست	mixed-up *adj* گیج شده
miserable *adj* بدبخت	mixer *n* مخلوط کن
misery *n* بدبختی	mixture *n* مخلوط
misfit *adj* نامناسب	mix-up *n* درهم و برهمی
misfortune *n* بدبختی	moan *v* زاری کردن
misgiving *n* شک	moan *n* ناله

mob v ازدحام کردن	**monastery** n دیر
mob n توده	**monastic** adj راهب
mobile adj سیار	**Monday** n دوشنبه
mobilize v متحرک کردن	**money** n پول
mobster n گانگستر	**money order** n حواله
mock v استهزاء کردن	**monitor** v اداره کردن
mockery n ریشخند	**monk** n راهب
mode n شیوه	**monkey** n میمون
model n مدل	**monogamy** n تك همسری
moderate adj ملایم	**monologue** n تك گویی
moderation n اعتدال	**monopoly** n انحصار
modern adj جدید	**monotonous** adj یکنواخت
modernize v نوین کردن	**monotony** n یکنواختی
modest adj متواضع	**monster** n هیولا
modesty n فروتنی	**monstrous** adj غول پیکر
modify v تغییر دادن	**month** n ماه
module n واحد	**monthly** adv ماهانه
moisten v نمدار کردن	**monument** n بنای یادبود
moisture n رطوبت	**monumental** adj یادگاری
molar n آسیای بزرگ	**mood** n حالت
mold v قالب گرفتن	**moody** adj دمدمی
mold n قالب	**moon** n ماه
moldy adj قالبی	**moor** v لنگر انداختن
mole n خال گوشتی	**moral** adj نتیجه اخلاقی
molecule n مولکول	**moral** n نتیجه اخلاقی
molest v مزاحم شدن	**morality** n اخلاقیات
mom n مادر	**more** adj بیشتر
moment n لحظه	**moreover** adv از این گذشته
momentarily adv برای یك لحظه	**morning** n صبح
momentous adj مهم	**moron** adj كودن
monarch n پادشاه	**morphine** n مرفین
monarchy n سلطنت	**morsel** n لقمه

M

M

mortal adj انسان	**mouse** n موش
mortality n فناپذیری	**mouth** n دهان
mortar n ملاط	**move** n حرکت
mortgage n رهن	**move** v جابجا شدن
mortification n خجلت	**move back** v عقب کشیدن
mortify v ریاضت دادن	**move forward** v جلو کشیدن
mortuary n سردخانه	**move out** v راه افتادن
mosaic n موزاییک	**move up** v بالا رفتن
mosque n مسجد	**movement** n حرکت
mosquito n پشه	**movie** n فیلم
moss n خزه	**mow** v علف چیدن
most adj بیشتر	**much** adv خیلی
mostly adv عمدتاً	**mucus** n بلغم
motel n متل	**mud** n گل
moth n شب پره	**muddle** n گیجی
mother n مادر	**muddy** adj گلی کنید
motherhood n مادری	**muffle** v خاموش کردن
mother-in-law n مادر همسر	**muffler** n صدا خفه کن
motion n حرکت	**mug** n لیوان دسته دار
motionless adj بی حرکت	**mug** v کتک زدن
motivate v تشویق کردن	**mugging** n کیف زنی
motive n انگیزه	**mule** n قاطر
motor n موتور	**multiple** adj چندگانه
motorcycle n موتورسیکلت	**multiplication** n ضرب
motto n شعار	**multiply** v ضرب کردن
mouldy adj کپک زده	**multitude** n تعدد
mount n پایه	**mummy** n مامان
mount v محکم کردن	**mumps** n اوریون
mountain n کوه	**munch** v جویدن
mountainous adj کوهستانی	**munitions** n مهمات
mourn v سوگواری کردن	**murder** n قتل
mourning n سوگواری	**murderer** n قاتل

murky *adj* تاريك	
murmur *v* زمزمه كردن	
murmur *n* زمزمه	**nag** *v* عيب جويى كردن
muscle *n* ماهيچه	**nagging** *adj* آزارنده
museum *n* موزه	**nail** *n* ناخن
mushroom *n* قارچ	**naive** *adj* ساده لوح
music *n* موسيقى	**naked** *adj* لخت
musician *n* موسيقى دان	**name** *n* نام
Muslim *adj* مسلمان	**namely** *adv* يعنى
must *iv* بايد	**nanny** *n* پرستار بچه
mustache *n* سبيل	**nap** *n* چرت
mustard *n* خردل	**napkin** *n* دستمال سفره
muster *v* فراخواندن	**narcotic** *n* ماده مخدر
mutate *v* تغيير دادن	**narrow** *adj* باريك
mute *adj* لال؛ خاموش	**narrowly** *adv* از نزديك
mutilate *v* معيوب كردن	**nasty** *adj* كثيف
mutiny *n* شورش	**nation** *n* ملت
mutually *adv* دوطرفه	**national** *adj* محلى
muzzle *v* پوزه بندزدن	**nationality** *n* مليت
muzzle *n* پوزه؛ دهانه	**nationalize** *v* ملى كردن
my *adj* مال من	**native** *adj* بومى
myopic *adj* نزديك بين	**natural** *adj* عادى
myself *pro* خودم	**naturally** *adv* به طور عادى
mysterious *adj* مرموز	**nature** *n* طبيعت
mystery *n* راز	**naughty** *adj* نافرمان
mystic *adj* استعارى	**nausea** *n* تهوع
mystify *v* گيچ كردن	**nave** *n* ناو كليسا
myth *n* اسطوره	**navel** *n* ناف
	navigate *v* هدايت كردن
	navigation *n* جهت يابى
	navy *n* نيروى دريايى

M
N

navy blue adj سرمه ای
near pre نزدیك
nearby adj نزدیك
nearly adv تقریباً
nearsighted adj نزدیك بین
neat adj تمیز
neatly adv به طور مرتب
necessary adj لازم
necessitate v ناگزیر ساختن
necessity n ملزوم
neck n گردن
necklace n گردنبند
necktie n کراوات
need v احتیاج داشتن
need n احتیاج
needle n سوزن
needless adj غیر ضروری
needy adj فقیر
negative adj منفی
neglect v فروگذار کردن
neglect n غفلت
negligence n غفلت
negligent adj مسامحه کار
negotiate v گفتگو کردن
negotiation n مذاکره
neighbor n همسایه
neighborhood n همسایگی
neither adj نه
neither adv نه
nephew n پسر عمه
nerve n عصب
nervous adj عصبانی

nest n آشیانه
net n خالص
Netherlands n هلند
network n شبکه
neurotic adj روان رنجور
neutral adj خنثی
neutralize v خنثی کردن
never adv هرگز
nevertheless adv هرگز
new adj جدید
newborn n نوزاد
newcomer n تازه وارد
newly adv به تازگی
newlywed adj تازه داماد؛ تاز
news n اخبار
newscast n پخش اخبار
newsletter n خبرنامه
newspaper n روزنامه
next adj بعدی
next door adj مجاور
nibble v گاز زدن
nice adj زیبا
nicely adv زیبا
nickel n نیکل
nickname n نام مستعار
nicotine n نیکوتین
niece n دختر خواهر
night n شب
nightfall n غروب
nightgown n پیراهن خواب
nightingale n بلبل
nightmare n کابوس

N

nine *adj* نه

nineteen *adj* نوزده

ninety *adj* نود

ninth *adj* نهم

nip *n* منگنه؛ گیره

nip *v* گاز گرفتن

nipple *n* نوک پستان

nitpicking *adj* عیب جویی

nitrogen *n* نیتروژن

no one *pro* هیچکس

nobility *n* اشراف

noble *adj* اشراف زاده

nobleman *n* اشراف زاده

nobody *pro* هیچکس

nocturnal *adj* شبانه

nod *v* سرتکان دادن

noise *n* سر و صدا

noisily *adv* باسروصدا

noisy *adj* شلوغ

nominate *v* کاندید کردن

none *pre* هیچکدام

nonetheless *c* با این همه

nonsense *n* چرند

nonsmoker *n* آدم غیرسیگاری

nonstop *adv* یکسره

noon *n* ظهر

noose *n* حلقه طناب

nor *c* نه

norm *n* معیار

normal *adj* عادی

normalize *v* طبیعی کردن

normally *adv* به طور عادی

north *n* روبه شمال

northeast *n* شمال شرق

northern *adj* شمالی

northerner *adj* اهل شمال

Norway *n* نروژ

Norwegian *adj* نروژی

nose *n* بینی

nosedive *v* شیرجه رفتن

nostalgia *n* حسرت گذشته

nostril *n* سوراخ بینی

nosy *adj* فضول

not *adv* نه

notable *adj* جالب توجه

notably *adv* به طور چشمگیر

notation *n* دستگاه علائم

note *v* یادداشت کردن

notebook *n* دفتر یادداشت

noteworthy *adj* درخورتوجه

nothing *n* هیچ چیز

notice *v* ملتفت شدن

notice *n* توجه؛ اخطار

noticeable *adj* محسوس

notification *n* اطلاع

notify *v* اطلاع دادن

notion *n* ایده

notorious *adj* رسوا

noun *n* اسم

nourish *v* غذا دادن

nourishment *n* خوراك

novel *n* رمان

novelist *n* داستان نویس

novelty *n* تازگی

N

November n نوامبر

novice n تازه وارد

now adv حالا

nowadays adv امروزه

nowhere adv هیچ کجا

noxious adj مضر

nuance n تفاوت ظریف

nuclear adj هسته ای

nude adj مدل برهنه

nudism n برهنه گرایی

nudist n برهنه گرا

nudity n برهنگی

nuisance n مزاحم

null adj هیچ

nullify v لغو کردن

numb adj کرخ

number n شماره

numbness n کرخی

numerous adj متعدد

nun n راهبه

nurse n پرستار

nurse v پروراندن

nursery n شیرخوارگاه

nurture v بزرگ کردن

nut n آجیل؛ مهر؛ خل

nutrition n تغذیه

nutritious adj مغذی

nutty adj دیوانه

oak n بلوط

oar n پارو

oasis n واحه

oath n قسم

oatmeal n غذای غلات

obedience n فرمانبرداری

obedient adj مطیع

obese adj فربه

obey v اطاعت کردن

object v اعتراض کردن

object n هدف

objection n اعتراض

objective n هدف

obligation n وظیفه

obligatory adj اجباری

oblige v مجبور کردن

obliged adj ملزم

oblique adj خط مورب

obliterate v محو کردن

oblivion n فراموشی

oblivious adj بی خبر

oblong adj مستطیل

obnoxious adj نامطبوع

obscene adj هرزه

obscenity n هرزگی

obscure adj تیره

obscurity n تیرگی

observation n مشاهده

observatory n رصدخانه

observe v رعایت کردن	offend v اذیت کردن
obsess v آزار دادن	offense n اهانت
obsession n دل مشغولی	offensive adj حمله
obsolete adj کهنه	offer v پیشکش کردن
obstacle n مانع	offer n پیشنهاد
obstinacy n لجاجت	offering n پیشنهاد
obstinate adj لجوج	office n دفتر
obstruct v مسدود کردن	officer n مامور
obstruction n انسداد	official adj مامور
obtain v به دست آوردن	officiate v اداره کردن
obvious adj آشکار	offset v جبران کردن
obviously adv آشکارا	offspring n فرزند
occasion n موقعیت	off-the-record adj خصوصی
occasionally adv گاهگاهی	often adv اغلب
occult adj علم غیبی	oil n نفت
occupant n ساکن	ointment n پماد
occupation n پیشه	okay adv درست
occupy v اشغال کردن	old adj قدیمی
occur v رخ دادن	old age n پیری
ocean n اقیانوس	old-fashioned adj سنتی
October n اکتبر	olive n زیتون
octopus n هشت پا	olympics n بازی های المپیک
ocurrence n رخداد	omelette n املت
odd adj عجیب	omen n شگون
oddity n عجیب	ominous adj شوم
odds n شانس	omission n حذف
odious adj نفرت انگیز	omit v حذف کردن
odometer n کیلومتر شمار	on pre روی
odor n بو	once adv یکبار
odyssey n سفر پرماجرا	once c یکبار
of pre از	one adj دیگری
off adv خاموش	oneself pre خود

ongoing adj جاری	**optimism** n خوش بینی
onion n پیاز	**optimistic** adj خوش بین
onlooker n ناظر	**option** n حق انتخاب
only adv تنها	**optional** adj اختیاری
onset n شروع	**opulence** n ثروت
onslaught n حمله بی امان	**or** c یا
onwards adv به بعد	**oracle** n معبد
opaque adj مات	**orally** adv به طور شفاهی
open v باز کردن	**orange** n پرتقال
open adj بازکنید	**orangutan** n اوانگوتان
open up v باز کردن	**orbit** n مدار
opening n بازکردن	**orchard** n باغ
open-minded adj روشنفکر	**orchestra** n ارکستر
openness n صداقت	**ordain** v ترتیب دادن
opera n اپرا	**ordeal** n عذاب
operation n کارکرد	**order** n سفارش
opinion n عقیده	**ordinarily** adv معمولی
opinionated adj جزمی	**ordinary** adj معمولی
opium n تریاک	**ordination** n رتبه بخشان
opponent n حریف	**ore** n سنگ معدن
opportune adj به جا	**organ** n اندام
opportunity n فرصت	**organism** n اورگانیسم
oppose v ضدیت کردن	**organist** n ارگ زن
opposite adj مقابل	**organization** n سازمان
opposite adv مقابل	**organize** v تشکیل دادن
opposite n مقابل	**orient** n سازگار
opposition n مخالفت	**oriental** adj شرقی
oppress v ستم کردن	**orientation** n جهت
oppression n مظلومیت	**oriented** adj دارای گرایش
opt for v طرفداری کردن	**origin** n منشا
optical adj نوری	**original** adj اصلی
optician n عینک ساز	**originally** adv اساساً

originate v ناشی شدن	outlaw v ممنوع ساختن
ornament n تزئین	outlet n خروجی؛ پریز
ornamental adj تزیینی	outline n خطوط اصلی
orphan n یتیم	outline v طرح ریزی کردن
orphanage n پرورشگاه	outlook n چشم انداز
orthodox adj سنتی	outmoded adj کهنه
ostentatious adj خودنما	outnumber v افزون بودن بر
ostrich n شترمرغ	outpatient n بیمار سرپائی
other adj دیگر	outpouring n برون ریزی
otherwise adv به طریق دیگری	output n خروجی
otter n سمور آبی	outrage n دست درازی
ought to iv باید	outrageous adj اهانت آمیز
ounce n اونس	outright adj کامل
our adj مال ما	outrun v پیش افتادن
ours pro مال ما	outset n آغاز
ourselves pro خودمان	outshine v پیشی گرفتن از
oust v برکنار کردن	outside adv بیرون
out adv خارج؛ بیرون	outsider n بیگانه
outbreak n شیوع	outskirts n حومه
outburst n ظهور ناگهانی	outspoken adj رک
outcast adj رانده شده	outstanding adj برجسته
outcome n حاصل	outstretched adj گشوده
outcry n نعره	outward adj به طرف خارج
outdated adj کهنه	outweigh v مهمتر بودن از
outdo v شکست دادن	oval adj بیضی
outdoor adv بیرون	ovary n تخمدان
outdoors adv بیرون	ovation n ابراز احساسات
outer adj برونی	oven n اجاق
outfit n مجهز	over pre بر روی
outgoing adj درحال رفتن	overall adv سراسر
outgrow v بزرگ تر شدن از	overbearing adj متکبر
outing n سفر تفریحی	overboard adv روی کشتی

overcast *adj* هوای ابری	**owing to** *adv* به علت
overcoat *n* پالتو	**owl** *n* جغد
overcome *v* غلبه کردن	**own** *v* مالک بودن
overcrowded *adj* شلوغ	**own** *adj* مال خودم
overdone *adj* بیش از حدپخته	**owner** *n* صاحب
overdue *adj* منقضی	**ownership** *n* مالکیت
overestimate *v* دست بالا گرفتن	**ox** *n* گاونر
overflow *v* سرشار شدن	**oxen** *n* گاوهای نر
overhaul *v* پیاده کردن	**oxygen** *n* اکسیژن
overlap *v* روی هم افتادن	**oyster** *n* صدف خوراکی
overlook *v* مسلط بودن بر	
overnight *adv* یك شبه	
overpower *v* فتح کردن	
overrate *v* زیاد اهمیت دادن	
override *v* پایمال کردن	
overrule *v* رد کردن	
overrun *v* تاخت و تاز کردن	
overseas *adv* خارجی	**pace** *v* گام زدن
oversee *v* سرکشی کردن	**pace** *n* قدم؛ سرعت
overshadow *v* تاریک کردن	**pacify** *v* آرام کردن
oversight *n* غفلت	**pack** *v* بسته کردن
overstate *v* اغراق آمیز کردن	**package** *n* بسته
overstep *v* تجاوز کردن	**pact** *n* پیمان
overtake *v* سبقت گرفتن بر	**pad** *v* پر کردن
overthrow *v* بهم زدن	**padding** *n* لایی
overthrow *n* براندازی	**paddle** *v* پارو زدن
overtime *adv* اضافه کار	**padlock** *n* قفل
overturn *v* واژگون/کردن	**pagan** *adj* کافر
overview *n* دیدکلی	**page** *n* صفحه؛ پادو
overweight *adj* اضافه وزن	**pail** *n* سطل
overwhelm *v* پایمال کردن	**pain** *n* درد
owe *v* بدهکار بودن	**painful** *adj* دردناك
	painkiller *n* مسکن

painless *adj* بی درد	**parable** *n* حکایت
paint *v* رنگ کردن	**parachute** *n* چتر
paint *n* رنگ	**parade** *n* رژه
paintbrush *n* قلم مو	**paradise** *n* بهشت
painter *n* نقاش	**paradox** *n* تضاد
painting *n* نقاشی	**paragraph** *n* پاراگراف
pair *n* جفت	**parakeet** *n* طوطی دم دراز
pajamas *n* لباس خواب	**parallel** *n* موازی
pal *n* رفیق	**paralysis** *n* فلج
palace *n* کاخ	**paralyze** *v* فلج کردن
palate *n* کام	**parameters** *n* عاملها
pale *adj* بی رنگ	**paramount** *adj* مهم
paleness *n* رنگ پریدگی	**paranoid** *adj* مجنون
palm *n* کف دست	**parasite** *n* انگل
palpable *adj* محسوس	**paratrooper** *n* چترباز
paltry *adj* ناچیز	**parcel** *n* بسته
pamper *v* به ناز پروردن	**parcel post** *n* بسته پستی
pamphlet *n* جزوه	**parch** *v* خشک کردن
pan *n* تشتک	**parchment** *n* کاغذ پوستی
pancreas *n* لوزالمعده	**pardon** *v* عفو کردن
pander *v* جاکشی کردن	**pardon** *n* بخشش
pang *n* درد شدید	**parenthesis** *n* پرانتز
panic *n* ناشی از وحشت	**parents** *n* والدین
panorama *n* منظره	**parish** *n* محله
panther *n* پلنگ	**parishioner** *n* مرید
pantry *n* آبدارخانه	**parity** *n* برابری
pants *n* شلوار	**park** *v* قرار دادن
pantyhose *n* جوراب شلواری	**park** *n* پارک
papacy *n* مقام پاپ	**parking** *n* جای پارک
paper *n* کاغذ	**parliament** *n* مجلس
paperclip *n* گیره کاغذ	**parochial** *adj* کوته فکر
paperwork *n* کاردفتری	**parrot** *n* طوطی

P

parsley n جعفری	**password** n رمز
parsnip n زردك	**past** adj گذشته
part v جداشدن	**paste** v چسباندن
part n قسمت	**paste** n چسب
partial adj جزئی	**pastime** n سرگرمی
partially adv به طور جزئی	**pastor** n كشیش
participate v شریک شدن	**pastoral** adj شعر شبانی
participation n مشاركت	**pastry** n نان شیرینی
participle n وجه وصفی	**pasture** n بچرانید
particle n ذره	**pat** n بلافاصله
particular adj خاص	**patch** v بهم پیوستن
particularly adv مخصوصاً	**patch** n وصله
parting n فرق	**patent** n پروانه ساخت
partisan n چریکی	**patent** adj پروانه ساخت
partition n بخش	**paternity** n پدری
partly adv تا حدی	**path** n مسیر
partner n شریک	**pathetic** adj ترحم انگیز
partnership n شراكت	**patience** n صبر
partridge n كبك	**patient** adj بیمار
party n مهمانی؛ حزب	**patio** n حیاط خلوت
pass n پاس؛ گذراندن	**patriarch** n مرد خانواده
pass v انتقال دادن	**patrimony** n ارث پدری
pass around v پاس دادن	**patriot** n میهن پرست
pass away v مردن	**patriotic** adj وطن پرست
pass out v ضعف كردن	**patrol** n گشت
passage n عبور و مرور	**patron** n حامی؛ مشتری
passenger n مسافر	**patronage** n حمایت
passer-by n عابر	**patronize** v تشویق كردن
passion n شور	**pattern** n نمونه
passionate adj احساساتی	**pavement** n پیاده رو
passive adj پذیرا	**pavilion** n غرفه
passport n گذرنامه	**paw** n پنجه

pawn v رهن دادن	**peer** n نظیر
pawnbroker n کارگشا	**pelican** n مرغ ماهی خوار
pay n پرداخت	**pellet** n گلوله
pay iv بپرداز	**pen** n قلم
pay back v بازپرداخت کردن	**penalize** v تنبیه کردن
pay off v پرداخت کردن	**penalty** n جریمه؛ پنالتی
payable adj قابل پرداخت	**penance** n توبه
paycheck n چک پرداخت	**penchant** n علاقه
payee n ذینفع	**pencil** n مداد
payment n پرداخت	**pendant** n گردنبند
payroll n لیست حقوق	**pending** adj معوق
payslip n فیش حقوق	**pendulum** n پاندول
pea n نخود	**penetrate** v نفوذ کردن
peace n صلح	**penguin** n پنگوئن
peaceful adj آرام	**penicillin** n پنی سیلین
peach n هلو	**peninsula** n شبه جزیره
peacock n طاوس	**penitent** n پشیمان
peak n اوج	**penniless** adj فقیر
peanut n بادام زمینی	**penny** n پنی
pear n گلابی	**pentagon** n پنج ضلعی
pearl n لولو	**pent-up** adj فروخورده
peasant n روستایی	**people** n مردم
pebble n ریگ	**pepper** n فلفل
peck v نوک زدن	**per** pre به ازاء هر
peck n نوک بزنید	**perceive** v درک کردن
peculiar adj خاص	**percent** adv درصد
pedagogy n آموزش وپرورش	**percentage** n درصد
pedal n پدالی	**perception** n ادراك
pedantic adj خشك	**perennial** adj گیاه چندساله
pedestrian n عابر پیاده	**perfect** adj کامل
peel v پوست انداختن	**perfection** n کمال
peel n پوست	**perforate** v درک کردن

P

perforation *n* سوراخ شدگی	**persuasion** *n* متقاعدسازی
perform *v* انجام دادن	**persuasive** *adj* قانع کننده
performance *n* اجرا؛ عملکرد	**pertain** *v* وابسته بودن
perfume *n* عطر	**pertinent** *adj* مناسب
perhaps *adv* شاید	**perturb** *v* ناراحت کردن
peril *n* خطر	**perverse** *adj* منحرف
perilous *adj* پرمخاطره	**pervert** *v* منحرف کردن
perimeter *n* محیط	**pervert** *adj* منحرف
period *n* دوره	**pessimism** *n* بدبینی
perish *v* هلاک شدن	**pessimistic** *adj* بدبین
perishable *adj* فاسدشدنی	**pest** *n* آفت
perjury *n* شهادت دروغ	**pester** *v* اذیت کردن
permanent *adj* دائم	**pesticide** *n* آفت کش
permeate *v* نفوذ کردن	**pet** *n* دست آموز
permission *n* اجازه	**petal** *n* گلبرگ
permit *v* اجازه دادن	**petite** *adj* ریزنقش
pernicious *adj* مضر	**petition** *n* استدعا
perpetrate *v* مرتکب شدن	**petrified** *adj* وحشت زده
persecute *v* اذیت کردن	**petroleum** *n* نفت خام
persevere *v* پشتکار داشتن	**pettiness** *n* ناچیزی
persist *v* سماجت کردن	**petty** *adj* کوچک؛ جزئی
persistence *n* سماجت	**pew** *n* نیمکت
persistent *adj* سمج	**phantom** *n* روح
person *n* شخص	**pharmacist** *n* داروساز
personal *adj* شخصی	**pharmacy** *n* داروسازی
personality *n* شخصیت	**phase** *n* مرحله
personify *v* شخصیت دادن	**pheasant** *n* قرقاول
personnel *n* کارکنان	**phenomenon** *n* پدیده
perspective *n* بعد نمایی	**philosopher** *n* فیلسوف
perspiration *n* تعریق	**philosophy** *n* فلسفه
perspire *v* عرق کردن	**phobia** *n* هراسی
persuade *v* وادار کردن	**phone** *n* تلفن

P

phone v تلفن زدن	**pile up** v جمع کردن
phoney adj آدم حقه باز	**pilfer** v کش رفتن
phosphorus n فسفر	**pilgrim** n مهاجر
photo n عکس	**pilgrimage** n زیارت
photocopy n فتوکپی	**pill** n قرص
photographer n عکاس	**pillage** v غارت کردن
photography n عکاسی	**pillar** n پایه
phrase n عبارت	**pillow** n بالش
physically adv فیزیکی	**pillowcase** n روبالشی
physician n پزشک	**pilot** n خلبان
physics n فیزیک	**pimple** n جوش
pianist n نوازنده پیانو	**pin** n سوزن
piano n پیانو	**pincers** n گازانبر
pick v انتخاب کردن	**pinch** v نیشگون گرفتن
pick up v برداشتن	**pinch** n نیشگون؛ گیره
pickpocket n جیب بر	**pine** n درخت کاج
pickup n جمع آوری	**pineapple** n آناناس
picture n تصویر	**pink** adj صورتی
picture v مجسم کردن	**pint** n پاینت
picturesque adj تماشایی	**pioneer** n پیشگام
pie n پای	**pious** adj پرهیزگار
piece n تکه	**pipe** n لوله
piecemeal adv تکه تکه	**pipeline** n خطلوله
pier n اسکله	**piracy** n دزدی دریایی
pierce v سوراخ کردن	**pirate** n غیرمجاز
piercing n تیز؛ نافذ	**pistol** n تپانچه
piety n پارسایی	**pit** n هسته
pig n خوک	**pitch-black** adj قیرگون
pigeon n کبوتر	**pitchfork** n چنگال
piggy bank n قلک	**pitiful** adj ترحم انگیز
pile v اندوختن	**pity** n ترحم
pile n پرزدار	**placard** n پلاکارد

P

placate *v* آرام کردن	pleasing *adj* خوشایند
place *n* مکان	pleasure *n* خوشی
placid *adj* آرام	pleat *n* پیله
plague *n* سرایت مرض؛ بلا	pleated *adj* پیلی دار
plain *n* جلگه	pledge *v* گرو گذاشتن
plain *adj* پهن؛ آشکار	pledge *n* قول
plainly *adv* به وضوح	plentiful *adj* فراوان
plaintiff *n* خواهان	plenty *n* مقدار زیاد
plan *v* طرح ریختن	pliable *adj* انعطاف پذیر
plan *n* طرح؛ برنامه ریزی	pliers *n* انبردست
plane *n* هواپیما	plot *v* رسم کردن
planet *n* سیاره	plot *n* توطئه
plant *v* کاشتن	plow *v* شخم زدن
plant *n* گیاه	ploy *n* دستاویز
plaster *n* گچ	pluck *v* چیدن
plaster *v* گچ زدن	plug *v* بستن؛ قاچ کردن
plastic *n* نرم	plug *n* درپوش؛ فیش
plate *n* بشقاب	plum *n* آلو
plateau *n* فلات	plumber *n* لوله کش
platform *n* سکو	plumbing *n* لوله کشی
platinum *n* طلای سفید	plummet *v* سرازیر شدن
platoon *n* دسته	plump *adj* فربه
plausible *adj* موجه	plunder *v* غارت کردن
play *v* بازی کردن	plunge *v* فرو رفتن
play *n* بازی؛ نمایش	plunge *n* گودال عمیق
player *n* بازیکن	plural *n* جمع
playful *adj* بازیگوش	plus *adj* باضافه
playground *n* زمین بازی	plush *adj* پارچه مخملی
plea *n* تقاضا	plutonium *n* پلوتونیم
plead *v* درخواست کردن	pneumonia *n* پنومونی
pleasant *adj* خوشایند	pocket *n* جیب
please *v* دلپذیر کردن	poem *n* شعر

P

poet n شاعر	**pomposity** n تکبر
poetry n شعر	**pond** n استخر
poignant adj غم انگیز	**ponder** v سنجیدن
point n نقطه؛ نکته	**pontiff** n پاپ
point v متوجه کردن	**pool** n استخر؛ بیلیارد
pointed adj نوک دار	**pool** v شریک شدن
pointless adj بی فایده	**poor** n ضعیف
poise n توازن؛ ثبات	**poorly** adv ضعیف
poison v مسموم کردن	**popcorn** n ذرت بوداده
poison n سم	**Pope** n پاپ
poisoning n مسمومیت	**poppy** n شقایق
poisonous adj سمی	**popular** adj عمومی
Poland n لهستان	**popularize** v مشهور کردن
polar adj قطبی	**populate** v ساکن شدن
pole n قطب	**population** n جمعیت
police n پلیس	**porcelain** n چینی
policeman n مامور پلیس	**porch** n هشتی
policy n خط مشی	**porcupine** n جوجه تیغی
Polish adj لهستانی	**pore** n اندیشه
polish n صیقل	**pork** n گوشت خوک
polish v صیقل دادن	**porous** adj متخلخل
polite adj مودب	**port** n بندر
politeness n ادب	**portable** adj قابل حمل
politician n سیاستمدار	**portent** n نشانه
politics n سیاست	**porter** n باربر
poll n صورت رأی	**portion** n قسمت
pollen n گرده	**portrait** n نقاشی
pollute v نجس کردن	**portray** v توصیف کردن
pollution n آلودگی	**Portugal** n پرتغال
polygamist adj چند زنه	**Portuguese** adj پرتغالی
polygamy n چند همسری	**pose** v مطرح کردن
pomegranate n انار	**pose** n تظاهر

P

posh *adj* شیك	**practise** *v* تمرین کردن
position *n* موضع	**practising** *adj* شاغل
positive *adj* مثبت	**pragmatist** *adj* عمل گرا
possess *v* دارا بودن	**prairie** *n* چمنزار
possession *n* مالکیت	**praise** *v* ستایش کردن
possibility *n* امکان	**praise** *n* تحسین
possible *adj* ممکن	**praiseworthy** *adj* قابل تحسین
post *n* پست؛ میله	**prank** *n* شوخی
post office *n* پستخانه	**prawn** *n* شاه میگو
postage *n* هزینه پست	**pray** *v* دعا کردن
postcard *n* کارت پستال	**prayer** *n* دعا گوینده
poster *n* پوستر	**preach** *v* موعظه کردن
posterity *n* آیندگان	**preacher** *n* واعظ
postman *n* نامه رسان	**preaching** *n* موعظه
postmark *n* مهرپست	**preamble** *n* مقدمه
postponement *n* عقب انداختن	**precarious** *adj* بی ثبات
pot *n* ظرف؛ دیگچه	**precaution** *n* احتیاط
potato *n* سیب زمینی	**precede** *v* مقدم بودن
potent *adj* قوی	**precedent** *n* سابقه
potential *adj* بالقوه	**preceding** *adj* پیش
pothole *n* چالاب	**precept** *n* دستور
poultry *n* طیور	**precious** *adj* گرانبها
pound *v* کوبیدن	**precipice** *n* سقوط ناگهانی
pound *n* پوند	**precipitate** *v* تسریع کردن
pour *v* ریختن	**precise** *adj* دقیق
poverty *n* فقر	**precision** *n* دقت
powder *n* پودر	**precocious** *adj* پیشرس
power *n* نیرو	**precursor** *n* مقدمه
powerful *adj* نیرومند	**predecessor** *n* سابق
powerless *adj* ضعیف	**predicament** *n* چگونگی
practical *adj* عملی	**predict** *v* پیشگویی کردن
practice *n* تمرین	**prediction** *n* پیش بینی

P

predilection n میل	**presentation** n ارائه
predisposed adj مستعد	**preserve** v نگاه داشتن
predominate v قاطع بودن	**preside** v ریاست کردن بر
preempt v قبضه کردن	**presidency** n ریاست جمهوری
prefabricate v پیس ساختن	**president** n رییس
preface n پیشگفتار	**press** n فشار ؛ پرس
prefer v ترجیح یافتن	**press** v فشار دادن
preference n اولویت	**pressing** adj فشار
prefix n پیشوند	**pressure** v فشردن
pregnancy n حاملگی	**pressure** n فشار
pregnant adj آبستن	**prestige** n آبرو
prehistoric adj ازپیش تاریخ	**presume** v فرض کردن
prejudice n تعصب	**presumption** n فرض
preliminary adj مقدماتی	**presupposition** n فرض
prelude n مقدمه	**pretend** v وانمود کردن
premature adj زودرس	**pretense** n وانمودسازی
premeditation n عمد	**pretension** n ادعا
premier adj نخست وزیر	**pretty** adj قشنگ
premise n مقدمه	**prevail** v شایع شدن
premises n دارایی	**prevalent** adj رایج
premonition n دلشوره	**prevent** v جلوگیری کردن
preoccupation n اشتغال ذهن	**prevention** n پیشگیری
preparation n آمادگی	**preventive** adj پیشگیر
prepare v آماده کردن	**preview** n پیش نمایش
preposition n حرف اضافه	**previous** adj قبلی
prerequisite n شرط لازم	**previously** adv قبلاً
prerogative n حق	**prey** n طعمه
prescribe v تجویز کردن	**price** n قیمت
prescription n نسخه	**pricey** adj گران
presence n حضور	**prick** v خراش دادن
present adj حاضر	**pride** n غرور
present v اهداء کردن	**priest** n روحانی

P

روحانی زن n **priestess**	عواید n **proceeds**
مقام کشیشی n **priesthood**	پردازش کردن v **process**
تفوق n **primacy**	فرآیند n **process**
در درجه اول adv **primarily**	حرکت n **procession**
نخست adj **prime**	اعلان کردن v **proclaim**
اولیه adj **primitive**	اعلان n **proclamation**
شاهزاده n **prince**	معوق گذراندن v **procrastinate**
شاهزاده خانم n **princess**	تولید کردن؛ زادن v **procreate**
اصلی adj **principal**	تهیه کردن v **procure**
اصل n **principle**	سک زدن v **prod**
چاپ کردن v **print**	عظیم adj **prodigious**
چاپ n **print**	نابغه n **prodigy**
چاپگر n **printer**	تولید کردن v **produce**
چاپ n **printing**	تولید n **produce**
پیشین adj **prior**	محصول n **product**
حق تقدم n **priority**	تولید n **production**
منشور n **prism**	بارآور adj **productive**
زندان n **prison**	کفر آمیز adj **profane**
زندانی n **prisoner**	اظهار کردن v **profess**
خصوصی n **privacy**	حرفه n **profession**
خصوصی adj **private**	حرفه ای adj **professional**
امتیاز n **privilege**	استاد n **professor**
جایزه n **prize**	مهارت n **proficiency**
احتمال n **probability**	ماهر adj **proficient**
احتمالی adj **probable**	نمایه n **profile**
بازرسی کردن v **probe**	سود بردن v **profit**
تحقیق n **probing**	سود n **profit**
مسئله n **problem**	سودآور adj **profitable**
دشوار adj **problematic**	عمیق adj **profound**
روش n **procedure**	برنامه n **program**
ادامه دادن v **proceed**	برنامه نویس n **programmer**
اقدامات n **proceedings**	پیشرفت کردن v **progress**

P

progress n پیشرفت	**proposition** n موضوع
progressive adj آدم مترقی	**prose** n نثر
prohibit v جلوگیری کردن	**prosecutor** n دادیار
prohibition n تحریم	**prospect** n دورنما
project v طرح کردن	**prosperity** n رفاه
project n پروژه؛ طرح	**prosperous** adj موفق
projectile n پرتابه	**prostate** n پروستات
prologue n مطلع	**prostrate** adj به خاک افتاده
prolong v طولانی کردن	**protect** v محافظت کردن
promenade n گردش	**protection** n محافظت
prominent adj برجسته	**protein** n پروتئین
promiscuous adj بی بندوبار	**protest** v اعتراض کردن
promise n قول	**protest** n اعتراض آمیز
promote v ترفیع دادن	**protocol** n معاهده
promotion n ترفیع	**prototype** n الگوی نخستین
prompt adj فوری	**protract** v طول دادن
prone adj مستعد	**protracted** adj طولانی
pronoun n ضمیر	**protrude** v تحمیل کردن
pronounce v حکم دادن	**proud** adj مفتخر
proof n اثبات	**proudly** adv با افتخار
propaganda n تبلیغات	**prove** v اثبات کردن
propagate v منتشر کردن	**proven** adj ثابت شده
propel v سوق دادن	**proverb** n مثل
propensity n کشش	**provide** v فراهم کردن
proper adj مناسب	**providence** n عنایت خداوند
properly adv به طور صحیح	**province** n استان
property n دارایی	**provision** n تهیه
prophecy n پیشگویی	**provisional** adj موقت
prophet n پیامبر	**provocation** n تحریک
proportion n نسبت	**provoke** v تحریک کردن
proposal n پیشنهاد	**prow** n دماغه کشتی
propose v پیشنهاد کردن	**prowl** v پرسه زدن

P

prowler n ولگرد	**pulsate** v تپیدن
proximity n نزدیکی	**pulse** n پالس
proxy n وکالت	**pulverize** v ساییدن
prudence n احتیاط	**pump** v پمپ کردن
prudent adj محتاط	**pump** n تلمبه
prune v هرس کردن	**pumpkin** n کدو تنبل
prune n آلو	**punch** v مشت زدن
prurient adj شهوانی	**punch** n منگنه؛ مشت
pseudonym n نام مستعار	**punctual** adj دقیق
psychiatrist n روان پزشک	**puncture** n پنچری
psychiatry n روان پزشکی	**punish** v تنبیه کردن
psychic adj واسطه	**punishable** adj سزاوار تنبیه
psychology n روان شناسی	**punishment** n تنبیه
psychopath n جنایت کارروانی	**pupil** n دانش آموز
puberty n بلوغ	**puppy** n توله سگ
public adj عمومی	**purchase** v خریداری کردن
publication n انتشار	**purchase** n خرید
publicity n تبلیغات	**pure** adj خالص
publicly adv علناً	**puree** n پوره
publish v منتشر کردن	**purgatory** n برزخ
publisher n ناشر	**purge** n تصفیه
pudding n پودینگ	**purge** v تهی کردن
puerile adj بچگانه	**purification** n تصفیه
puff n پک	**purify** v خالص کردن
puffy adj پف دار	**purity** n خلوص
pull v کشیدن	**purple** adj رنگ ارغوانی
pull ahead v جلو کشیدن	**purpose** n منظور
pull down v پائین کشیدن	**purposely** adv عمداً
pull out v بیرون کشیدن	**purse** n کیف پول
pulley n قرقره	**pursue** v تعقیب کردن
pulp n خمیره	**pursuit** n تعقیب؛ پیشه
pulpit n منبر	**pus** n چرک

P

push v فشار دادن	**quarter** n ربع
pushy adj سمج	**quarterly** adj سه ماه یکبار
put iv بگذار	**quarters** n ربعها
put aside v کنار گذاشتن	**quash** v نقض کردن
put away v مردود ساختن	**queen** n ملکه
put off v به تأخیر انداختن	**queer** adj غیر عادی
put out v بیرون گذاشتن	**quell** v فرونشاندن
put up v پیشنهاد کردن	**quench** v فرونشاندن
put up with v تحمل کردن	**quest** n جستجو
putrid adj گندیده	**question** v پرسیدن
puzzle n پازل؛ جورچین	**question** n سوال
puzzling adj گیج کننده	**questionable** adj سوال برانگیز
pyramid n هرم	**questionnaire** n پرسش نامه
python n اژدرمار	**queue** n ردیف
	quick adj سریع
	quicken v تسریع کردن
	quickly adv به سرعت
	quicksand n ماسه بادی

Q

	quiet adj آرام
	quietness n سکوت
	quilt n لحاف
	quit iv ترک کن
	quite adv کاملاً
quagmire n باتلاق	**quiver** v لرزیدن
quail n بلدرچین	**quiz** v آزمایش کردن
quake v لرزیدن	**quotation** n نقل قول
qualify v واجد شرایط شدن	**quotient** n بهر
quality n کیفیت	
qualm n عذاب وجدان	
quandery n سرگردانی	
quantity n کمیت	
quarrel v منازعه	
quarrel n دعوا	
quarrelsome adj دعوایی	
quarry n استخراج	

P
Q

R

خاخام **rabbi** n
خرگوش **rabbit** n
بیماری هاری **rabies** n
راکون **raccoon** n
مسابقه دادن **race** v
نژاد؛ مسابقه **race** n
نژادپرستی **racism** n
نژادپرست **racist** adj
راکت **racket** n
باجگیری **racketeering** n
رادار **radar** n
تابش **radiation** n
رادیاتور **radiator** n
ریشه **radical** adj
رادیویی **radio** n
تربچه **radish** n
شعاع **radius** n
قرعه کشی **raffle** n
کلک **raft** n
کهنه **rag** n
خشم **rage** n
پاره پوره **ragged** adj
حمله؛ کمین **raid** n
هجوم آوردن **raid** v
مهاجم **raider** n
دست انداز **rail** n
خط راه آهن **railroad** n
باران بیایید **rain** n
باریدن **rain** v

رنگین کمان **rainbow** n
بارانی **raincoat** n
بارندگی **rainfall** n
بارانی **rainy** adj
بلند کردن **raise** n
تربیت کردن **raise** v
کشمش **raisin** n
شن کش **rake** n
قوچ **ram** n
با فشار راندن **ram** v
انشعاب **ramification** n
سراشیبی **ramp** n
وحشیگری کردن **rampage** v
شایع **rampant** adj
نوعی سیر **ramson** n
مزرعه **ranch** n
کینه **rancor** n
به طور اتفاقی **randomly** adv
حیطه؛ محدوده **range** n
نامطبوع؛ رتبه **rank** n
رتبه بندی کردن **rank** v
جستجو کردن **ransack** v
تجاوز جنسی کردن **rape** v
تجاوز به عنف **rape** n
تند **rapid** adj
متجاوز جنسی **rapist** n
حسن تفاهم **rapport** n
کم **rare** adj
بندرت **rarely** adv
آدم رذل **rascal** n
دانه **rash** n
تمشک جنگلی **raspberry** n

rat n موش	**really** adv واقعاً
rate n ارزیابی؛ رتبه بندی	**realm** n قلمرو
rather adv تا حدی	**realty** n املاك
ratification n تصویب	**reap** v درو کردن
ratify v تصویب کردن	**reappear** v دوباره ظاهر شدن
ratio n نسبت	**rear** v تربیت کردن
ration v تخصیص دادن	**rear** n عقبی
ration n سهمیه	**rear** adj عقبی
rational adj عقلی	**reason** v دلیل آوردن
rationalize v تفسیر کردن	**reason** n دلیل
rattle v تغ تغ کردن	**reasonable** adj معقول
ravage v غارت کردن	**reasoning** n استدلال
ravage n نابود	**rebate** n استرداد
rave v دیوانه شدن	**rebel** v شورش کردن
raven n کلاغ سیاه	**rebel** n طغیان
ravine n دره عمیق و باریک	**rebellion** n شورش
raw adj خام	**rebirth** n تجدیدحیات
ray n شعاع؛ پرتو	**rebound** v برگشتن؛ پس زدن
raze v ویران کردن	**rebuff** v جلوگیری کردن
razor n تیغ	**rebuff** n منع
reach v رسیدن	**rebuild** v دوباره ساختن
reach n دسترسی	**rebuke** v سرزنش کردن
reaction n واکنش	**rebuke** n توبیخ
read iv بخوان	**rebut** v رد کردن؛ پس زدن
reader n خواننده	**recall** v فراخواندن
readiness n آمادگی	**recant** v انکار کردن
reading n خواندن	**recap** v روکش زدن
ready adj آماده	**recapture** v پس گرفتن
real adj واقعی	**recede** v کنار کشیدن
realism n رئالیسم	**receipt** n دریافت
reality n واقعیت	**receive** v دریافت کردن
realize v درک کردن	**recent** adj اخیر

R

reception *n* پذیرش	**recourse** *n* توسل
receptionist *n* متصدی پذیرش	**recover** *v* بهبود یافتن
receptive *adj* پذیرا	**recovery** *n* بهبود
recess *n* تنفس	**recreate** *v* تفریح کردن
recession *n* کسادی	**recreation** *n* سرگرمی
recharge *v* دوباره شارژ کردن	**recruit** *v* استخدام کردن
recipe *n* دستور عمل	**recruit** *n* نیروی تازه گرفتن
reciprocal *adj* دوجانبه	**recruitment** *n* استخدام
recital *n* گزارش	**rectangle** *n* مستطیل
recite *v* از بر خواندن	**rectangular** *adj* مستطیل
reckless *adj* بی احتیاط	**rectify** *v* اصلاح کردن
reckon *v* شمردن	**rector** *n* کشیش منطقه
reckon on به حساب آوردن	**rectum** *n* راست روده
reclaim احیاء کردن	**recuperate** *v* بهبود یافتن
recline *v* تکیه کردن	**recur** *v* تکرار شدن
recluse *n* گوشه گیر	**recurrence** *n* تکرار
recognition *n* بازشناسی	**recycle** *v* بازیافت کردن
recognize *v* تشخیص دادن	**red** *adj* قرمز
recollect به خاطر آوردن	**red tape** *n* نوار باریک قرمز
recollection *n* یادآوری	**redden** *v* قرمز کردن
recommend *v* توصیه کردن	**redeem** بازخرید کردن
recompense *v* غرامت پرداختن	**redemption** *n* رستگاری
recompense *n* پاداش	**red-hot** *adj* عصبانی
reconcile *v* وفق دادن	**redo** *v* از نو انجام دادن
reconsider *v* تجدید نظر کردن	**redouble** *v* دو چندان کردن
reconstruct *v* از نو ساختن	**reduce** *v* کاهش دادن
record *v* ضبط کردن	**redundant** *adj* تکراری
record *n* سابقه؛ رکورد؛ ثبت	**reed** *n* نی
recorder *n* ثبات	**reef** *n* آبسنگ
recording *n* ضبط	**reel** *n* قرقره؛ طبلک
recount *n* نقل	**reenactment** *n* بازآفرینی
recourse *v* مراجعه کردن	**reentry** *n* ورود مجدد

R

refer to v ارجاع دادن به	**regeneration** n احیا
referee n داور	**regent** n نایب السلطنه
reference n اشاره	**regime** n رژیم
referendum n همه پرسی	**regiment** n هنگ
refill v دوباره پر کردن	**region** n منطقه
refinance v از نو تجارت کردن	**regional** adj منطقه ای
refine v تصفیه کردن	**register** v ثبت کردن
refinery n پالایشگاه	**registration** n ثبت
reflect v بازتاب یافتن	**regret** v افسوس خوردن
reflection n انعکاس	**regret** n تأسف
reflexive adj انعکاسی	**regrettable** adj تاسف آور
reform v اصلاح کردن	**regularity** n نظم
reform n اصلاح	**regularly** adv مرتباً
refrain v اجتناب کردن	**regulate** v تنظیم کردن
refresh v تجدید کردن	**regulation** n آیین نامه
refreshing adj نیروبخش	**rehabilitate** v نوتوان کردن
refreshment n تازگی	**rehearsal** n تمرین
refrigerate v خنک کردن	**rehearse** v تمرین کردن
refuge n پناه	**reign** v سلطنت کردن
refugee n پناهنده	**reign** n سلطنت
refund v مجدداً پرداختن	**reimburse** v مسترد کردن
refund n بازپرداخت	**reimbursement** n بازپرداخت
refurbish v روشن و تازه کردن	**rein** v افسار کردن
refusal n امتناع	**rein** n مهار
refuse v قبول نکردن	**reindeer** n گوزن شمالی
refuse n جواب رد	**reinforce** v تقویت کردن
regain v بازیافتن	**reinforcements** n تقویتها
regal adj شاهانه	**reiterate** v تکرار کردن
regard v اعتنا کردن	**reject** v رد کردن
regarding pre راجع به	**rejection** n رد
regardless adv بدون توجه	**rejoice** v شادی کردن
regards n تبریکات	**rejoin** v پاسخ دفاعی کردن

R

rejuvenate v دوباره جوان کردن	remains n مانده
relapse n بازگشت	remake v بازساختن
related adj مربوط	remark v اظهار داشتن
relationship n رابطه	remark n اظهارنظر
relative adj خویشاوند	remarkable adj به یاد ماندنی
relative n خویشاوند	remedy v درمان کردن
relax v تمدد اعصاب کردن	remedy n درمان
relaxation n آرامش	remember v به یاد آوردن
relaxing adj آرامش بخش	remembrance n یادآوری
relay v اعلام خبر کردن	remind v یادآوری کردن
release v ترخیص کردن	reminder n یادآور
relegate v واگذار کردن	remission n عفو
relent v پشیمان شدن	remit v وجه فرستادن
relentless adj بی رحم	remittance n وجه
relevant adj مربوط	remnant n ته مانده
reliable adj قابل اعتماد	remodel v تعمیر کردن
reliance n اعتماد	remorse n پشیمانی
relic n اثر	remorseful adj پشیمان
relief n تسکین	remote adj دور
relieve v خلاص کردن	removal n انتقال
religion n دین	remove v جابجا کردن
religious adj دینی	remunerate v تاوان دادن
relinquish v چشم پوشیدن	renew v تجدید کردن
relish v با رغبت خوردن	renewal n تجدید
relocate v جابجا کردن	renounce v انکار کردن
relocation n نقل مکان	renovate v از سر گرفتن
reluctant adj بی میل	renovation n نوسازی
reluctantly adv کراهاً	renowned adj مشهور
rely on v استناد کردن	rent v اجاره کردن
remain v باقی ماندن	rent n اجاره
remainder n بقیه	repair v تعمیر کردن
remaining adj باقیمانده	reparation n جبران

R

repay v برگرداندن	reproach n سرزنش
repayment n بازپرداخت	reproduce v تکثیر کردن
repeal v لغو کردن	reproduction n تولید مثل
repeal n لغو	reptile n خزنده
repeat v تکرار کردن	republic n جمهوری
repel v مقابله کردن	repudiate v انکار کردن
repent v اصلاح شدن	repugnant adj نفرت انگیز
repentance n پشیمانی	repulse v دفع کردن
repetition n تکرار	repulse n دفع
replace v جایگزین کردن	repulsive adj نفرت انگیز
replacement n جایگزینی	reputation n شهرت
replay n پخش دوباره	reputedly adv ظاهراً
replenish v مجدداً پر کردن	request v درخواست کردن
replete adj سیر	request n درخواست
replica n مدل	require v نیاز داشتن
replicate v تکرار کردن	requirement n نیاز
reply v پاسخ دادن	rescue v نجات دادن
reply n پاسخ	rescue n نجات
report v گزارش دادن	research v تحقیق کردن
report n گزارش	research n تحقیق
reportedly adv ظاهراً	resemblance n شباهت
reporter n گزارشگر	resemble v شباهت داشتن
repose v استراحت کردن	resent v رنجیدن
repose n تکیه	resentment n رنجش
represent v نمایندگی کردن	reservation n ذخیره
repress v باز فشردن	reserve v ذخیره کردن
repression n سرکوبی	reservoir n مخزن
reprieve n لغو حکم اعدام	reside v اقامت داشتن
reprint v از نو چاپ کردن	residence n اقامت
reprint n تجدید چاپ	residue n باقیمانده
reprisal n تلافی	resign v استعفا دادن
reproach v سرزنش کردن	resignation n استعفا

R

resilient *adj* ارتجاعی	**resume** *v* از سر گرفتن
resist *v* مقاومت کردن	**resumption** *n* ازسرگیری
resistance *n* مقاومت	**resurrection** *n* احیا
resolute *adj* مصمم	**resuscitate** *v* زنده کردن
resolution *n* راه حل	**retain** *v* احراز کردن
resolve *v* حل کردن	**retaliate** *v* تلافی کردن
resounding *adj* پرطنین	**retaliation** *n* معامله به مثل
resource *n* منابع	**retarded** *adj* عقب مانده
respect *v* احترام گذاشتن	**retention** *n* نگهداری
respect *n* احترام	**retire** *v* بازنشسته شدن
respectful *adj* مودب	**retirement** *n* بازنشستگی
respective *adj* مربوطه	**retract** *v* منقبض کردن
respiration *n* تنفس	**retreat** *v* عقب زدن
respite *n* استراحت	**retreat** *n* عقب نشینی
respond *v* پاسخ دادن	**retrieval** *n* بازیابی
response *n* پاسخ	**retrieve** *v* بازیافتن
responsibility *n* مسئولیت	**retroactive** *adj* معطوف به گذشته
responsible *adj* مسئول	**return** *v* بازگشتن
responsive *adj* حساس	**return** *n* بازگشت
rest *v* استراحت کردن	**reunion** *n* تجدید دیدار
rest *n* استراحت	**reveal** *v* آشکار کردن
rest room *n* توالت	**revealing** *adj* افشاگرانه
restaurant *n* رستوران	**revel** *v* شادی کردن
restful *adj* آرام بخش	**revelation** *n* رازگشایی
restitution *n* استرداد	**revenge** *v* انتقام گرفتن
restless *adj* بی قرار	**revenge** *n* انتقام
restoration *n* استرداد	**revenue** *n* درآمد
restore *v* اعاده کردن	**reverence** *n* حرمت
restrain *v* جلوگیری کردن	**reversal** *n* معکوس
restraint *n* محدودیت	**reverse** *n* معکوس
restrict *v* محدود کردن	**reversible** *adj* قابل تغییر
result *n* نتیجه	**revert** *v* رجوع کردن

R

review v بازدید کردن	**right** adv راست
review n مرور؛ بازبینی	**right** adj راست؛ درست
revise v بازبینی کردن	**right** n راست
revision n تجدیدنظر	**rigid** adj سخت
revive v زنده شدن	**rigor** n سخت گیری
revoke v فسخ کردن	**rim** n دوره؛ کناره
revolt v قیام کردن	**ring** iv احاطه کن
revolt n قیام؛ جنبش	**ring** n احاطه؛ حلقه
revolting adj تنفرآور	**ringleader** n سردسته
revolve v تغییر کردن	**rinse** v شستشو دادن
revue n جنگ شادی	**riot** v شورش کردن
revulsion n انزجار	**riot** n آشوب
reward v پاداش دادن	**rip** v پاره کردن
reward n پاداش	**rip apart** v پاره کردن
rewarding adj ارزنده	**rip off** v دزدی کردن
rheumatism n روماتیسم	**ripe** adj رسیده
rhinoceros n کرگدن	**ripen** v کامل شدن
rhyme n قافیه	**ripple** n موج
rhythm n ریتم	**rise** iv بالا بیا
rib n دنده	**risk** v خطر کردن
ribbon n نوار	**risk** n احتمال خطر
rice n برنج	**risky** adj خطرناک
rich adj غنی	**rite** n آیین
rid of iv نجات بده از	**rival** n رقیب
riddle n غربال	**rivalry** n رقابت
ride iv بران؛ سوار شو	**river** n رودخانه
ridge n پشته	**rivet** v پرچ کردن
ridicule v استهزا کردن	**riveting** adj جذاب
ridicule n تمسخر	**road** n جاده
ridiculous adj خنده دار	**roam** v گردش کردن
rifle n تفنگ	**roar** v داد کشیدن
rift n شکاف	**roar** n فریاد

R

roast v کباب کردن	**rousing** adj شورانگیز
roast n کباب	**route** n مسیر
rob v دزدیدن	**routine** n امور روزمره
robber n سارق	**row** v به خط کردن
robbery n سرقت	**row** n ردیف
robe n لباس بلند و گشاد	**rowdy** adj شر
robust adj صحیح	**royal** adj سلطنتی
rock n سنگ	**royalty** n سلطنت
rocket n موشك	**rub** v مالیدن
rocky adj سنگی	**rubber** n لاستیك
rod n میله	**rubbish** n آشغال
rodent n جونده	**rubble** n قلوه سنگ
roll v غلت خوردن	**ruby** n یاقوت
romance n افسانه	**rudder** n سكان
roof n سقف	**rude** adj بی تربیت
room n اتاق؛ انبار	**rudeness** n گستاخی
roomy adj جادار	**rudimentary** adj ابتدایی
rooster n خروس	**rug** n فرش
root n ریشه	**ruin** v از بین بردن
rope n طناب	**ruin** n خرابی
rosary n تسبیح	**rule** v فرمانروایی کردن
rose n گل سرخ	**rule** n حكم
rosy adj گلگون	**ruler** n خطكش؛ حاكم
rot v فاسد کردن	**rum** n عرق نیشكر
rot n پوسید	**rumble** v غریدن
rotate v چرخیدن	**rumble** n غرش
rotation n چرخش	**rumor** n شایعه
rotten adj پوسیده	**run** iv اجرا کن
rough adj ناهمواری	**run away** v فرار کردن
round adj گرد	**run into** v برخورد کردن
roundup n خلاصه اخبار	**run out** v به آخر رسیدن
rouse v به هیجان درآوردن	**run over** v لبریز شدن

R

run up v شلیک کردن	**sadden** v غمگین کردن
runner n دونده	**saddle** n زین
runway n باند	**sadist** n آزارگر
rupture n شکستگی	**sadness** n غم
rupture v گسستن	**safe** adj امن
rural adj روستایی	**safeguard** n حفاظ
ruse n حیله	**safety** n ایمنی
rush v عجله کردن	**sail** n قایقرانی
Russia n روسیه	**sailboat** n قایق بادبانی
Russian adj روسی	**sailor** n ملوان
rust v زنگ زدن	**saint** n مقدس
rust n زنگ زده	**salad** n سالاد
rustic adj روستایی	**salary** n حقوق
rust-proof adj ضد زنگ	**sale** n فروش
rusty adj زنگ زده	**sale slip** n رسید فروش
ruthless adj ظالم	**salesman** n فروشنده
rye n دشت	**saliva** n بزاق
	salmon n ماهی آزاد
	saloon n سالن
	salt n نمك
	salty adj شور

S

sabotage v خرابکاری کردن	**salvage** v نجات دادن
sabotage n خرابکاری	**salvation** n نجات
sack v اخراج کردن	**same** adj همان
sack n کیسه؛ تخت	**sample** n نمونه
sacrament n آیین مقدس	**sanctify** v تقدیس کردن
sacred adj مقدس	**sanction** v جریمه کردن
sacrifice n فداکاری	**sanction** n اجازه
sacrilege n بی حرمتی	**sanctity** n تقدس
sad adj غمگین	**sanctuary** n مکان مقدس
	sand n ماسه
	sandal n صندل

R
S

سنباده sandpaper n	داربست scaffolding n
ساندویچ sandwich n	آب پز کردن scald v
عاقل sane adj	مقیاس کردن scale v
سلامت عقل sanity n	مقیاس scale n
نقب بزنید sap n	پوست سر scalp n
شیره کشیدن sap v	نقشه scam n
یاقوت کبود saphire n	کاوش کردن scan v
طعنه sarcasm n	رسوایی scandal n
کنایه دار sarcastic adj	رسوا کردن scandalize v
ساردین sardine n	سپربلا scapegoat n
شیطانی satanic adj	اثرزخم scar n
ماهواره satellite n	کمیاب scarce adj
طنز satire n	بسختی scarcely adv
رضایت satisfaction n	کمیابی scarcity n
رضایتبخش satisfactory adj	ترساندن scare v
خشنود کردن satisfy v	بترسید scare n
اشباع کردن saturate v	ترساندن scare away v
شنبه Saturday n	روسری scarf n
سس sauce n	ترسناك scary adj
ماهی تابه saucepan n	پراکنده کردن scatter v
نعلبکی saucer n	فیلم نامه scenario n
سوسیس sausage n	صحنه؛ مرحله scene n
آدم وحشی savage adj	منظره scenery n
وحشیگری savagery n	نمایشی scenic adj
نجات دادن save v	بو scent n
پس انداز savings n	شكاك sceptic adj
نجات دهنده savior n	زمانبندی کردن schedule v
فهمیدن savor v	برنامه زمانی schedule n
اره کن saw iv	طرح scheme n
اره saw n	دودستگی schism n
بگو say iv	محقق scholar n
گفتن saying n	بورس scholarship n

S

school *n* مدرسه	screw *v* پیچ کردن
science *n* علم	screw *n* پیچ
scientific *adj* علمی	screwdriver *n* پیچ گوشتی
scientist *n* دانشمند	scribble *v* با شتاب نوشتن
scissors *n* قیچی	script *n* دستخط
scoff *v* تمسخر کردن	scroll *n* طوماری
scold *v* پرحرفی کردن	scrub *v* خراشیدن
scolding *n* پرخاش	scruples *n* وجدانها
scooter *n* روروک بچه ها	scrupulous *adj* شریف
scope *n* حدود	scrutiny *n* بررسی
scorch *v* سوزاندن	scuffle *n* زدوخورد
score *n* امتیاز	sculptor *n* مجسمه ساز
score *v* امتیاز گرفتن	sculpture *n* مجسمه سازی
scorn *v* استهزا کردن	sea *n* دریا
scornful *adj* تحقیرآمیز	seafood *n* غذای دریایی
scorpion *n* عقرب	seagull *n* کاکایی
scoundrel *n* آدم رذل	seal *v* آب بندی کردن
scour *v* پاک کردن	seal *n* مهر؛ آب بند
scourge *n* شلاق	seal off ممنوع الورود کردن
scout *n* دیده ور	seam *n* درز
scramble *v* در هم آمیختن	seamless *adj* بدون درز
scrambled *adj* رمزی شده	seamstress *n* خیاط زنانه
scrap *n* تکه	search *v* جستجو کردن
scrap *v* دور ریختن	search *n* جستجو
scrape *v* تراشیدن	seashore *n* ساحل
scratch *v* خط زدن	seasick *adj* دریازده
scratch *n* خراش	seaside *adj* کناردریا
scream *v* جیغ کشیدن	season *n* فصل
scream *n* جیغ	seasonal *adj* فصلی
screech *v* جیغ کشیدن	seasoning *n* ادویه
screen *n* صفحه؛ غربال	seat *n* صندلی
screen *v* جدا کردن	seated *adj* نشسته

S

secede *v* کناره گیری کردن	selection *n* انتخاب
secluded *adj* منزوی	self-esteem *n* احترام به خود
seclusion *n* انزوا	self-evident *adj* بدیهی
second *n* دوم	self-interest *n* منفعت شخصی
secondary *adj* ثانوی	selfish *adj* خودخواه
secrecy *n* پنهانی	selfishness *n* خودخواهی
secret *n* راز	self-respect *n* شرافت نفس
secretary *n* منشی	sell *iv* بفروش
secretly *adv* پنهانی	seller *n* فروشنده
sect *n* فرقه	sellout *n* فروش کامل
section *n* بخش	semblance *n* ظاهر
sector *n* بخش	semester *n* نیمسال تحصیلی
secure *v* محکم نگهداشتن	seminary *n* مدرسه مذهبی
secure *adj* محفوظ	senate *n* سنا
security *n* امنیت	senator *n* سناتور
sedate *v* تسکین دادن	send *iv* بفرست
sedation *n* مسکن	sender *n* فرستنده
seduce *v* گمراه کردن	senile *adj* پیری
seduction *n* اغوا	senior *adj* ارشد
see *iv* ببین	seniority *n* ارشدیت
seed *n* دانه	sensation *n* احساس
seedless *adj* بی دانه	sense *v* حس کردن
seedy *adj* پرتخم	sense *n* حس؛ مفهوم
seek *iv* جستجو کن	senseless *adj* بی احساس
seem *v* به نظر آمدن	sensible *adj* باشعور
segment *n* بخش	sensitive *adj* حساس
segregate *v* سوا کردن	sensual *adj* شهوانی
segregation *n* جدایی	sentence *v* محکوم کردن
seize *v* ربودن؛ درک کردن	sentence *n* جمله؛ حکم
seizure *n* تصرف	sentiment *n* احساس
seldom *adv* بندرت	sentimental *adj* عاطفی
select *v* انتخاب کردن	sentry *n* نگهبان

S

separate v جدا کردن	settlement n اسکان؛ تسویه
separate adj جدا	settler n مهاجر مقیم
separation n جدایی	setup n تنطیم
September n سپتامبر	seven adj هفت
sequel n نتیجه	seventeen adj هفده
sequence n تسلسل	seventh adj هفتم
serenade n آواز عاشقانه	seventy adj هفتاد
serene adj آرام	sever v جدا کردن
serenity n آرامش	several adj چندین
sergeant n گروهبان	severance n قطع؛ تفکیک
series n مجموعه	severe adj سخت؛ شدید
serious adj جدی؛ خطرناک	severity n سختی
seriousness n جدیت؛ وقار	sew v دوختن
sermon n وعظ	sewage n فاضلاب
serpent n مار	sewer n فاضلاب
serum n خونابه	sewing n خیاطی
servant n خدمتکار	sexuality n جنسیت
serve v خدمت کردن	shabby adj کهنه
service n خدمت	shack n آلونك
service v خدمت کردن	shackle n مانع
session n نشست	shade n سایه؛ سایبان
set n مجموعه	shadow n سایه
set iv ردیف کن	shady adj سایه دار
set about v حمله کردن	shake iv تکان بده
set off v جلوه دادن	shaken adj یکه خورده
set out v عهده دار شدن	shaky adj لرزان
set up v راه اندازی کردن	shallow adj کم عمق
setback n مانع	sham n ساختگی
setting n تنطیم	shambles n آشفتگی
settle v تسویه کردن	shame v خجالت دادن
settle down v آرام شدن	shame n شرم
settle for v راضی شدن به	shameful adj شرم آور

S

shameless adj بی شرم

shape v شکل دادن

shape n شکل

share n سهم؛ فرض

shareholder n سهام دار

shark n کوسه

sharp adj تیز؛ زیرک

sharpen v تیز کردن

sharpener n تیزکن

shatter v خرد کردن

shattering adj تکان دهنده

shave v تراشیدن

she pro او

shear iv ببر

shed iv جاری کن

sheep n گوسفند

sheets n برگه ها

shelf n قفسه

shell n پوسته

shellfish n صدف دار

shelter v پناه گرفتن

shelter n پناهگاه

shelves n قفسه ها

shepherd n چوپان

sherry n شری

shield v محافظت کردن

shield n سپر

shift n شیفت کاری

shift v تغییر دادن

shine iv بدرخش

shiny adj براق

ship n کشتی

shipment n محموله

shipwreck n شکستن کشتی

shirk v شانه خالی کردن از

shirt n پیراهن

shiver v لرزیدن

shiver n لرزش

shock v تکان دادن

shock n تکان؛ شوک

shocking adj تکان دهنده

shoddy adj شلخته

shoe n کفش

shoelace n بندکش

shoepolish n واکس کفش

shoot iv شلیک کن

shoot down v با گلوله کشتن

shop v خریدن

shop n مغازه

shoplifting n دزدی از مغازه

shopping n خرید

shore n ساحل

short adj کوتاه؛ خلاصه

shortage n کمبود

shortcoming n عیب

shortcut n میانبر

shorten v کوتاه کردن

shorthand n تندنویسی

shortlived adj کم عمر

shortly adv به زودی

shorts n شورت

shortsighted adj نزدیک بین

shot n گلوله

shotgun n تفنگ شکاری

S

shoulder *n* شانه	sick *adj* بیمار
shout *v* فریاد کشیدن	sicken *v* مریض کردن
shout *n* فریاد	sickening *adj* بیمارکننده
shouting *n* فریاد	sickle *n* داس
shove *v* پرتاب کردن	sickness *n* ناخوشی
shove *n* هل	side *n* طرف
shovel *n* بیل	sideburns *n* خطریش
show *iv* نشان بده	sidestep *v* گریز کردن
show off *v* خودنمائی کردن	sidewalk *n* پیاده رو
show up *v* حضور یافتن	sideways *adv* با
showdown *n* رویارویی نهایی	siege *n* محاصره
shower *n* دوش	siege *v* محاصره کردن
shrapnel *n* ترکش	sift *v* الک زدن
shred *v* پاره کردن	sigh *n* آه
shred *n* باریکه	sigh *v* آه کشیدن
shrewd *adj* زرنگ	sight *n* منظر
shriek *n* فریاد	sightseeing *v* دیدن
shrimp *n* میگو	sign *v* امضاء کردن
shrine *n* زیارتگاه	sign *n* امضا؛ علامت
shroud *n* کفن	signal *n* برجسته
shrouded *adj* لفاف دار	signature *n* امضا
shrub *n* بوته	significance *n* اهمیت
shrug *v* منقبض کردن	significant *adj* معنی دار
shudder *n* لرزش	signify *v* دلالت کردن
shudder *v* لرزیدن	silence *n* سکوت
shuffle *v* به هم آمیختن	silence *v* ساکت کردن
shun *v* پرهیز کردن	silent *adj* ساکت
shut *iv* ببند	silhouette *n* ضدنور
shut off *v* پایان دادن	silk *n* ابریشم
shut up *v* ساکت بودن	silly *adj* ابله
shy *adj* کمرو	silver *n* نقره ای
shyness *n* کمرویی	silverplated *adj* نقره اندود

S

silversmith n نقره کار	**siren** n آژیر
silverware n نقره آلات	**sirloin** n گوشت راسته
similar adj مشابه	**sissy** adj سوسول
similarity n همانندی	**sister** n خواهر
simmer v آهسته جوشیدن	**sister-in-law** n خواهر زن
simple adj ساده	**sit** iv بنشین
simplicity n سادگی	**site** n سایت
simplify v ساده کردن	**sitting** n نشسته
simply adv به سادگی	**situated** adj واقع
simultaneous adj هم زمان	**situation** n وضع
sin v معصیت کردن	**six** adj شش
sin n گناه	**sixteen** adj شانزده
since c ازوقتی که	**sixth** adj ششم
since pre از انجائیکه	**sixty** adj شصت
since then adv از آن موقع	**sizable** adj قابل توجه
sincere adj اصیل	**size** n اندازه
sincerity n صداقت	**size up** ارزیابی کردن
sinful adj گناهکار	**skate** n اسکیت
sing iv بخوان	**skeleton** n استخوان بندی
singer n خواننده	**skeptic** adj شکاک
single n مجرد	**sketch** v رسم کردن
single adj مجرد؛ تک	**sketch** n نقشه تقریبی
singlehanded adj دست تنها	**sketchy** adj سردستی
singleminded adj امین؛ با اراده	**ski** v اسکی کردن
singular adj صیغه مفرد	**skill** n مهارت
sinister adj بدیمن	**skillful** adj ماهر
sink iv فرو ببر	**skim** v شنا کردن
sink in v آهسته فراگرفتن	**skin** v لخت کردن
sinner n گناه کار	**skin** n پوست
sip v چشیدن	**skinny** adj پوستی
sip n جرعه	**skip** v پریدن؛ رد کردن
sir n آقا	**skip** n بپرید

S

skirmish *n* درگیری	**slide** *iv* لیز بخور
skirt *n* دامن لباس	**slightly** *adv* اندکی
skull *n* جمجمه	**slim** *adj* لاغر؛ نازک
sky *n* آسمان	**slip** *v* لغزیدن
skylight *n* نورگیر سقف	**slip** *n* لیز خوردن
skyscraper *n* آسمان خراش	**slipper** *n* دمپایی
slab *n* صفحه	**slippery** *adj* لغزنده
slack *adj* بی توجه	**slit** *iv* چاك بده
slacken *v* سست کردن	**slob** *adj* آدم بیعار
slacks *n* شلوار راحتی	**slogan** *n* شعار
slam *v* به هم کوفتن	**slope** *n* شیب
slander *n* افترا	**sloppy** *adj* خیس
slanted *adj* مایل	**slot** *n* سوراخ
slap *n* سیلی	**slow** *adj* آهسته
slap *v* سیلی زدن	**slow down** کند کردن
slash *n* برش	**slow motion** *n* حرکت آهسته
slash *v* شکاف دادن	**slowly** *adv* آهسته
slate *n* سنگ لوح	**sluggish** *adj* کند
slaughter *v* کشتار کردن	**slum** *n* محله فقیرنشین
slaughter *n* کشتار	**slump** *v* سقوط کردن
slave *n* برده	**slump** *n* سقوط
slavery *n* بردگی	**sly** *adj* فریب کار
slay *iv* بکش	**smack** *n* ماچ کنید
sleazy *adj* کثیف	**smack** *v* کتک زدن
sleep *iv* بخواب	**small** *adj* کوچك
sleep *n* بخوابید	**small print** *n* چاپ ریز
sleeve *n* آستین	**smallpox** *n* آبله مرغان
sleeveless *adj* بی آستین	**smart** *adj* باهوش
sleigh *n* سورتمه	**smash** *v* خرد شدن
slender *adj* باریك	**smear** *n* آلودن
slice *v* قاش کردن	**smear** *v* آغشتن
slice *n* برش	**smell** *iv* بو کن

S

smelly adj بدبو	**snub** v سرزنش کردن
smile v لبخند زدن	**snub** n منع
smile n لبخند	**soak** v خیساندن
smith n فلزکار	**soak in** v خیس شدن در
smoke v سیگار کشیدن	**soar** v بلند پروازی کردن
smoked adj دودزده	**sob** v هق هق کردن
smoker n آدم سیگاری	**sob** n هق هق
smoking gun n تفنگ سیگاری	**sober** adj عاقل
smooth v نرم کردن	**so-called** adj نامیده شده
smooth adj صاف	**sociable** adj اجتماعی
smoothly adv به آرامی	**socialism** n سوسیالیسم
smoothness n نرمی	**socialist** adj سوسیالیست
smother v خفه کردن	**socialize** v اجتماعی کردن
smuggler n قاچاقچی	**society** n جامعه
snail n حلزون	**sock** n ضربه مشت
snake n مار	**sod** n چمن
snapshot n عکس	**soda** n سودا
snare v به دام انداختن	**sofa** n کاناپه
snare n بند؛ کمند	**soft** adj نرم
snatch v ربودن	**softly** adv به نرمی
sneeze v عطسه کردن	**softness** n نرمی
sneeze n عطسه	**soggy** adj خیس خیس
sniff v استشمام کردن	**soil** v آلودن
sniper n تیرانداز	**soil** n خاک
snitch v کش رفتن	**soiled** adj خاکی شده
snooze v چرت زدن	**solace** n تسکین
snore v خرناس کشیدن	**solar** adj خورشیدی
snore n خر و پف	**solder** v جوش دادن
snow v برف باریدن	**soldier** n سرباز
snow n برف	**sold-out** adj فروخته شده
snowfall n بارش برف	**sole** n منحصربفرد
snowflake n دانه برف	**sole** adj منحصربفرد

S

solely adv صرفا

solemn adj سنگین

solicit v درخواست کردن

solid adj سخت

solidarity n همبستگی

solitary adj تنها

solitude n انزوا

soluble adj حل شدنی

solution n راه حل

solve v حل کردن

solvent adj حلال

somber adj تیره

some adj مقداری

somebody pro کسی

someday adv یک روز

somehow adv بطریقی

someone pro کسی

something pro چیزی

sometimes adv بعضی اوقات

someway adv یک جوری

somewhat adv تا اندازه ای

son n پسر

song n آواز

son-in-law n داماد

soon adv بزودی

soothe v آرام کردن

sorcerer n جادوگر

sorcery n جادوگری

sore n سخت

sore adj سخت

sorrow n غم

sorrowful adj متاسف

sorry adj متاسف

sort n نوع

sort out v رده بندی کردن

soul n روح

sound n صدا؛ بی عیب

sound v به صدا درآوردن

soup n سوپ

sour adj ترش

source n منبع

south n جنوب

southbound adv جنوبی

southeast n جنوب شرقی

southern adj جنوبی

southerner n جنوبی

southwest n جنوب غرب

souvenir n یادگاری

sovereign adj حکومت

sovereignty n حاکمیت

soviet adj شورا

sow iv بکار

space n فضا

space out v خیره شدن

spacious adj وسیع

spade n بیل

Spain n اسپانیا

span v اندازه گرفتن

span n چشمه

Spaniard n اسپانیولی

Spanish adj اسپانیایی

spank v درکونی زدن

spanking n کتک

spare v دریغ داشتن

S

spare adj اضافی	**spelling** n هجی
spare part n قطعه یدکی	**spend** iv صرف کن
sparingly adv با صرفه جویی	**spending** n گذراندن
spark n جرقه	**sperm** n اسپرم
spark plug n شمع موتور	**sphere** n کره
sparkle v درخشیدن	**spice** n ادویه
sparrow n پرنده	**spicy** adj پرادویه
sparse adj نامتراکم	**spider** n عنکبوت
spasm n انقباض عضلانی	**spiderweb** n تارعنکبوت
speak iv صحبت کن	**spill** iv سرازیر شو
speaker n سخنگو؛ بلندگو	**spill** n میله؛ توپی
spear n نیزه	**spin** iv بچرخ؛ بچرخان
spearhead v رهبری کردن	**spine** n ستون فقرات
special adj مخصوص	**spinster** n پیر دختر
specialize v تخصص یافتن	**spirit** n روح
specialty n تخصص	**spiritual** adj روحانی
species n گونه ها	**spit** iv تف کن
specific adj خاص	**spite** n بغض؛ بدخواهی
specimen n نمونه	**spiteful** adj بدخواه
speck n ذره	**splash** v ترکیدن
spectacle n عینکی	**splendid** adj باشکوه
spectator n تماشاچی	**splendor** n شکوه
speculate v سوداگری کردن	**splinter** n خردبشوید
speculation n حدس	**splinter** v متلاشی شدن
speech n سخنرانی	**split** n شکافته
speechless adj بی جواب	**split** iv شکافته کن
speed iv سرعت بده	**split up** v پاره شدن
speed n سرعت	**spoil** v غارت کردن
speedily adv باسرعت	**spoils** n غنیمت؛ یغما
speedy adj سریع	**sponge** n اسفنج
spell iv بیان کن	**sponsor** n حامی
spell n افسون	**spontaneity** n خودبخودی

S

spontaneous *adj* خودبخود	**squeaky** *adj* جیرجیری
spooky *adj* شبح وار	**squeamish** *adj* زودرنج
spool *n* قرقره	**squeeze** *v* فشردن
spoon *n* قاشق	**squid** *n* ماهی مرکب
sporadic *adj* پراکنده	**squirrel** *n* سنجاب
sport *n* ورزش	**stab** *v* خنجر شدن
sportman *n* ورزشکار	**stab** *n* زخم چاقو
sporty *adj* اهل ورزش	**stability** *n* دوام
spot *v* کشف کردن	**stable** *adj* ثابت
spot *n* نقطه؛ محل	**stable** *n* ثابت
spotless *adj* بدون لك	**stack** *v* کومه کردن
spotlight *n* چراغ نورافکن	**stack** *n* توده
spouse *n* همسر	**staff** *n* کارکنان
sprain *v* رگ به رگ کردن	**stage** *n* مرحله
sprawl *v* پهن نشستن	**stage** *v* اجرا کردن
spray *v* پاشیدن	**stagger** *v* تلو تلو خوردن
spread *iv* پهن کن	**staggering** *adj* گیج کننده
spring *iv* بپر؛ ظاهر شو	**stagnant** *adj* راکد
spring *n* بهار؛ فنر	**stagnate** *v* راکد کردن
springboard *n* تخته پرش	**stagnation** *n* رکود
sprinkle *v* ترشح کردن	**stain** *v* لکه دار کردن
sprout *v* جوانه زدن	**stain** *n* لکه
spruce up *v* آراسته کردن	**stair** *n* پله
spur *v* مهمیز زدن	**staircase** *n* پله کان
spur *n* سیخ؛ آبشکن	**stairs** *n* پله ها
spy *v* جاسوسی کردن	**stake** *n* تیر؛ میخ چوبی
spy *n* جاسوس	**stake** *v* محکم کردن
squalid *adj* کثیف	**stale** *adj* کهنه
squander *v* ولخرجی کردن	**stalemate** *n* پات
square *adj* مربع	**stalk** *v* خرامیدن
square *n* مربع؛ میدان	**stalk** *n* تعقیب
squash *v* له کردن	**stall** *v* طفره زدن

S

stammer v لکنت پیدا کردن

stamp v مهر زدن

stamp n مهر

stamp out v فرونشاندن

stampede n رم؛ لگد

stand iv بایست

stand n پایه

stand for v داوطلب بودن

stand out v برجسته بودن

stand up v روی پا ایستادن

standard n استاندارد

standardize v متعارف کردن

standing n دائمی

standpoint n دیدگاه

standstill adj وقفه

staple v منگنه زدن

staple n محصول عمده

stapler n ماشین دوخت

star n ستاره

starch n نشاسته

starchy adj نشاسته ای

stare v خیره شدن

stark adj خشک

start v آغاز کردن

start n شروع

startle v از جا پراندن

startled adj بهت زده

starvation n گرسنگی

starve v گرسنگی کشیدن

state n بیان؛ ایالت

state v عنوان کردن

statement n اظهار

station n ایستگاه

stationary adj ثابت

stationery n نوشت افزار

statistic n آماری

statue n مجسمه

status n وضعیت؛ پایگاه

statute n قانون

staunch adj بندبیاورید

stay v ماندن

stay n بمانید

steady adj محکم؛ استوار

steak n استیك

steal iv بدزد

stealthy adj بی سروصدا

steam n بخاری

steel n فولاد

steep adj خیس

stem n اصلی

stem v ساقه دار کردن

stench n بوی گند

step n قدم؛ پله

step down v کم کردن

step out v خارج شدن

step up v برخاستن

stepbrother n برادر ناتنی

step-by-step adv گام به گام

stepdaughter n نادختری

stepfather n ناپدری

stepladder n نردبان آهنی

stepmother n نامادری

stepsister n ناخواهری

stepson n ناپسری

S

sterile adj سترون	**stir** v تکان دادن
sterilize v گندزدایی کردن	**stir up** v بهم زدن
stern n دنباله	**stitch** v بخیه زدن
stern adj دنباله	**stitch** n بخیه بزنید
sternly adv با تحکم	**stock** v انبار کردن
stew n تاس کباب	**stock** n کالا؛ انبار
stewardess n مهماندارزن	**stocking** n جوراب
stick n چوب بازی هاکی	**stockpile** n ذخیره
stick iv بچسب	**stockroom** n انبار
stick around v درنگ کردن	**stoic** adj رواقی
stick out v اصرار کردن	**stomach** n شکم
stick to v اهمیت دادن به	**stone** n سنگ
sticker n برچسب	**stone** v سنگسار کردن
sticky adj چسبناك	**stool** n چهارپایه
stiff adj کامل	**stop** v متوقف کردن
stiffen v سفت کردن	**stop** n توقف
stiffness n خشکی	**stop by** v سر زدن
stifle v خفه کردن	**store** v ذخیره کردن
stifling adj خفه کننده	**store** n محل ذخیره
still adj هنوز	**stork** n لك لك
still adv هنوز	**storm** n طوفان
stimulant n ماده محرك	**stormy** adj توفانی
stimulate v تحریک کردن	**story** n داستان؛ طبقه
stimulus n محرك	**stove** n اجاق
sting iv نیش بزن	**straight** adj مستقیم
sting n نیش؛ سوزش	**straighten out** v مرتب کردن
stinging adj گزنده	**strain** v کرنش کردن
stingy adj کنس	**strain** n کشیدگی
stink iv بوی تعفن بده	**strained** adj نگران
stink n بوی تعفن	**strainer** n صافی
stinking adj خیلی بد	**strait** n تنگه
stipulate v پیمان بستن	**stranded** adj سرگردان

S

strange *adj* عجیب	**strip** *v* چاک دادن
stranger *n* غریبه	**stripe** *n* نوار
strangle *v* سرگردان شدن	**striped** *adj* راه راه
strap *n* تسمه	**strive** *iv* تلاش کن
strategy *n* راهبرد	**stroke** *n* ضربه با کنترل
straw *n* کاه	**stroll** *v* قدم زدن
strawberry *n* توت فرنگی	**strong** *adj* قوی
stray *adj* سرگردان	**structure** *n* ساختار
stray *v* ولگردی کردن	**struggle** *v* تلاش کردن
stream *n* جریان آب؛ جویبار	**struggle** *n* نبرد
street *n* خیابان	**stub** *n* کنده؛ ریشه
streetcar *n* تراموای شهری	**stubborn** *adj* یک دنده
streetlight *n* چراغ خیابان	**student** *n* دانشجو
strength *n* مقاومت؛ قدرت	**study** *v* مطالعه کردن
strengthen *v* قوی کردن	**stuff** *n* چرخش توپ
strenuous *adj* پرزور	**stuff** *v* پر کردن
stress *n* نیرو؛ اضطراب	**stuffing** *n* لایی
stressful *adj* تنش زا	**stuffy** *adj* خفه
stretch *n* کشش	**stumble** *v* لغزیدن
stretch *v* کشش	**stun** *v* سراسیمه کردن
stretcher *n* برانکار	**stunning** *adj* عالی
strict *adj* سختگیر	**stupendous** *adj* شگفت انگیز
stride *iv* گام بردار	**stupid** *adj* احمق
strife *n* مبارزه	**stupidity** *n* حماقت
strike *n* اعتصابی	**sturdy** *adj* خوش بنیه
strike *iv* ضربه بزن	**stutter** *v* لکنت داشتن
strike out *v* خارج شدن	**style** *n* روش
strike up *v* نواختن	**subdue** *v* مطیع کردن
striking *adj* چشمگیر	**subdued** *adj* آرام
string *n* رشته؛ نخ	**subject** *v* مطیع کردن
stringent *adj* سخت	**subject** *n* موضوع؛ متهم
strip *n* باریکه؛ نوار	**sublime** *adj* والا

S

submerge v زیر آب کردن	**suddenly** adv ناگهان
submissive adj سلطه پذیر	**sue** v تعقیب قانونی کردن
submit v ارسال کردن	**suffer** v رنج بردن
subpoena n احضاریه	**suffer from** v رنج بردن از
subscribe v شرکت کردن	**suffering** n درد
subscription n اشتراك	**sufficient** adj کافی
subsequent adj بعدی	**suffocate** v خفه کردن
subsidiary adj شرکت وابسته	**sugar** n شکر
subsidize v کمک خرج دادن	**suggest** v پیشنهاد کردن
subsidy n یارانه	**suggestion** n توصیه
subsist v زیست کردن	**suggestive** adj دلالت کننده
substance n ماده	**suicide** n خودکشی
substandard adj نامرغوب	**suit** n جامه
substantial adj قابل توجه	**suitable** adj مناسب
substitute v تعویض کردن	**suitcase** n چمدان
substitute n جانشین	**sullen** adj اخمو
subtitle n عنوان فرعی	**sulphur** n گوگرد
subtle adj ظریف	**sum** n جمع
subtract v کم کردن	**sum up** v جمع کردن
subtraction n تفریق	**summarize** v خلاصه کردن
suburb n حومه	**summary** n خلاصه
subway n راهروی زیرزمینی	**summer** n تابستان
succeed v موفق شدن	**summit** n قله
success n موفقیت	**sumptuous** adj شاهانه
successful adj موفق	**sun** n خورشید
successor n جانشین	**sunblock** n کرم ضدآفتاب
succulent adj گوشتی	**sunburn** n آفتاب سوختگی
succumb v از پا درآمدن	**Sunday** n یکشنبه
such adj چنان	**sundown** n غروب
suck v مکیدن	**sunglasses** n عینك آفتابی
sucker adj مکنده	**sunken** adj فرورفته
sudden adj ناگهانی	**sunny** adj آفتابی

S

طلوع آفتاب *n* **sunrise**	نام خانوادگی *n* **surname**
غروب آفتاب *n* **sunset**	پیش افتادن از *v* **surpass**
عالی *adj* **superb**	مازاد *n* **surplus**
اضافی *adj* **superfluous**	متعجب کردن *v* **surprise**
بالاتر *adj* **superior**	غیرمترقبه *n* **surprise**
برتری *n* **superiority**	تسلیم شدن *v* **surrender**
فروشگاه بزرگ *n* **supermarket**	تسلیم *n* **surrender**
ابرقدرت *n* **superpower**	احاطه کردن *v* **surround**
لغو کردن *v* **supersede**	محیط *n* **surroundings**
خرافه *n* **superstition**	نظارت *n* **surveillance**
سرپرستی *n* **supervision**	ارزیابی *n* **survey**
شام *n* **supper**	بقا *n* **survival**
نرم *adj* **supple**	نجات دادن *v* **survive**
تامین کننده *n* **supplier**	بازمانده *n* **survivor**
ملزومات *n* **supplies**	حساس *adj* **susceptible**
فراهم کردن *v* **supply**	بدگمان شدن *v* **suspect**
پشتیبانی کردن *v* **support**	مظنون *n* **suspect**
حامی *n* **supporter**	معلق کردن *v* **suspend**
فرض کردن *v* **suppose**	بندجوراب *n* **suspenders**
بفرض اینکه *c* **supposing**	تعلیق *n* **suspense**
فرض *n* **supposition**	تعلیق *n* **suspension**
منکوب کردن *v* **suppress**	بدگمانی *n* **suspicion**
برتری *n* **supremacy**	مشکوک *adj* **suspicious**
برتر *adj* **supreme**	نگهداشتن *v* **sustain**
اضافه بار *n* **surcharge**	معاش *n* **sustenance**
مطمئن *adj* **sure**	قورت دادن *v* **swallow**
بطور قطع *adv* **surely**	باتلاق *n* **swamp**
موج سواری کردن *v* **surf**	غرق شده *adj* **swamped**
سطح *n* **surface**	قو *n* **swan**
موج *n* **surge**	جانشین کردن *v* **swap**
جراح *n* **surgeon**	معاوضه *n* **swap**
جراحی *adv* **surgical**	دسته زیاد *n* **swarm**

S

sway v تاب خوردن	sword n شمشیر
swear iv قسم بخور	swordfish n شمشیر ماهی
sweat n عرق	syllable n مقطع
sweat v عرق کردن	symbol n نماد
sweater n ژاکت	symbolic adj نمادی
Sweden n سوئد	symmetry n تقارن
Sweedish adj سوئدی	sympathize v همدردی کردن
sweep iv جارو کن	sympathy n همدردی
sweet adj شیرین	symphony n سمفونی
sweeten v شیرین کردن	symptom n نشانه
sweetheart n دلبر	synagogue n کنیسه
sweetness n شیرینی	synchronize v هم زمان کردن
sweets n شیرینها	synonym n مترادف
swell iv بزرگ شو	synthesis n ترکیب
swelling n تورم	syphilis n سیفیلیس
swift adj سریع	syringe n سرنگ
swim iv شنا کن	syrup n شربت
swimmer n شناگر	system n سیستم
swimming n شنا	systematic adj منظم
swindle v گول زدن	
swindle n فریب	
swindler n شیاد	
swing iv تاب بده	
swing n تاب؛ نوسان	
Swiss adj سوئیس	

T

switch v تعویض کردن	table n میز
switch n جایگزینی؛ کلید	tablecloth n رومیزی
switch off v خاموش کردن	tablespoon n قاشق غذاخوری
switch on v روشن کردن	tablet n قرص؛ لوحه
Switzerland n سوئیس	tack n پونز
swivel v نوسان کردن	tackle v از عهده برآمدن
swollen adj متورم	tact n ظرافت

tactful adj باظرافت	**tapestry** n فرشینه
tactical adj تاکتیکی	**tar** n قطران
tactics n تاکتیک	**tarantula** n رتیل
tag n برچسب	**tardy** adv کند
tail n دم	**target** n هدف؛ مقصد
tail v تعقیب کردن	**tariff** n تعرفه
tailor n خیاط	**tarnish** v تیره کردن
tainted adj فاسد	**tart** n تارت
take iv بگیر	**tartar** n جرم
take apart v شرکت کردن	**task** n عمل
take away v گرفتن	**taste** v مزه کردن
take back v پس گرفتن	**taste** n مزه
take in v تو گذاشتن	**tasteful** adj باسلیقه
take off v جهش کردن	**tasteless** adj بی مزه
take out v بیرون آوردن	**tasty** adj خوشمزه
take over v تحویل گرفتن	**tavern** n میخانه
tale n قصه	**tax** n مالیات
talent n استعداد	**tea** n چای
talk v صحبت کردن	**teach** iv درس بده
talkative adj پرحرف	**teacher** n آموزگار
tall adj بلند	**team** n تیم
tame v رام کردن	**teapot** n قوری
tangent n مماس	**tear** iv پاره کن
tangerine n نارنگی	**tear** n اشک
tangible adj ملموس	**tearful** adj گریان
tangle n گره	**tease** v آزار دادن
tank n مخزن	**technical** adj تخصصی
tanned adj برنزه شده	**technicality** n جنبه فنی
tantamount to adj معادل به	**technician** n کاردان فنی
tantrum n عصبانیت	**technique** n فن
tap n شیر	**technology** n فن آوری
tape n نوار	**tedious** adj کسل کننده

tedium *n* ملالت	**tenth** *n* دهمین
teenager *n* نوجوان	**tenuous** *adj* ظریف
teeth *n* دندانها	**tepid** *adj* ولرم
telegram *n* تلگرام	**term** *n* دوره
telepathy *n* دورآگاهی	**terminate** *v* پایان دادن
telephone *n* تلفن	**terminology** *n* اصطلاحات
telescope *n* تلسکوپ	**termite** *n* موریانه
television *n* تلویزیون	**terms** *n* ضوابط
tell *iv* بگو	**terrace** *n* مهتابی
teller *n* گوینده	**terrain** *n* زمین
telling *adj* بازگویی	**terrestrial** *adj* زمینی
temper *n* خلق	**terrible** *adj* هولناك
temperature *n* درجه حرارت	**terrific** *adj* هولناك
tempest *n* طوفان	**terrify** *v* وحشت زده کردن
temple *n* پرستشگاه	**terrifying** *adj* وحشتناك
temporary *adj* موقت	**territory** *n* قلمرو
tempt *v* اغوا کردن	**terror** *n* وحشت
temptation *n* اغواگری	**terrorism** *n* تروریسم
tempting *adj* وسوسه انگیز	**terrorist** *n* تروریست
ten *adj* ده	**terrorize** *v* ارعابگری کردن
tenacity *n* سفتی	**terse** *adj* مختصر
tenant *n* مستاجر	**test** *v* آزمایش کردن
tendency *n* گرایش	**test** *n* آزمایش
tender *adj* نرم؛ نازک	**testament** *n* شاهد
tenderness *n* مهر؛ دلسوزی	**testify** *v* تصدیق کردن
tennis *n* تنیس	**testimony** *n* شهادت
tenor *n* تنور	**text** *n* متن
tense *adj* عصبی	**textbook** *n* کتاب درسی
tension *n* تنش	**texture** *n* بافت
tent *n* چادر	**thank** *v* تشکر کردن
tentacle *n* شاخك	**thankful** *adj* متشکر
tentative *adj* آزمایشی	**thanks** *n* تشکر

T

that *adj* آن	thirty *adj* سی
thaw *v* گداختن	this *adj* این
thaw *n* آب بشوید	thorn *n* خار
theater *n* تئاتر	thorny *adj* خاردار
theft *n* دزدی	thorough *adj* کامل
theme *n* موضوع	those *adj* آنها
themselves *pro* خودشان	though *c* معهذا
then *adv* در آنوقت	thought *n* فکر
theologian *n* دین شناس	thoughtful *adj* متفکر
theology *n* دین شناسی	thousand *adj* هزار
theory *n* نظریه	thread *v* نخ کردن
therapy *n* درمان	thread *n* رشته
there *adv* آنجا	threat *n* تهدید
therefore *adv* بنابراین	threaten *v* تهدید کردن
thermometer *n* گرماسنج	three *adj* سه
thermostat *n* دمایا	threshold *n* آستانه
these *adj* اینها	thrifty *adj* صرفه جو
thesis *n* رساله	thrill *v* به هیجان درآوردن
they *pro* آنها	thrill *n* هیجان
thick *adj* ضخیم؛ تیره	thrive *v* پیشرفت کردن
thicken *v* ضخیم کردن	throat *n* گلو
thickness *n* ضخامت	throb *n* تپش
thief *n* دزد	throb *v* تپیدن
thigh *n* ران	thrombosis *n* ترومبوز
thin *adj* نازک؛ لاغر	throne *n* تخت
thing *n* چیز	throng *n* گروه
think *iv* فکر کن	through *pre* از طریق
thinly *adv* به صورت نازک	throw *iv* بیانداز
third *adj* سوم	throw away *v* دور انداختن
thirst *v* تشنه بودن	throw up *v* بالا انداختن
thirsty *adj* تشنه	thug *n* شرور
thirteen *adj* سیزده	thumb *n* شست

T

thumbtack *n* پونز	**tin** *n* قلع
thunder *n* تندر	**tiny** *adj* ریز
thunderbolt *n* رعدوبرق	**tip** *n* نوك؛ نكته
thunderstorm *n* توفان تندری	**tiptoe** *n* سرانگشت
Thursday *n* پنج شنبه	**tired** *adj* خسته
thus *adv* بنابراین	**tiredness** *n* خستگی
thwart *v* بی نتیجه گذاردن	**tireless** *adj* خستگی ناپذیر
thyroid *n* تیروئید	**tiresome** *adj* خسته کننده
tickle *v* غلغلك دادن	**tissue** *n* بافت
tickle *n* غلغلک	**title** *n* عنوان
ticklish *adj* دقیق	**to** *pre* به
tidal wave *n* موج جزر و مدی	**toad** *n* وزغ
tide *n* جزر و مد	**toast** *n* برشته
tidy *adj* مرتب	**toaster** *n* تستر
tie *v* گره زدن	**tobacco** *n* توتون
tie *n* گره؛ کروات	**today** *adv* امروز
tiger *n* ببر	**toddler** *n* بچه نوپا
tight *adj* محکم	**toe** *n* پنجه
tighten *v* سفت کردن	**toenail** *n* ناخن پا
tile *n* کاشی؛ سفال	**together** *adv* با همدیگر
till *adv* تا	**toil** *v* زحمت کشیدن
till *v* کشت کردن	**toilet** *n* توالت
tilt *v* نوسان کردن	**token** *n* نشان
timber *n* الوار	**tolerable** *adj* قابل تحمیل
time *n* زمان	**tolerance** *n* تحمل
time *v* زمان دادن	**tolerate** *v* تحمل کردن
timeless *adj* ابدی	**toll** *n* عوارض راهداری
timely *adj* بموقع	**toll** *v* زنگ زدن
times *n* دوره	**tomato** *n* گوجه فرنگی
timetable *n* جدول زمانی	**tomb** *n* آرامگاه
timid *adj* ترسو	**tombstone** *n* سنگ قبر
timidity *n* حجب	**tomorrow** *adv* فردا

T

ton n تن	**touching** adj تماس
tone n طنین	**tough** adj محکم
tongs n انبر	**toughen** v سخت کردن
tongue n زبان	**tour** n تور
tonic n داروی تقویت	**tourism** n جهانگردی
tonight adv امشب	**tourist** n جهانگرد
tonsil n لوزه	**tow** v کشیدن
too adv همچنین	**towards** pre بطرف
tool n ابزار	**towel** n حوله
tooth n دندان	**tower** n برج
toothache n دندان درد	**towering** adj بلند
toothpick n خلال دندان	**town** n شهر
top n بالا	**town hall** n شهرداری
topic n سرفصل	**toxic** adj سمی
topple v از سر افتادن	**toxin** n سم
torch n چراغ قوه	**toy** n اسباب بازی
torment v زجر داد	**track** n خط سیر
torment n عذاب	**track** v دنبال کردن
torrent n سیلاب	**traction** n کشش
torrid adj داغ	**tractor** n تراکتور
torso n تنه	**trade** n تجارت
tortoise n لاک پشت	**trade** v معاوضه کردن
torture v شکنجه دادن	**trademark** n علامت تجارتی
torture n شکنجه	**trader** n بازرگان
toss v پرتاب کردن	**tradition** n سنت
total adj جمع	**traffic** n آمد و شد
totalitarian adj تک حزبی	**traffic** v قاچاق کردن
totality n کلیت	**tragedy** n تراژدی
touch n لمس	**tragic** adj حزن انگیز
touch v لمس کردن	**trail** n دنباله
touch on v رسیدن به	**trailer** n گیاه خزنده
touch up v بهبود دادن	**train** n تربیت؛ قطار

T

trigger

train v آموزش دادن	**travel** v مسافرت کردن
trainee n کارآموز	**traveler** n مسافر
trainer n مربی	**tray** n سینی
training n آموزش	**treacherous** adj خائن
trait n ویژگی	**treachery** n خیانت
traitor n خائن	**tread** iv برو
trajectory n مسیر گلوله	**treason** n خیانت
tram n تراموا	**treasure** n گنج
trample v پایمال کردن	**treasurer** n خزانه دار
trance n خلسه	**treat** v رفتار کردن
tranquility n آرامش	**treat** n رفتار؛ خوراک رایگان
transaction n انجام	**treatment** n رفتار؛ تدبیر
transcend v برتری یافتن	**treaty** n معاهده
transcribe v رونویسی کردن	**tree** n درخت
transfer v انتقال دادن	**tremble** v لرزیدن
transfer n انتقال	**tremendous** adj عظیم
transform v تغییر شکل دادن	**tremor** n لرزش
transformation n دگرگونی	**trench** n مجرا
transfusion n انتقال خون	**trend** n گرایش
transient adj مسافر	**trendy** adj اهل مد
transit n عبور	**trespass** v تعدی کردن
transition n انتقال	**trial** n آزمایش؛ دادرسی
translate v ترجمه کردن	**triangle** n مثلث
translator n مترجم	**tribe** n قبیله
transmit v انتقال دادن	**tribulation** n غم
transparent adj شفاف	**tribunal** n جایگاه قاضی
transplant v نشا کردن	**tribute** n ستایش
transport v حمل و نقل کردن	**trick** v حیله زدن
trap n تله	**trick** n خطوط؛ نیرنگ
trash n آشغال	**trickle** v چکانیدن
trash can n سطل آشغال	**tricky** adj فریبکار
traumatic adj ضربه ای	**trigger** v راه انداختن

T

راه اندازی **trigger** *n*	امتحان کردن **try** *v*
چیدن **trim** *v*	لگن **tub** *n*
دوره سه ماهه **trimester** *n*	سل **tuberculosis** *n*
آرایه ها **trimmings** *n*	سه شنبه **Tuesday** *n*
سفر **trip** *n*	شهریه **tuition** *n*
مسافرت کردن **trip** *v*	گل لاله **tulip** *n*
سه برابر **triple** *adj*	پرداخت کردن **tumble** *v*
سه پایه **tripod** *n*	شکم **tummy** *n*
پیروزی **triumph** *n*	غده **tumor** *n*
پیروز **triumphant** *adj*	غوغا **tumult** *n*
بدیهی؛ مبتذل **trivial** *adj*	جنجالی **tumultuous** *adj*
بی اهمیت کردن **trivialize** *v*	تن **tuna** *n*
چرخ دستی **trolley** *n*	کوک؛ صدا **tune** *n*
گروه **troop** *n*	میزان کردن **tune** *v*
جایزه **trophy** *n*	تنظیم کردن موتور **tune up** *v*
مدار **tropic** *n*	تونیک **tunic** *n*
استوایی **tropical** *adj*	تونل **tunnel** *n*
مشکل **trouble** *n*	توربین **turbine** *n*
آزار دادن **trouble** *v*	اغتشاش **turbulence** *n*
پرزحمت **troublesome** *adj*	چمن **turf** *n*
شلوار **trousers** *n*	ترک **Turk** *adj*
ماهی قزل آلا **trout** *n*	ترکیه **Turkey** *n*
آتش بس موقت **truce** *n*	آشوب **turmoil** *n*
کامیون **truck** *n*	نوبت؛ چرخش **turn** *n*
راننده کامیون **trucker** *n*	چرخیدن **turn** *v*
نادرست **trumped-up** *adj*	برگشتن **turn back** *v*
شیپور **trumpet** *n*	رد کردن **turn down** *v*
تنه؛ سیم اصلی **trunk** *n*	ارسال کردن **turn in** *v*
اعتماد کردن به **trust** *v*	خاموش کردن **turn off** *v*
اطمینان **trust** *n*	روشن کردن **turn on** *v*
حقیقت **truth** *n*	تولید کردن **turn out** *v*
راستگو **truthful** *adj*	تغییر جهت دادن **turn over** *v*

turn up v ظاهر شدن
turret n برجك هرمی
turtle n لاك پشت
tusk n عاج
tutor n معلم خصوصی
tweezers n موچین
twelfth adj دوازدهمی
twelve adj دوازده
twentieth adj بیستم
twenty adj بیست
twice adv دوبار
twilight n تاریك روشن
twin n دوقلو
twinkle v چشمک زدن
twist v پیچاندن
twist n چرخش
twisted adj مچاله
twister n آدم نادرست
two adj دو
tycoon n بازرگان مهم
type n نوع؛ تایپ کردن
type v تایپ کردن
typical adj نمونه
tyranny n استبداد

U

ugliness n زشتی
ugly adj زشت
ulcer n زخم
ultimate adj نهایت
ultimatum n اتمام حجت
ultrasound n فراصوت
umbrella n چتر
umpire n داور
unable adj ناتوان
unanimity n اتفاق
unarmed adj بی سلاح
unassuming adj خالی از تظاهر
unattached adj مستقل
unavoidable adj غیرقابل اجتناب
unaware adj بی خبر
unbearable adj غیرقابل تحمل
unbeatable adj شکست ناپذیر
unbelievable adj باورنکردنی
unbiased adj بی طرف
unbroken adj چموش
unbutton v گشودن دکمه
uncertain adj ناپایدار
uncle n عمو
uncomfortable adj ناراحت
uncommon adj نامتعارف
unconscious adj بی هوش
uncover v معلوم کردن
undecided adj مردد
undeniable adj غیرقابل انکار

T
U

under *pre* زیر	**uneventful** *adj* عادی
undercover *adj* مخفی	**unfailing** *adj* همیشگی
underdog *n* بازنده	**unfair** *adj* دور از انصاف
undergo *v* تحمل کردن	**unfairness** *n* بی عدالتی
underground *adj* زیرزمین	**unfaithful** *adj* عهدشکن
underlying *adj* نهفته	**unfamiliar** *adj* ناشناس
undermine *v* تحلیل بردن	**unfasten** *v* باز کردن
underneath *pre* زیر	**unfavorable** *adj* نامطلوب
underpass *n* زیرگذر	**unfit** *adj* نامناسب
understand *v* درک کردن	**unfold** *v* آشکار کردن
understandable *adj* قابل فهم	**unforeseen** *adj* غیرمترقبه
understanding *n* درك	**unfounded** *adj* بی اساس
undertake *v* عهده دار شدن	**unfriendly** *adj* غیردوستانه
underwear *n* لباس زیر	**unfurnished** *adj* بدون مبلمان
underwrite *v* تعهد کردن	**ungrateful** *adj* ناسپاس
undeserved *adj* ناحق	**unhappiness** *n* غم
undesirable *adj* نامطلوب	**unhappy** *adj* ناخشنود
undisputed *adj* انکارناپذیر	**unharmed** *adj* صحیح وسالم
undo *v* خنثی کردن فعالیت	**unhealthy** *adj* ناسالم
undoubtedly *adv* بی تردید	**unheard-of** *adj* بی سابقه
undress *v* لباس کندن	**unhurt** *adj* صحیح وسالم
undue *adj* بیش از اندازه	**unification** *n* اتحاد
unearth *v* حفاری کردن	**uniform** *n* یونیفرم
uneasiness *n* نگرانی	**uniformity** *n* همسانی
uneasy *adj* ناراحت	**unify** *v* متحد کردن
uneducated *adj* تحصیل نکرده	**unilateral** *adj* یك طرفه
unemployed *adj* بیکار	**union** *n* اتحاد
unemployment *n* بیکاری	**unique** *adj* منحصر بفرد
unending *adj* بی پایان	**unit** *n* واحد
unequal *adj* نابرابر	**unite** *v* متحد کردن
unequivocal *adj* صریح	**unity** *n* وحدت
uneven *adj* نابرابر	**universal** *adj* جهانی

U

universe *n* جهان	**unrest** *n* ناآرامی
university *n* دانشگاه	**unsafe** *adj* خطرناک
unjust *adj* غیر عادلانه	**unselfish** *adj* از خودگذشته
unjustified *adj* ناموجه	**unspeakable** *adj* وصف ناپذیر
unknown *adj* ناشناخته	**unstable** *adj* ناپایدار
unlawful *adj* غیرقانونی	**unsteady** *adj* سست
unleaded *adj* بدون سرب	**unsuccessful** *adj* ناموفق
unleash *v* از بند رها کردن	**unsuitable** *adj* نامناسب
unless *c* مگر اینکه	**unsuspecting** *adj* بی خبر
unlike *adj* ناهمانند	**unthinkable** *adj* غیرقابل تصور
unlikely *adj* بعید	**untie** *v* باز کردن
unlimited *adj* نامحدود	**until** *pre* تا
unload *v* بار خالی کردن	**untimely** *adj* بی موقع
unlock *v* باز کردن قفل	**untouchable** *adj* دور از دسترس
unlucky *adj* بدشانس	**untrue** *adj* دروغ
unmarried *adj* مجرد	**unusual** *adj* غیرعادی
unmask *v* نقاب برداشتن	**unveil** *v* حجاب برداشتن
unmistakable *adj* غیرقابل تردید	**unwillingly** *adv* با بی میلی
unnecessary *adj* غیرضروری	**unwind** *v* بی کوک کردن
unnoticed *adj* بدون جلب توجه	**unwise** *adj* نابخردانه
unoccupied *adj* خالی	**unwrap** *v* واپیچیدن
unpleasant *adj* ناخوشایند	**upbringing** *n* تربیت
unplug *v* از برق جدا کردن	**upcoming** *adj* آینده
unpopular *adj* غیر مشهور	**upgrade** *v* ترقی دادن
unprofitable *adj* ناسودآور	**upheaval** *n* اغتشاش
unprotected *adj* بی حفاظ	**uphill** *adv* به طرف بالا
unravel *v* از هم باز کردن	**uphold** *v* حمایت کردن
unreal *adj* غیرواقعی	**upholstery** *n* روکش
unrealistic *adj* غیرواقع بین	**upkeep** *n* نگهداری
unreasonable *adj* نامعقول	**upon** *pre* تا
unrelated *adj* بی ارتباط	**upper** *adj* رویه
unreliable *adj* غیرقابل اعتماد	**upright** *adj* تیر عمودی

U

شورش **uprising** n
غوغا **uproar** n
ریشه کن کردن **uproot** v
مضطرب کردن **upset** v
وارونه **upside-down** adv
طبقه دوم **upstairs** adv
ناراحت **uptight** adj
جدیدترین **up-to-date** adj
روبه بالا **upwards** adv
شهری **urban** adj
میل؛ اصرار **urge** n
ترغیب کردن **urge** v
فوریت **urgency** n
فوری **urgent** adj
ادرار کردن **urinate** v
ادرار **urine** n
خاکستردان **urn** n
به ما **us** pro
مصرف **usage** n
استفاده کردن **use** v
استفاده؛ کاربرد **use** n
سابقاً **used to** adj
مفید **useful** adj
سودمندی **usefulness** n
غیرقابل استفاده **useless** adj
استفاده کننده **user** n
راهنما **usher** n
عادی **usual** adj
غصب کردن **usurp** v
ابزار **utensil** n
رحم **uterus** n
بکار بردن از **utilize** v

بیشترین **utmost** adj
ادا کردن **utter** v

جای خالی **vacancy** n
خالی **vacant** adj
تعطیل کردن **vacate** v
تعطیلات **vacation** n
واکسن زدن به **vaccinate** v
واکسن **vaccine** n
دودل بودن **vacillate** v
ولگرد **vagrant** n
مبهم **vague** adj
بیهوده **vain** adj
با بیهودگی **vainly** adv
شجاع **valiant** adj
معتبر **valid** adj
معتبر ساختن **validate** v
اعتبار **validity** n
دره **valley** n
ارزشمند **valuable** adj
ارزش **value** n
دریچه **valve** n
بکن **vampire** n
وانت **van** n
آدم مخرب **vandal** n
تخریب **vandalism** n
خرابگری کردن **vandalize** v

vanguard n پیشتاز	**verbatim** adv کلمه به کلمه
vanish v ناپدید شدن	**verdict** n رای
vanity n تکبر	**verge** n حاشیه
vanquish v در هم شکستن	**verification** n صحت
vaporize v تبخیر شدن	**verify** v تأئید کردن
variable adj متغیر	**versatile** adj انعطاف پذیر
varied adj گوناگون؛ متنوع	**verse** n شعر
variety n تنوع	**versed** adj ماهر
various adj گوناگون	**version** n نگارش
varnish v لاک زدن	**versus** pre در مقابل
varnish n روغن جلا	**vertebra** n مهره پشت
vary v نوسان دادن	**very** adv خیلی
vase n گلدان	**vessel** n ظرف
vast adj وسیع	**vest** n جلیقه
veal n گوشت گوساله	**vestige** n رد؛ جای پا
veer v پس دادن	**veteran** n سرباز قدیمی
vegetation n گیاه	**veterinarian** n دامپزشک
vehicle n وسیله نقلیه	**veto** v رای مخالف دادن
veil n پوشش	**viaduct** n پل راه بر
vein n سیاهرگ	**vibrant** adj درحال جنبش
velocity n سرعت	**vibrate** v لرزیدن
velvet n مخمل	**vibration** n ارتعاش
venerate v تکریم کردن	**vice** n معاون
vengeance n انتقام	**vicinity** n حول و حوش
venison n گوشت آهو	**vicious** adj بیرحم
venom n زهر	**victim** n قربانی
vent n هواکش	**victimize** v طعمه کردن
ventilate v تهویه کردن	**victor** n فاتح
ventilation n تهویه	**victorious** adj برنده
venture n مشارکت	**victory** n پیروزی
verb n فعل	**view** n منظر
verbally adv به طور شفاهی	**view** v مشاهده کردن

viewpoint *n* دیدگاه	**visualize** *v* تجسم کردن
vigil *n* بیدارمانی	**vital** *adj* حیاتی
village *n* روستا	**vitality** *n* سرزندگی
villager *n* روستایی	**vitamin** *n* ویتامین
villain *n* آدم شرور	**vivacious** *adj* شاد
vindictive *adj* انتقام جویانه	**vivid** *adj* روشن
vine *n* تاك	**vocabulary** *n* فرهنگ لغات
vinegar *n* سرکه	**vocation** *n* احساس وظیفه
vineyard *n* تاکستان	**vogue** *n* مد
violate *v* تخلف کردن از	**voice** *n* صدا
violence *n* خشونت	**void** *adj* تهی؛ باطل
violent *adj* خشن	**volatile** *adj* بی ثبات
violet *n* بنفشه	**volcano** *n* آتشفشان
violin *n* ویولن	**volleyball** *n* والیبال
violinist *n* نوازنده ویولن	**voltage** *n* ولتاژ
viper *n* افعی	**volume** *n* حجم؛ بلندی صدا
virgin *n* دوشیزه	**volunteer** *n* داوطلب
virginity *n* بکارت	**vomit** *v* استفراغ کردن
virile *adj* نیرومند	**vomit** *n* استفراغ
virility *n* قدرت جنسی	**vote** *v* رای دادن
virtually *adv* واقعاً	**vote** *n* رأی
virtue *n* پرهیزگاری	**voting** *n* رأی دادن
virtuous *adj* شریف	**vouch for** *v* ضمانت کردن
virulent *adj* کشنده	**voucher** *n* سند
virus *n* ویروس	**vow** *v* عهد کردن
visibility *n* دید	**vowel** *n* مصوت
visible *adj* قابل رویت	**voyage** *n* سفر دریایی
vision *n* بینش	**voyager** *n* مسافر کشتی
visit *n* دیدار	**vulgar** *adj* زشت
visit *v* دیدن کردن از	**vulgarity** *n* هرزگی
visitor *n* بازدید کننده	**vulnerable** *adj* آسیب پذیر
visual *adj* دیدنی	**vulture** *n* کرکس

wafer n ویفر	warehouse n انبار
wag v جنباندن	warfare n جنگ
wage n دستمزد	warm adj گرم
wagon n گاری	warm up v گرم کردن
wail v شیون کردن	warmth n گرمی
wail n ناله	warn v هشدار دادن
waist n کمر	warning n اخطار
wait v منتظر ماندن	warp v تاب دادن
waiter n پیشخدمت	warped adj منحرف
waiting n منتظر	warrant v تضمین کردن
waitress n پیشخدمت زن	warrant n تعهد
waive v صرفنظر کردن از	warranty n ضمانت
wake up iv بیدار شو	warrior n مبارز
walk v راه رفتن	warship n رزمناو
walk n گام	wart n زگیل
walkout n اعتصاب	wary adj مواظب
wall n دیوار	wash v شستن
wallet n کیف بغلی	washable adj قابل شستشو
walnut n گردو	wasp n زنبور
walrus n فیل دریایی	waste v ضایع کردن
waltz n موزیک و رقص	waste n باطله
wander v سرگردان بودن	waste basket n سبد باطله
wanderer n سرگردان	wasteful adj مسرف
wane v به آخر رسیدن	watch n تماشا
want v خواستن	watch v دیدن
war n جنگ	watch out v مواظب بودن
ward n بخش	watchful adj گوش به زنگ
warden n رئیس	watchmaker n ساعت ساز
wardrobe n قفسه	water n آب
	water v آب دادن
	water down v رقیق کردن
	waterfall n آبشار

waterheater n آب گرم کن	**Wednesday** n چهارشنبه
watermelon n هندوانه	**weed** n هرز گیاه
waterproof adj ضدآب	**weed** v وجین کردن
watershed n آب پخشان	**week** n هفته
watertight adj نفوذناپذیر	**weekday** adj روزکار
watery adj آبکی	**weekly** adv هفته ای یکبار
watt n وات	**weep** iv اشک ریز
wave n موج؛ هیجان	**weigh** v وزن کردن
waver v متزلزل شدن	**weight** n وزن
wavy adj موج دار	**weird** adj عجیب و غریب
wax n واکس	**welcome** v خوش آمد گفتن
way n راه؛ روش	**welcome** n خوش آیند
way in n راه دخول	**weld** v جوش دادن
way out n راه خروج	**welder** n جوشکار
we pro ما	**welfare** n رفاه
weak adj ضعیف	**well** n خوب
weaken v سست کردن	**well-known** adj شناخته شده
weakness n ضعف	**well-to-do** adj ثروتمند
wealth n ثروت	**west** n غرب
wealthy adj ثروتمند	**westbound** adv مسافر
weapon n سلاح	**western** adj غربی
wear n سایش؛ پوشاک	**westerner** adj غربی
wear iv بپوش	**wet** adj خیس
wear down v از پا درآوردن	**whale** n بال
wear out v پوسیدن	**wharf** n اسکله
weary adj خسته	**what** adj چه
weather n آب و هوا	**whatever** adj هرچه
weave iv بباف	**wheat** n گندم
web n وب؛ تار عنکبوت	**wheel** n چرخ
wed iv ازدواج کن	**wheelbarrow** n فرقون
wedding n عروسی	**wheelchair** n صندلی چرخ دار
wedge n گوه	**wheeze** v خس خس کردن

W

when adv کی	**wicked** adj رذل
whenever adv هر وقت	**wickedness** n شرارت
where adv کجا	**wide** adj گسترده
whereabouts n محل	**widely** adv کاملاً
whereas c درحالی که	**widen** v عریض کردن
whereupon c که در نتیجه آن	**widespread** adj شایع
wherever c هرجا	**widow** n بیوه
whether c اگر	**widower** n بیوه مرد
which adj کدام	**width** n پهنا
while c زمانیکه	**wield** v گرداندن
whim n هوس	**wife** n همسر
whine v نالیدن	**wig** n کلاه گیس
whip v تازیانه زدن؛	**wiggle** v وول خوردن
whip n شلاق	**wild** adj وحشی
whirl v چرخاندن	**wild boar** n گراز
whirlpool n گرداب	**wilderness** n بیابان؛ صحرا
whiskers n سبیل	**wildlife** n طبیعت وحشی
whisper v نجوا کردن	**will** n آرزو؛ مشیت
whisper n نجوا کردن	**willfully** adv از روی لجبازی
whistle v سوت زدن	**willing** adj راغب
whistle n سوت	**willingly** adv از روی میل
white adj سفید	**willingness** n تمایل
whiten v سفید کردن	**willow** n بید
whittle v بریدن	**wily** adj حیله گر
who pro که آن	**wimp** adj ضعیف و ترسو
whoever pro هرکس	**win** iv پیروز شو
whole adj درست	**win back** v پس گرفتن
wholehearted adj صمیمی	**wind** n باد
wholesale n عمده فروشی	**wind** iv بچرخان
wholesome adj سالم	**wind up** v پایان دادن
whom pro که او	**winding** adj مارپیچی
why adv چرا	**windmill** n آسیای بادی

window *n* پنجره	wizard *n* سحرآمیز ؛ نابغه
windpipe *n* نای	wobble *v* لنگ بودن
windy *adj* طوفانی	woes *n* اندوه ها
wine *n* شراب	wolf *n* گرگ
wing *n* بال	woman *n* زن
wink *n* چشمک	womb *n* رحم
wink *v* چشمک زدن	women *n* زن ها
winner *n* برنده	wonder *v* در شگفت شدن
winter *n* زمستان	wonder *n* تعجب
wipe *v* خشک کردن	wonderful *adj* عالی
wipe out *v* محو کردن	wood *n* چوب
wire *n* سیم	wooden *adj* چوبی
wireless *adj* بی سیم	wool *n* پشم
wisdom *n* عقل	woolen *adj* پشمی
wise *adj* خردمند	word *n* کلمه
wish *v* آرزو کردن	wording *n* عبارت
wish *n* آرزو	work *n* کار
wit *n* عقل	work *v* کار کردن
witch *n* جادوگر	work out *v* حل کردن
witchcraft *n* جادوگری	workable *adj* کارکن
with *pre* با	workbook *n* کتابچه راهنما
withdraw *v* صرفنظر کردن	worker *n* کارگر
withdrawal *n* عقب نشینی	workshop *n* کارگاه
withdrawn *adj* درخودفرورفته	world *n* جهان
wither *v* پژمرده کردن	worldly *adj* مادی
withhold *iv* امتناع کن	worldwide *adj* جهانی
within *pre* در مدت	worm *n* کرم
without *pre* بدون	worn-out *adj* خسته و کوفته
withstand *v* تاب آوردن	worrisome *adj* نگران کننده
witness *n* شاهد	worry *v* نگران کردن
witty *adj* شوخ	worry *n* نگرانی
wives *n* همسرها	worse *adj* بدتر

W

worsen v بدتر کردن	**wrong** adj ناصحیح
worship n پرستش	
worst adj بدترین	
worth adj ارزش	
worthless adj بی ارزش	
worthwhile adj ارزنده	
worthy adj درخور	**X-mas** n کریسمس
would-be adj خواستار	**X-ray** n اشعه ایکس
wound n جرح	
wound v زخمی کردن	
woven adj بافته	
wrap v پیچیدن	
wrap up v خاتمه یافتن	
wrapping n لفاف	
wrath n خشم	
wreath n تاج گل	**yard** n یارد
wreck v خراب کردن	**yarn** n نخ
wreckage n تکه پاره ها	**yawn** n خمیازه
wrench n آچار	**yawn** v خمیازه کشیدن
wrestle v کشتی گرفتن	**year** n سال
wrestler n کشتی گیر	**yearly** adv سالانه
wrestling n کشتی	**yearn** v آرزو کردن
wretched adj نگون بخت	**yeast** n مخمر
wring iv بپیچان	**yell** v فریاد زدن
wrinkle n چین خوردگی	**yellow** adj زرد
wrist n مچ	**yes** adv بلی
write iv بنویس	**yesterday** adv دیروز
write down v نوشتن	**yet** c هنوز
writer n نویسنده	**yield** v تولید کردن
writhe v به خود پیچیدن	**yield** n بازدهی
writing n نوشتن	**yoke** n یوغ
written adj نوشته	

W
X
Y

yolk *n* زرده

you *pro* شما

young *adj* جوان

youngster *n* بچه

your *adj* مال تو؛ مال شما

yours *pro* مال تو؛ مال شما

yourself *pro* خودت

youth *n* جوان

youthful *adj* جوان

Z

zeal *n* اشتیاق

zealous *adj* غیور؛ مجاهد

zebra *n* گوراسب

zero *n* صفر

zest *n* رغبت؛ میل

zinc *n* روی

zip code *n* کدپستی

zipper *n* زیپ

zone *n* منطقه

zoo *n* باغ وحش

zoology *n* جانورشناسی

Y
Z

Farsi-English

Bilingual Dictionaries, Inc.

Abbreviations

a - article
n - noun
e - exclamation
pro - pronoun
adj - adjective
adv - adverb
v - verb
iv - irregular verb
pre - preposition
c - conjunction

connection *n* اتصال
contingent *adj* اتفاق
unanimity *n* اتفاق
come about *v* اتفاق افتادن
arise *v* اتفاق بیافت
coincidental *adj* اتفاقی
atom *n* اتم
ultimatum *n* اتمام حجت
atomic *adj* اتمی
accusation *n* اتهام
iron *v* اتو کردن
bus *n* اتوبوس
auto, car *n* اتومبیل
proof *n* اثبات
demonstrate *v* اثبات کردن
effect, relic *n* اثر
fingerprint *n* اثر انگشت
scar *n* اثر زخم
affect *v* اثر کردن
lease, rent *n* اجاره
lease *v* اجاره دادن
rent *v* اجاره کردن
charter *n* اجاره نامه
permission *n* اجازه
let *v* اجازه بده
let out *v* اجازه خروج دادن
authorize *v* اجازه دادن
let in *v* اجازه دخول دادن
admittance *n* اجازه ورود

ا

coalition *n* ائتلاف
rudimentary *adj* ابتدایی
banality *n* ابتذال
ingenuity *n* ابتکار
infection *n* ابتلا
mastermind *v* ابداع کردن
everlasting *adj* ابدی
immortality *n* ابدیت
eternity *n* ابدیت وازلیت
cloud, foam *n* ابر
ovation *n* ابراز احساسات
superpower *n* ابرقدرت
eyebrow *n* ابرو
cloudy *adj* ابری
silk *n* ابریشم
utensil, tool *n* ابزار
cancellation *n* ابطال
silly *adj* ابله
demon *n* ابلیس
opera *n* اپرا
room *n* اتاق
bedroom *n* اتاق خواب
dining room *n* اتاق ناهارخوری
living room *n* اتاق نشیمن
union *n* اتحاد
pursue *v* اتخاذ کردن

احساس خارش n itchiness	اجاق n oven, stove
احساس کردن v appreciate	اجبار n coercion, force
احساس کن v feel	اجباری adj compulsory
احساس وظیفه n vocation	اجتماع n community
احساسات n feelings	اجتماعی adj sociable
احساساتی adj passionate	اجتماعی کردن v socialize
احضار کردن v evoke	اجتناب n avoidance
احضاریه n subpoena	اجتناب پذیر adj avoidable
احمق adj idiot, fool	اجتناب کردن v refrain
احمقانه adj idiotic	اجتناب کردن از v elude
احیا n regeneration	اجتناب ناپذیر adj inevitable
احیاء کردن v reclaim	اجرا n performance
اخاذی n extortion	اجرا کردن v enforce
اخبار n news	اجرا کن v run
اختراع n invention	اجرت n fee
اختراع کردن v invent	احاطه n ring
اخترشناس n astronomer	احاطه کردن v circle, surround
اخترشناسی n astronomy	احاطه کن v beset, ring
اختصار n abbreviation	احترام n honor, respect
اختصاص دادن v allocate	احترام به خود n self-esteem
اختلاف n disagreement	احترام گذاشتن v respect
اختلال n disruption	احتمال n likelihood
اختیاری adj optional	احتمال خطر n risk
اخراج n expulsion	احتمالی adj probable
اخراج کردن v sack	احتیاج n need
اخطار n warning,	احتیاج داشتن v need
اخلاق n ethics	احتیاط n precaution
اخلاق ستیزی n immorality	احراز کردن v retain
اخلاقی adj ethical	احساس n feeling

morality n اخلاقیات	communication, liaison n ارتباط
frown v اخم کردن	resilient adj ارتجاعی
sullen adj اخمو	heresy n ارتداد
recent adj اخیر	army n ارتش
lately adv اخیراً	marshal n ارتشبد
charade n ادا	vibration n ارتعاش
utter v ادا کردن	altitude, height n ارتفاع
mannerism n ادا و اصول	elevation n ارتقا
bureau n اداره	patrimony n ارث پدری
manage, wield v اداره کردن	hereditary adj ارثی
continuation n ادامه	refer to v ارجاع دادن به
continue, go on v ادامه دادن	duck n اردک
discontinue v ادامه ندادن	expedition n اردو
homage n ادای احترام	camp v اردو زدن
politeness n ادب	currency n ارز
literature n ادبیات	inexpensive adj ارزان
urine n ادرار	worth, value n ارزش
urinate v ادرار کردن	valuable adj ارزشمند
perception n ادراک	worthwhile adj ارزنده
allegation n ادعا	appraise v ارزیابی کردن
claim v ادعا کردن	rate, survey n ارزیابی
merger n ادغام کننده	evaluate v ارزیابی کردن
crust n ادم جسور	dispatch v ارسال کردن
seasoning n ادویه	senior adj ارشد
fuss n اذیت	seniority n ارشدیت
harass, pester v اذیت کردن	terrorize v ارعابگری کردن
presentation n ارائه	orchestra n ارکستر
cart n ارابه	organist n ارگ زن
lordship n اربابی	saw n اره

اره برقی chainsaw n	از سر گرفتن renovate v
اره کن saw v	از شکل افتادگی deformity n
اره مویی jigsaw n	از طرف behalf (on) adv
اروپا Europe n	از طریق through pre
اروپایی European adj	از عهده برآمدن tackle v
اروغ زدن belch v	از عهده بربیا deal v
از of, from pre	از قید رها کردن emancipate v
از این گذشته moreover adv	از کار افتادن crash v
از آن موقع since then adv	از موقع گذشته belated adj
از آنجائیکه since pre	از میان بردن abolish v
از بر خواندن recite v	از نزدیک narrowly adv
از برق جدا کردن unplug v	از نظر روانی mentally adv
از بند رها کردن unleash v	از نو انجام دادن redo v
از بین بردن ruin v	از نو تجارت کردن refinance v
از بین رفتن decay v	از نو چاپ کردن reprint v
از پا درآمدن succumb v	از نو ساختن reconstruct v
از پا درآوردن wear down v	از هم باز کردن unravel v
از پوست درآوردن thresh v	از وقتی که since c
از پیش تاریخ prehistoric adj	ازدحام crowd n
از پیش خبر دادن foreshadow v	ازدحام کردن crowd, mob n
از جا پراندن startle v	ازدواج marriage n
از خط خارج کردن derail v	ازدواج کردن marry v
از خود گذشته unselfish adj	ازدواج کن wed v
از دست دادن miss v	ازسرگیری resumption n
از راه فرعی رفتن bypass v	اژدرمار python n
از روی لجبازی willfully adv	اژدها dragon n
از روی میل willingly adv	اسارت captivity n
از ریشه کندن eradicate v	اساس basis n
از سر افتادن topple v	اساساً originally adv

استدلال n reasoning	اساسی adj basic
استراحت n respite, rest	اسب n horse
استراحت کردن v repose, rest	اسباب n appliance
استرداد n restitution	اسباب اثاثیه n belongings
استرداد مجرم n extradition	اسباب بازی n toy
استشمام کردن v sniff	اسباب و اثاثیه n furnishings
استطاعت داشتن v afford	اسپانیا n Spain
استعاره n metaphor	اسپانیایی adj Spanish
استعاری adj mystic	اسپانیولی n Spaniard
استعداد n aptitude	اسپرم n sperm
استعفا n resignation	استاد n professor
استعفا دادن v resign	استان n province
استعمال کردن v exercise	استاندارد n standard
استفاده n use	استبداد n tyranny
استفاده کردن v use	استبدادی adj dictatorial
استفاده کننده n user	استتار n camouflage
استفاده نابجا n misuse	استثناء n exception
استفراغ n vomit	استثنایی adj exceptional
استفراغ کردن v vomit	استخدام n recruitment
استقرار n deployment	استخدام کردن v recruit
استقلال n independence	استخر n pool, pond
استناد کردن v rely on	استخراج n quarry
استنباط کردن v deduce	استخراج کردن v extract
استنتاج کردن v infer	استخوان n bone
استنشاق کردن v inspire	استخوان بندی n skeleton
استهزا کردن v ridicule, scorn	استخوان ترقوه n collarbone
استهزاء کردن v mock	استخوان گونه n cheekbone
استهلاک n merger	استدعا n petition
استوار adj consistent, steady	استدعا کن v beseech

استوانه cylinder n	اشتباه mistaken adj
استوایی tropical adj	اشتباه بزرگ blunder n
استیک steak n	اشتباه چاپی literal adj
اسراف کردن lavish v	اشتباه کردن goof v
اسطوره myth n	اشتباه کن mistake v
اسفنج sponge n	اشتراک subscription n
اسقف bishop n	اشتعال combustion n
اسقف اعظم archbishop n	اشتغال employment n
اسکان settlement n	اشتغال ذهن preoccupation n
اسکله pier, wharf n	اشتها appetite n
اسکن کردن scan v	اشتها آور appetizer n
اسکنه chisel n	اشتیاق enthusiasm n
اسکورت convoy n	اشراف nobility n
اسکی کردن ski v	اشراف زاده aristocrat n
اسکیت skate n	اشراف سالاری aristocracy n
اسلامی Islamic adj	اشعه ایکس X-ray n
اسلحه گرم firearm n	اشغال کردن occupy v
اسم noun n	اشک tear n
اسم عام generic adj	اشک بریز weep, tear v
اسم فعل gerund n	اشنا کردن acquaint v
اسهال diarrhea n	اصرار کردن stick out v
اسید acid n	اصرار ورزیدن insist v
اسیر captive n	اصطکاک friction n
اسیر کردن captivate v	اصطلاح idiom n
اشاره reference, hint n	اصطلاحات terminology n
اشاره کردن mention, hint v	اصل authentic adj
اشباع glut n	اصل principle n
اشباع کردن saturate v	اصل متعارف axiom n
اشتباه error, mistake n	اصلاح reform n

اصلاح شدن v repent

اصلاح کردن v rectify, amend

اصلاح ناپذیر adj incorrigible

اصلی adj principal, main

اصلی ها n initials

اصول n basics

اصول دین n catechism

اصیل adj sincere

اضافه بار n surcharge

اضافه کار adv overtime

اضافه کردن v add

اضافه وزن adj overweight

اضافی adj additional

اضطراب n stress, anxiety

اطاعت n compliance

اطاعت کردن v obey

اطاق زیرشیروانی n attic

اطراف pre around

اطلاع n notification

اطلاع دادن v notify

اطلاعات n information

اطمینان نکردن به v mistrust

اطمینان n certainty

اطمینان دادن v assure

اطمینان کردن v confide

اظهار n statement

اظهار داشتن v declare

اظهار عشق کردن v court

اظهار کردن v affirm

اظهار نظر n remark

اظهاریه n comment

اعاده کردن v restore

اعانه دادن v contribute

اعتبار n credit, validity

اعتبار دادن v authenticate

اعتدال n moderation

اعتراض n objection

اعتراض آمیز n protest

اعتراض کردن v protest, object

اعتراف n confession

اعتراف شده adj avowed

اعتراف کردن v confess

اعتراف گاه n confessional

اعتصاب n walkout

اعتصاب کن v strike

اعتصابی n strike

اعتماد n confidence

اعتماد کردن به v trust

اعتماد نداشتن v distrust

اعتنا کردن v heed, regard

اعتیاد n addiction

اعشاری adj decimal

اعطا n concession

اعطا کردن v award

اعطائیه n grant

اعلام n declaration

اعلام خبر کردن v relay

اعلام خطر کردن v call out

اعلام کردن v herald	افسونگر enchanting adj
اعلان n proclamation	افشاگرانه revealing adj
اعلان کردن v proclaim	افعی n viper
اعمال کردن v exert	افق n horizon
اغتشاش n chaos	افقی horizontal adj
اغراق آمیز کردن v overstate	اقامت n residence
اغفال کردن v blind	اقامت داشتن v reside
اغلب often adv	اقامه کردن raise, allege v
اغما n coma	اقامه کردن دلیل account for v
اغوا n enticement	اقتدار طلب authoritarian adj
اغوا کردن v tempt	اقتصاد economy n
اغواگری n temptation	اقتصادی economical adj
افتادن v fall down	اقدام کردن برای apply for v
افتتاح کردن v inaugurate	اقدامات n proceedings
افتخار n glory	اقرار کردن v admit
افترا n slander, calumny	اقلیت minority n
افزایش increment, increase n	اقیانوس ocean n
افزایش دادن v increase	اکتبر October n
افزایش یابنده increasing adj	اکتساب acquisition n
افزون بودن بر v outnumber	اکثریت majority n
افسار n bridle	اکراه grudge n
افسار کردن v rein	اکسیژن oxygen n
افسانه n fable, legend	اگر if, whether c
افسردگی n depression	اگرچه although c
افسرده downcast adj	اگهی دادن announce v
افسرده شدن v languish	الاغ donkey n
افسوس خوردن v regret	التهاب inflammation n
افسون n spell	التهاب مفصل arthritis n
افسون کردن charm, bewitch v	الحاد atheism n

constraint *n* الزام	sign *v* امضاء كردن
annulment *n* الغاء	possibility *n* امكان
alphabet *n* الفبا	realty *n* املاك
sift *v* الك زدن	omelette *n* املت
electronic *adj* الكترونيكى	safe *adj* امن
electric *adj* الكتريكى	security *n* امنيت
electrify *v* الكتريكى كردن	routine *n* امور روزمره
alcoholic *adj* الكلى	hope *n* اميد
alcoholism *n* الكليسم	hopeful *adj* اميد
prototype *n* الگوى نخستين	hopefully *adv* اميدوارانه
diamond *n* الماس	singleminded *adj* امين
inspiration *n* الهام	pomegranate *n* انار
goddess *n* الهه	warehouse *n* انبار
timber *n* الوار	stock *v* انبار كردن
divinity *n* الوهيت	accumulate *v* انباشتن
but *c* اما	laden *adj* انباشته
emperor *n* امپراتور	tongs *n* انبر
empire *n* امپراتورى	pliers *n* انبردست
imperialism *n* امپرياليسم	choice *n* انتخاب
examine *v* امتحان كردن	elect, pick *v* انتخاب كردن
refusal *n* امتناع	choose *v* انتخاب كن
withhold *v* امتناع كن	election *n* انتخابات
franchise, privilege *n* امتياز	adoptive *adj* انتخابى
score *v* امتياز گرفتن	publication *n* انتشار
today *adv* امروز	appointment *n* انتصاب
nowadays *adv* امروزه	anticipation *n* انتظار
tonight *adv* امشب	expect *v* انتظار داشتن
sign, signature *n* امضا	review *v* انتقاد كردن
endorse *v* امضا كردن	transfer, shift *n* انتقال

transfusion *n* انتقال خون	energy *n* انرژی
transmit *v* انتقال دادن	revulsion *n* انزجار
vengeance *n* انتقام	seclusion *n* انزوا
vindictive *adj* انتقام جویانه	human, mortal *adj* انسان
revenge *v* انتقام گرفتن	human being *n* انسان
transaction *n* انجام	cohesion *n* انسجام
do *v* انجام بده	obstruction *n* انسداد
accomplish *v* انجام دادن	ramification *n* انشعاب
freezing *adj* انجماد	fairness *n* انصاف
association *n* انجمن	lapse *n* انصراف
aberration *n* انحراف	annexation *n* انضمام
monopoly *n* انحصار	adaptation *n* انطباق
corner *n* انحصار موقتی	discipline *n* انظباط
depravity *n* انحطاط	gratuity *n* انعام
drop *v* انداختن	flexible *adj* انعطاف پذیر
drop in *v* انداختن در	coagulation *n* انعقاد
size *n* اندازه	reflection *n* انعکاس
fit *v* اندازه بودن	reflexive *adj* انعکاسی
downsize *v* اندازه را کم کردن	eruption, explosion *n* انفجار
measure *v* اندازه گرفتن	contraction *n* انقباض
measurement *n* اندازه گیری	spasm *n* انقباض عضلانی
organ *n* اندام	expiration *n* انقضا
hive *n* اندختن	denial *n* انکار
lean *adj* اندک	deny, recant *v* انکار کردن
slightly *adv* اندکی	undisputed *adj* انکارناپذیر
pile *v* اندوختن	finger *n* انگشت
distress *n* اندوه	parasite *n* انگل
woes *n* اندوه ها	England *n* انگلستان
pore *n* اندیشه	English *adj* انگلیسی

انگور grape *n*	اولی former *adj*
انگیزه motive *n*	اولین اجرا debut *n*
انهدام annihilation *n*	اولیه primitive *adj*
انیمیشن animation *n*	اونس ounce *n*
اهانت offense *n*	ایالت state *n*
اهانت آمیز outrageous *adj*	ایتالیا Italy *n*
اهدا dedication *n*	ایتالیایی Italian *adj*
اهدا کردن dedicate *v*	ایجاد حریق arson *n*
اهدا کننده donor *n*	ایجادحریق عمدی arsonist *n*
اهداء کردن present *v*	ایده idea, notion *n*
اهرم lever *n*	ایرلند Ireland *n*
اهل شمال northerner *adj*	ایرلندی Irish *adj*
اهل مد trendy *adj*	ایست قلبی cardiac arrest *n*
اهل ورزش sporty *adj*	ایستادن cease *v*
اهلی کردن domesticate *v*	ایستگاه station *n*
اهمال کار lax *adj*	ایما واشاره gesture *n*
اهمیت significance *n*	ایمان faith *n*
اهمیت دادن به stick to *v*	ایمن immune *adj*
اهمیت داشتن concern *v*	ایمنی safety *n*
او he, she *pro*	این this *adj*
اوانگوتان orangutan *n*	اینجا here *adv*
اوت August *n*	اینچ inch *n*
اوج peak *n*	اینها these *adj*
اوج خوشبختی heyday *n*	
اوج، قله climax *n*	
اورگانیسم organism *n*	
اوریون mumps *n*	
اول first *adj*	
اولویت preference *n*	

آ

آئین نماز n liturgy
آب n water
آب بند n mole; seal, floodgate
آب بندی کردن v seal
آب پخشان n watershed
آب پز کردن v scald
آب دادن v water
آب شدن v melt
آب کردن v dissolve
آب کردن یخ v defrost
آب گرم کن n waterheater
آب مروارید n cataract
آب نبات n candy
آب و هوا adj climatic
آب و هوا n weather
آباره n aqueduct
آبجو n beer
آبجوسازی n brewery
آبدار adj juicy
آبدارخانه n pantry
آبدره n fjord
آبرو n prestige
آبستن adj pregnant
آبسنگ n reef
آبشار n waterfall
آبشار بزرگ n cataract
آبشکن n spur

آبفشان n geyser
آبکی adj watery
آبله جوجه n chicken pox
آبله مرغان n smallpox
آبی adj blue
آبیاری n irrigation
آبیاری کردن v irrigate
آپارتمان n apartment
آپوستروف n apostrophe
آتش n bonfire
آتش بازی n fireworks
آتش بس n cease-fire
آتش بس موقت n truce
آتش زدن v ignite
آتش نشان n firefighter
آتشدان n hearth
آتشفشان n volcano
آتشی کردن v infuriate
آجر n brick
آجیل n nut
آچار n wrench
آخر زمان n apocalypse
آخرین n end
آخرین adj later, latest
آخور n manger
آداب n manners
آداب معاشرت n etiquette
آداب و رسوم n customs
آدامس n gum

bubble gum *n* آدامس بادکنکی	peaceful *adj* آرام
jerk *n* آدم احمق و نادان	restful *adj* آرام بخش
extremist *adj* آدم افراطی	calm down *v* آرام شدن
innocent *adj* آدم بی گناه	pacify, soothe *v* آرام کردن
slob *adj* آدم بیعار	serenity *n* آرامش
coward *n* آدم ترسو	relaxing *adj* آرامش بخش
phoney *adj* آدم حقه باز	tomb *n* آرامگاه
kidnap *v* آدم دزدی کردن	makeup *n* آرایش
abduction *n* آدم ربایی	garnish *v* آرایش دادن
rascal *n* آدم رذل	embellish *v* آرایش کردن
smoker *n* آدم سیگاری	barber *n* آرایشگر
villain *n* آدم شرور	hairdo *n* آرایشگر زنانه
layman *n* آدم غیرحرفه ای	array *n* آرایه
nonsmoker *n* آدم غیرسیگاری	trimmings *n* آرایه ها
eccentric *adj* آدم غیرعادی	artichoke *n* آرتیشو
hunchback *n* آدم قوزپشت	flour *n* آرد
midget *n* آدم کوتاه	wish, will *n* آرزو
progressive *adj* آدم مترقی	yearn, crave, aspire *v* آرزو کردن
bigot *adj* آدم متعصب	arsenic *n* آرسنیک
vandal *n* آدم مخرب	archive *n* آرشیو
drunk *adj* آدم مست	badge *n* آرم
celebrity *n* آدم مشهور	elbow *n* آرنج
twister *n* آدم نادرست	jaw *n* آرواره
benefactor *n* آدم نیکوکار	belch, burp *n* آروغ
savage *adj* آدم وحشی	burp *v* آروغ زدن
cannibal *n* آدمخوار	free *adj* آزاد
decorate *v* آذین کردن	liberate *v* آزاد کردن
equip *v* آراستن	freeway *n* آزادراه
spruce up *v* آراسته کردن	liberation *n* آزادسازی

freedom n آزادی	molar n آسیای بزرگ
obsess, bug v آزار دادن	damage, harm n آسیب
masochism n آزارطلبی	hurt v آسیب برسان
sadist n آزارگر	vulnerable adj آسیب پذیر
nagging adj آزارنده	hurt adj آسیب دیده
afflict v آزردن	damaging adj آسیب رساننده
experiment, test n آزمایش	injure v آسیب زدن
quiz, test v آزمایش کردن	beverage n آشامیدنی
lab n آزمایشگاه	cook n آشپز
tentative adj آزمایشی	kitchen n آشپزخانه
siren n آژیر	cuisine n آشپزی
easy adj آسان	conciliatory adj آشتی جویانه
facilitate v آسان کردن	junk, trash n آشغال
indulgent adj آسان گیر	confusion n آشفتگی
elevator n آسانسور	chaotic adj آشفته
ease n آسانی	plain, obvous adj آشکار
comfort n آسایش	reveal v آشکار کردن
aspirin n آسپیرین	obviously adv آشکارا
threshold n آستانه	familiar adj آشنا
coat, lining n آستر	acquaintance n آشنایی
sleeve n آستین	riot, turmoil n آشوب
asphalt n آسفالت	nest n آشیانه
asthma n آسم	outset n آغاز
sky n آسمان	start v آغاز کردن
skyscraper n آسمان خراش	smear v آغشتن
celestial adj آسمانی	embrace n آغوش
mill n آسیاب	pest n آفت
grind v آسیاب کن	pesticide n آفت کش
windmill n آسیای بادی	bask v آفتاب خوردن

آفتاب سوختگی sunburn n	آمادگی readiness n
آفتابی sunny adj	آماده ready adj
آفرینش creation n	آماده کردن prepare v
آفرینندگی creativity n	آماری statistic n
آفریننده creator n	آمبولانس ambulance n
آقا sir n	آمد و شد traffic n
آقای mister n	آمدن coming adj
آقای محترم gentleman n	آمدن coming n
آکادمیک academic adj	آمدن از come from v
آکاردئون accordion n	آمریکایی American adj
آکواریوم aquarium n	آمفی تئاتر amphitheater n
آگاه aware adj	آموختن indoctrinate v
آگاهی awareness n	آموزاندن instruct v
آگاهی دادن inform v	آموزش training n
آگاهی دهنده informant n	آموزش دادن train v
آگهی دادن advertise v	آموزش و پرورش pedagogy n
آلرژی allergic adj	آموزشی educational adj
آلرژی allergy n	آموزگار teacher n
آلمان Germany n	آمونیاک ammonia n
آلمانی German adj	آمیختن mingle v
آلو plum, prune n	آن that adj
آلودگی pollution n	آناً instantly adv
آلودن smear n	آناناس pineapple n
آلودن soil v	آنجا there adv
آلوده impure adj	آنژین angina n
آلوده کردن defile, contaminate v	آنسوی beyond adv
آلومینیوم aluminum n	آنفلوآنزا influenza n
آلونک shack n	آنگاه else adv
آلیاژ alloy n	آنها they pro

آ
ب

آنها	those *adj*
آه	sigh *n*
آه کشیدن	sigh *v*
آهسته	slow *adj*
آهسته	slowly *adv*
آهسته جوشیدن	simmer *v*
آهسته فراگرفتن	sink in *v*
آهنگ ساز	composer *n*
آهنگر	blacksmith *n*
آهنگین	melodic *adj*
آهنی	iron *n*
آواز	song *n*
آواز عاشقانه	serenade *n*
آوریل	April *n*
آویزان کردن	dangle *v*
آویزان کن	hang *v*
آویزه	hanger *n*
آیندگان	posterity *n*
آینده	future *n*
آینده	hereafter *adv*
آینده	upcoming *adj*
آینده نگری	foresight *n*
آینه	mirror *n*
آیین	rite *n*
آیین مقدس	sacrament *n*
آیین نامه	regulation *n*
آیینه	looking glass *n*

ب

با	sideways *adv*
با	with *pre*
با ابهت	imposing *adj*
با اتوبوس رفتن	bus *v*
با احتیاط	careful *adj*
با استعداد	gifted *adj*
با افتخار	proudly *adv*
با اکراه	grudgingly *adv*
با این همه	nonetheless *c*
با برق کشتن	electrocute *v*
با بی میلی	distasteful *adj*
با بیهودگی	vainly *adv*
با پای برهنه	barefoot *adj*
با پست فرستادن	mail *v*
با تحکم	sternly *adv*
با خشونت	harshly *adv*
با رغبت خوردن	relish *v*
با سر اشاره کردن	nod *v*
با سر و صدا	noisily *adv*
با سرعت	speedily *adv*
با سلیقه	tasteful *adj*
با شادی	joyfully *adv*
با شتاب	hurriedly *adv*
با شتاب نوشتن	scribble *v*
با شدت کم	lowkey *adj*
با صراحت	expressly *adv*
با صرفه جویی	sparingly *adv*

ب

با ظرافت tactful *adj*	بادکنک balloon *n*
با عصبانیت furiously *adv*	باده گساری drunkenness *n*
با فشار راندن ram *v*	باده نوشی کردن toast *v*
با کندی bluntness *n*	بادوام lasting *adj*
با گاری بردن cart *v*	بار load, cargo *n*
با گلوله کشتن shoot down *v*	بار خالی کردن unload *v*
با ملاحظه considerate *adj*	بار شده loaded *adj*
با ناآزمودگی clumsiness *n*	بار کردن load *v*
با نگاه از رو بردن look down *v*	باران rain *n*
با نوار بستن bandage *v*	بارانداز depot *n*
با هم زیستن coexist *v*	بارانی raincoat *n*
با هم کار کردن collaborate *v*	بارانی rainy *adj*
با همدیگر together *adv*	بارآور productive *adj*
با وجود اینکه despite *c*	باربر porter *n*
بابا dad *n*	بارداری gestation *n*
بابا بزرگ granddad *n*	بارش برف snowfall *n*
باتری battery *n*	بارش رادیواکتیو fallout *n*
باتلاق swamp, bog *n*	بارندگی rainfall *n*
باتوم baton *n*	باروت gunpowder *n*
باجگیری racketeering *n*	بارور fertile *adj*
باجه kiosk *n*	بارور کردن fertilize *v*
باحال cool *adj*	باروری fertility *n*
باد wind *n*	باریدن rain *v*
باد کردن bloat *v*	باریک narrow *adj*
باد کرده baggy *adj*	باریکه shred, strip *n*
بادام almond *n*	باز open *adj*
بادام زمینی peanut *n*	باز buzzard *n*
بادبادک kite *n*	باز شدن break open *v*
بادخور کردن air *v*	باز فشردن repress *v*

ب

باز کردن open, untie v	**بازگشت** return n
باز کردن opening n	**بازگشتن** return v
باز کردن قفل unlock v	**بازگویی** telling adj
باز گرفتن withdraw v	**بازمانده** survivor n
بازار market n	**بازمانده ها** debris n
بازآفرینی reenactment n	**بازنده** loser n
بازبینی review n	**بازنشستگی** retirement n
بازبینی کردن revise v	**بازنشسته شدن** retire v
بازپرداخت refund n	**بازنمود کردن** manifest v
بازپرداخت کردن pay back v	**بازو** arm n
بازپرسی کردن interrogate v	**بازوبند** bracelet n
بازتاب feedback n	**بازی** game, play n
بازتاب یافتن reflect v	**بازی کردن** perform v
بازخرید کردن redeem v	**بازی های المپیک** olympics n
بازداشت deterrence n	**بازیابی** retrieval n
بازداشت کردن curb v	**بازیافت کردن** recycle v
بازداشتن deter v	**بازیافتن** regain v
بازدهی yield n	**بازیکن** player n
بازدید کردن review v	**بازیگوش** playful adj
بازدید کننده visitor n	**باستان شناسی** archaeology n
بازرس inspector n	**باسواد** literate adj
بازرسی inspection n	**باش** be v
بازرسی کردن inspect v	**باشعور** sensible adj
بازرگان businessman n	**باشکوه** glorious adj
بازرگان مهم tycoon n	**باشگاه** club n
بازرگانی commerce n	**باضافه** plus adj
بازرگانی commercial adj	**باطل** void adj
بازساختن remake v	**باطل کردن** quash v
بازشناسی recognition n	**باطله** waste n

ب

cause *n* باعث	fin *n* باله
impressive *adj* باعظمت	flaunt *v* بالیدن
garden *n* باغ	exemplify *v* بامثال فهماندن
zoo *n* باغ وحش	affectionate *adj* بامحبت
gardener *n* باغبان	meaningful *adj* بامعنی
bed *n* باغچه	runway *n* باند
texture, tissue *n* بافت	airstrip *n* باند موقت
knit *v* بافتن	influential *adj* بانفوذ
woven *adj* بافته	bank *n* بانک
remain *v* باقی ماندن	crow *n* بانگ خروس
remaining *adj* باقیمانده	crow *v* بانگ زدن
bacteria *n* باکتری	cute *adj* بانمک
baguette *n* باگت	lady *n* بانو
wing, whale *n* بال	smart *adj* باهوش
above *pre* بالا	believe *v* باور کردن
high *adj* بالا	credible *adj* باور کردنی
top *n* بالا	incredible *adj* باور نکردنی
throw up *v* بالا انداختن	faithful *adj* باوفا
enhance *v* بالا بردن	bias *n* بایاس
rise *v* بالا بیا	must *v* باید
go up *v* بالا رفتن	have to *v* بایستن
hoist *n* بالابر	file *n* بایگانی
superior *adj* بالاتر	weave *v* بباف
improvise *v* بالبداهه ساختن	cut, shear *v* ببر
pillow *n* بالش	tiger *n* ببر
grown-up *n* بالغ	shut *v* ببند
amount to *v* بالغ شدن بر	see *v* ببین
potential *adj* بالقوه	spring, leap *v* بپر
balcony *n* بالکن	pay *v* بپرداز

بپوش wear v	بخاطر سپردن memorize v
بپیچان wring v	بخت fortune n
بت idol n	بخت آزمایی lottery n
بت پرستی idolatry n	بخر buy v
بترک burst v	بخش sector, fraction n
بتوان can v	بخشایش forgiveness n
بتون concrete adj	بخشش pardon n
بتون concrete n	بخشنامه circular adj
بجز except pre	بخشندگی mercy n
بچرخ spin v	بخشنده merciful adj
بچرخان spin v	بخشودگی impunity n
بچسب cling, stick v	بخشودنی forgivable adj
بچگانه childish adj	بخشیدن absolve v
بچگی childhood n	بخواب sleep v
بچه youngster, child n	بخوان read, sing v
بچه حرام زاده illegitimate adj	بخود انحصار دادن monopolize v
بچه دزد kidnapper n	بخور eat v
بچه دزدی kidnapping n	بخیه stitch n
بچه گربه kitten n	بخیه زدن stitch v
بچه نوپا toddler n	بد bad adj
بچه ها children n	بد اداره کردن mismanage v
بحث discussion n	بد تعبیر کردن misconstrue v
بحث انگیز controversial adj	بد خلقی کردن grouch v
بحث کردن argue v	بد رفتاری mistreatment n
بحران crisis n	بد رفتاری کردن misbehave v
بحرانی acute adj	بد شکل کردن disfigure v
بخار دادن fumigate v	بد گویی کردن knock v
بخاری heater n	بداخلاق grumpy adj
بخاری دیواری fireplace n	بداخم disagreeable adj

ب

بدبخت miserable adj	بدهکار debtor n
بدبختی misery n	بدهکار بودن owe v
بدبو smelly, fetid adj	بدهی debt, debit n
بدبین pessimistic adj	بدون without pre
بدبینی pessimism n	بدون ابر cloudless adj
بدتر worse adj	بدون توجه regardless adv
بدتر کردن worsen v	بدون جلب توجه unnoticed adj
بدترین worst adj	بدون درز seamless adj
بدجور badly adv	بدون سرب unleaded adj
بدخلق grouchy adj	بدون صلاحیت incompetent adj
بدخواه spiteful adj	بدون لک spotless adj
بدخواهی کردن malign v	بدون مبلمان unfurnished adj
بدرخش shine v	بدیمن sinister adj
بدرفتاری کردن mistreat v	بدین وسیله hereby adv
بدزد steal v	بدیهی self-evident adj
بدشانس unlucky adj	بر روی over pre
بدشکل کردن deface v	بر هم زدن disband v
بدعمل کردن malfunction v	برابر equivalent adj
بدقضاوت کردن misjudge v	برابر بودن correspond v
بدگمان distrustful adj	برابر کردن contrast v
بدگمان شدن suspect v	برابری equality n
بدگمانی distrust n	برادر brother n
بدم blow v	برادر زن brother-in-law n
بدن body n	برادر ناتنی stepbrother n
بدنام infamous adj	برادران brethren n
بدنام کردن smear, blemish v	برادرانه brotherly adj
بدنه chest n	برادری fraternity n
بدنی bodily adj	برازنده elegant adj
بده give v	براق shiny adj

ب

برداشتن v pick up	بران v drive, ride
بردباری n meekness	برانداختن v exterminate
بردگی n slavery	برانداز کردن v glance
برده n slave	براندازی n overthrow
بررسی n scrutiny	برانکار n stretcher
بررسی کردن v canvas	برانگیختن v instigate
برزخ n purgatory	برانگیزنده adj irritating
برس n brush	برای pre for
برس مو n hairbrush	برای یک لحظه adv momentarily
برسید adj mellow	برآشفتن v excite
برش n slice, slash	برآمدگی n bulge
برش کار n cutter	برپا adj erect
برشته adj crusty, crispy	برپا کردن v erect
برشته n toast	برتر adj supreme
برشته کردن v parch	برتری n superiority
برصندلی نشاندن v chair	برتری داشتن بر v excel
برطرف کردن v dispel	برتری یافتن v transcend
بر عکس adv conversely	برج n tower
برف n snow	برج ناقوس n belfry
برف باریدن v snow	برجسته adj outstanding
برق n electricity	برجسته n signal
برقکار n electrician	برجسته بودن v stand out
برکنار کردن v oust	برجک هرمی n turret
برگ n card	برچسب n label, tag
برگرداندن v avert, repay	برخاستن v step up
برگزیده adj favorite	برخورد n clash, impact
برگشت n drawback	برخورد کردن v clash
برگشتن v go back, rebound	برخورد کردن با v bump into
برگه ها n sheets	برخورد کردن به v come across

ب

برنامه program n	بزاق saliva n
برنامه تبلیغاتی scheme n	بزدلی cowardice n
برنامه زمانی schedule n	بزرگ great, huge adj
برنامه مسافرت itinerary n	بزرگ تر شدن از outgrow v
برنامه نویس programmer n	بزرگ جلوه کردن loom v
برنج rice n	بزرگ شدن grow up v
برنده victorious adj	بزرگ شو swell v
برنده winner n	بزرگ کردن enlarge v
برنز bronze n	بزرگراه highway n
برنزه شده tanned adj	بزرگسال adult n
بره lamb n	بزرگی magnitude n
برهنگی nudity n	بزن beat, hit v
برهنه گرا nudist n	بزهکارانه delinquent adj
برهنه گرایی nudism n	بزهکاری delinquency n
برو go, tread v	بزودی soon adv
بروشور brochure n	بساز build, make v
برون ریزی outpouring n	بسازید make n
برون گرا demonstrative adj	بساوایی touch n
برونشیت bronchitis n	بستر مرگ deathbed n
برونگرا extroverted adj	بستری کردن hospitalize v
برونی outer adj	بستگی hinge n
بری از اشتباه infallible adj	بستن curdle, plug v
بریتانیا Britain n	بستن کمربند buckle up v
بریتانیایی British adj	بستنی ice cream n
بریدگی incision n	بسته package n
بریدن intercept, cut off v	بسته پستی parcel post n
بز goat n	بسته کردن pack v
بز کوهی antelope n	بسختی scarcely adv
بزا breed v	بسر بردن get along v

ب

بسرعت رفتن dash v	بعدازظهر afternoon n
بسط extension n	بعدی next adj
بسط دادن expand v	بعضی اوقات sometimes adv
بسط یافتن hold out v	بعید unlikely adj
بسکتبال basketball n	بغض spite n
بسوزان burn v	بغل hug n
بسیار dearly adv	بغلامی درآوردن enthrall v
بسیار دقیق meticulous adj	بغلط تفسیر کردن misinterpret v
بسیار سرد frigid, icy adj	بفرست send v
بسیار مهم crucial adj	بفرض اینکه supposing c
بسیاربزرگ immense adj	بفروش sell v
بسیارسرد arctic adj	بقا survival n
بشر mankind n	بقایای آتش embers n
بشریت humankind n	بقیه remainder n
بشقاب plate n	بکار sow v
بشکن break v	بکار بردن از utilize v
بشکه barrel n	بکارت virginity n
بشناس know v	بکش slay v
بشنو hear v	بکن dig v
بشو become v	بگذار put v
بطری bottle n	بگریز flee v
بطور خلاصه briefly adv	بگو say, tell v
بطور صریح frankly adv	بگیر take, get v
بطور قطع surely adv	بلافاصله pat n
بعد dimension n	بلبل nightingale n
بعد از after pre	بلدرچین quail n
بعد از آن afterwards adv	بلژیک Belgium n
بعد نمایی perspective n	بلژیکی Belgian adj
بعداً later adv	بلسان balm n

بلعیدن gulp down v	**بند جوراب** suspenders n
بلعیدن devour v	**بندباز** acrobat n
بلغم mucus n	**بندر** port n
بلند aloud adv	**بندرت** seldom adv
بلند long, tall adj	**بندکش** shoelace n
بلند پروازی کردن soar v	**بنزین** gasoline n
بلند شدن lift-off n	**بنشین** sit v
بلند کردن heighten, lift v	**بنفشه** violet n
بلند مدت long-term adj	**بنگر** behold v
بلندگو speaker, loudspeaker n	**بنوش** drink v
بلندی Highness n	**بنویس** write v
بلندی صدا volume n	**بنیاد** foundation n
بلوار boulevard n	**بنیاد گذاشتن** institute v
بلور crystal n	**بنیادی** drastic adj
بلوز blouse n	**به** to pre
بلوط acorn, oak n	**به ارث گذاشتن** hand down v
بلوغ maturity n	**به ازاء هر** per pre
بلوک block n	**به او** her adj
بلی yes adv	**به اوج رسیدن** culminate v
بمان be v	**به این دلیل** hence adv
بمب bomb n	**به آخر رسیدن** run out v
بمباران bombing n	**به آرامی** smoothly adv
بمباران کردن bomb v	**به آسانی** easily adv
بن بست dead end n	**به آغوش کشیدن** squeeze v
بن بست deadlock adj	**به بعد** onwards adv
بنا bricklayer n	**به پایان رساندن** finalize v
بنابراین therefore adv	**به پشت** backwards adv
بنای یادبود monument n	**به تازگی** newly adv
بند snare, article n	**به تأخیر انداختن** put off v

ب

به تعویق انداختن v adjourn	به شوخی adv jokingly
به جا adj opportune	به صدا درآوردن v sound
به جای n lieu	به صورت نازک adv thinly
به چنگ آوردن v grasp	به طرف pre towards
به حدکافی adv enough	به طرف بالا adv uphill
به حساب آوردن v reckon on	به طرف خارج adj outward
به خاطر pre because of	به طریق دیگری adv otherwise
به خاطر آوردن v recollect	به طریقی adv somehow
به خاک افتاده adj prostrate	به طور اتفاقی adv incidentally
به خصوص adv especially	به طور جدی adv earnestly
به خط شدن v line up	به طور جزئی adv partially
به خط کردن v row	به طور چشمگیر adv notably
به خطر انداختن v jeopardize	به طور رسمی adv formally
به خواب رفتن v drop off	به طور شفاهی adv orally
به خود پیچیدن v writhe	به طور صحیح adv properly
به دار آویختن v crucify	به طور عادی adv normally
به دام انداختن v snare	به طور غیر رسمی adv unofficially
به دست آوردن v acquire	به طور کلی adv broadly
به دقت دیدن v look through	به طور مرتب adv neatly
به زودی adv shortly	به طور ناشایست adv badly
به زور adv forcibly	به عقب adj backward
به زور گرفتن v extort	به علت adv owing to
به ساحل adv ashore	به قتل رساندن v assassinate
به سادگی adv simply	به کار انداختن v exploit
به سرعت adv quickly	به گناه متهم کردن v incriminate
به سلامتی n cheers	به ما pro us
به سمت داخل adv inwards	به مبارزه طلبیدن v defy
به سوی شرق adv eastward	به مخاطره انداختن v endanger
به شرط اینکه آن c providing that	به موقع adv duly

timely *adj*	**به موقع**
pamper *v*	**به ناز پروردن**
fall through *v*	**به نتیجه نرسیدن**
barely *adv*	**به ندرت**
lightly *adv*	**به نرمی**
embroil *v*	**به نزاع انداختن**
seem *v*	**به نظر آمدن**
sound *v*	**به نظر رسیدن**
anyhow *pro*	**به هرحال**
shuffle *v*	**به هم آمیختن**
slam *v*	**به هم کوفتن**
flush *v*	**به هیجان آمدن**
thrill *v*	**به هیجان درآوردن**
clearly *adv*	**به وضوح**
remember *v*	**به یاد آوردن**
remarkable *adj*	**به یاد ماندنی**
glimpse *v*	**به یک نظر دیدن**
spring *n*	**بهار**
excuse *n*	**بهانه**
recovery *n*	**بهبود**
touch up *v*	**بهبود دادن**
recover *v*	**بهبود یافتن**
improve *v*	**بهبودی دادن**
consternation *n*	**بهت**
awe *n*	**بهت زده**
startled *adj*	**بهت زده**
better *adj*	**بهتر**
best *adj*	**بهترین**
crowning *n*	**بهترین**

hygiene *n*	**بهداشت**
quotient *n*	**بهر**
however *c*	**بهرحال**
explotation, exploit *n*	**بهره برداری**
heaven *n*	**بهشت**
heavenly *adj*	**بهشتی**
convalescent *adj*	**بهگرا**
link *v*	**بهم پیوستن**
mess *n*	**بهم ریختگی**
overthrow *v*	**بهم زدن**
compression *n*	**بهم فشردگی**
impact *v*	**بهم فشردن**
avalanche *n*	**بهمن**
odor, scent *n*	**بو**
smell	**بو کن**
bush, shrub *n*	**بوته**
budget *n*	**بودجه**
being *n*	**بودن**
blizzard *n*	**بوران**
bourgeois *adj*	**بورژوا**
scholarship *n*	**بورس**
blow *v*	**بوز**
kiss *n*	**بوسه**
kiss *v*	**بوسیدن**
by *pre*	**بوسیله**
honk *v*	**بوق زدن**
bowl *n*	**بولینگ**
ecology *n*	**بوم شناسی**
domestic *adj*	**بومی**

ب

بی تربیت rude _adj_	بوی تعفن stink _n_
بی تردید undoubtedly _adv_	بوی تعفنبده stink _v_
بی تصمیمی indecision _n_	بوی گند stench _n_
بی تفاوتی apathy _n_	بویه buoy _n_
بی توجه mindless _adj_	بی اثر کردن foil, defuse _v_
بی ثبات volatile _adj_	بی احترامی disrespect _n_
بی ثباتی instability _n_	بی احتیاط reckless _adj_
بی ثمر barren _adj_	بی احتیاطی indiscretion _n_
بی جان lifeless _adj_	بی احساس senseless _adj_
بی جواب speechless _adj_	بی ادب impolite _adj_
بی حد و حصر boundless _adj_	بی ادبی discourtesy _n_
بی حرکت motionless _adj_	بی ارتباط unrelated _adj_
بی حرمت کردن desecrate _v_	بی ارزش worthless _adj_
بی حرمتی sacrilege _n_	بی اساس unfounded _adj_
بی حس کردن amortize _v_	بی اعتبار invalid _n_
بی حفاظ exposed _adj_	بی اعتبار ساختن discredit _v_
بی حفاظ گذاردن expose _v_	بی اعتمادی mistrust _n_
بی حوصلگی boredom _n_	بی اعتنا indifferent _adj_
بی خانمان homeless _adj_	بی اعتنایی indifference _n_
بی خبر unaware, oblivious _adj_	بی اهمیت کردن trivialize _v_
بی خبری ignorance _n_	بی آب کردن dehydrate _v_
بی خوابی insomnia _n_	بی آبرو disgrace _n_
بی خیال frivolous _adj_	بی آستین sleeveless _adj_
بی دانه seedless _adj_	بی باک bold _adj_
بی درد painless _adj_	بی بندوبار promiscuous _adj_
بی دفاع defenseless _adj_	بی بهره کردن deprive _v_
بی دقت careless _adj_	بی پایان endless _adj_
بی دقتی carelessness _n_	بی پرده blunt _adj_
بی دولتی anarchy _n_	بی تجربه inexperienced _adj_

بی **دین** godless adj	بی **معنی** meaningless, dumb adj
بی **رحم** atrocious adj	بی **موقع** untimely adj
بی **رنگ** pale adj	بی **میل** reluctant adj
بی **ریا** folksy adj	بی **میلی** distaste n
بی **ریسمان** cordless adj	بی **میلی نشانبده** shrink v
بی **سابقه** unheard-of adj	بی **نتیجه** ineffective adj
بی **سروصدا** stealthy adj	بی **نتیجه گذاردن** thwart v
بی **سلاح** unarmed adj	بی **نظمی** disorder n
بی **سواد** illiterate adj	بی **نقص** flawless adj
بی **سیم** wireless adj	بی **نوک** blunt adj
بی **شرم** shameless adj	بی **هدف** aimless adj
بی **شکل** amorphous adj	بی **هوش** unconscious adj
بی **شمار** innumerable adj	بی **وقفه** incessant adj
بی **صبر** impatient adj	بیا come v
بی **صبری** impatience n	بیاب find v
بی **ضرر** harmless adj	بیابان desert n
بی **طرف** impartial adj	بیافت fall v
بی **عدالتی** injustice n	بیان expression n
بی **عیب** impeccable adj	بیان **کردن** express v
بی **عیب** sound n	بیان **کن** spell v
بی **غم** carefree adj	بیانداز throw, cast v
بی **فایده** pointless adj	بیاور bring v
بی **فرزند** childless adj	بیابان wilderness n
بی **قرار** restless adj	بیایست stand v
بی **کوک کردن** unwind v	بید willow n
بی **گناه** blameless adj	بیدار awake adj
بی **گناهی** innocence n	بیدار **شدن** get up v
بی **مزه** insipid adj	بیدار **شو** awake v
بی **مصرف کردن** dismantle v	بیدار **کردن** arouse v

vigil n بیدارمانی	unemployment n بیکاری
awakening n بیداری	outsider n بیگانه
vicious adj بیرحم	shovel, spade n بیل
cruelty n بیرحمی	pool, billiards n بیلیارد
get out v بیرن رفتن	billion n بیلیون
exterior adj بیرون	billionaire n بیلیونر
outside adv بیرون	ailing, sick adj بیمار
expel v بیرون انداختن	leper n بیمار جذامی
come out v بیرون آمدن	lunatic adj بیمار روانی
take out v بیرون آوردن	outpatient n بیمار سرپائی
draw v بیرون بکش	incurable adj بیمار علاج ناپذیر
give out v بیرون دادن	hospital n بیمارستان
go out v بیرون رفتن	sickening adj بیمارکننده
fire, eject v بیرون کردن	disease n بیماری
pull out v بیرون کشیدن	diabetes n بیماری قند
put out v بیرون گذاشتن	rabies n بیماری هاری
aversion n بیزاری	epidemic n بیماری همه گیر
baseball n بیسبال	insurance n بیمه
twenty adj بیست	insure v بیمه کردن
twentieth adj بیستم	among pre بین
biscuit n بیسکویت	compromise n بینابین
undue adj بیش از اندازه	eyesight n بینایی
excessive adj بیش از حد	vision n بینش
overdone adj بیش از حد پخته	nose n بینی
chiefly adv بیشتر	futility n بیهودگی
more adj بیشتر	futile, vain adj بیهوده
utmost adj بیشترین	anesthesia n بیهوشی
oval adj بیضی	widow n بیوه
idle, jobless adj بیکار	widower n بیوه مرد

ب

پ

پا n feet, foot, leg

پائیز n fall

پائین adv down

پائین adj low

پائین آمدن v come down

پائین رفتن از v go down

پائین کشیدن v pull down

پاپ n pontiff, Pope

پات n stalemate

پاداش n reward

پاداش دادن v reward

پادزهر n antidote

پادزیست n antibiotic

پادشاه n king

پادشاهی n kingdom

پادگان n garrison

پاراگراف n paragraph

پارچ n jug

پارچه n cloth

پارچه سفید n garnish

پارچه مخملی adj plush

پارسایی n piety

پارک n park

پاره پوره adj ragged

پاره شدن v split up

پاره کردن v rip, shred

پاره کن v tear

پارو n oar

پارو زدن v paddle

پازل n puzzle

پاس n pass

پاس دادن v pass around

پاستوریزه کردن v pasteurize

پاسخ n reply

پاسخ دادن v respond, answer

پاشنه پا n heel

پاشیدن v spray

پافشاری n insistence

پاک adj immaculate

پاک کردن v erase, clear

پاکت n envelope

پاکسازی n clearance

پالایشگاه n refinery

پالتو n overcoat

پالس n pulse

پاندول n pendulum

پانزده adj fifteen

پای n pie

پایا adj long-standing

پایان n ending

پایان دادن v end up

پایتخت n capital

پایداری n constancy

پایگاه n status

پایگاه داده ها n database

پایمال کردن v overwhelm

پایمردی fortitude *n*	پر از گرد و خاک dusty *adj*
پاینت pint *n*	پر پیچ و خم devious *adj*
پایه base, pillar *n*	پر جنب و جوش dashing *adj*
پاییز autumn *n*	پر چین و شکنج convoluted *adj*
پایین bottom *n*	پر زرق و برق flashy *adj*
پایین آمدن descend *v*	پر زور strenuous *adj*
پایینی lower *adj*	پر کردن fill, stuff, cram *v*
پتو blanket *n*	پرادویه spicy *adj*
پختن cook *v*	پراکندگی کردن dissipate *v*
پختن cooking *n*	پراکنده sporadic *adj*
پخش broadcast *n*	پراکنده شدن disperse *v*
پخش اخبار newscast *n*	پراکنده کردن scatter *v*
پخش دوباره replay *n*	پرانتز parenthesis *n*
پخش شدن diffuse *v*	پربوده شده infested *adj*
پخش کردن hand out *v*	پرپشت lush *adj*
پدالی pedal *n*	پرتاب توپ delivery *n*
پدر father *n*	پرتاب کردن hurl, toss *v*
پدر زن father-in-law *n*	پرتابه projectile *n*
پدرانه fatherly *adj*	پرتخم seedy *adj*
پدربزرگ grandfather *n*	پرتغال Portugal *n*
پدری fatherhood *n*	پرتغالی Portuguese *adj*
پدیدار شدن emerge *v*	پرتقال orange *n*
پدیده phenomenon *n*	پرتکاپو hectic *adj*
پذیرا passive, receptive *adj*	پرجمعیت crowded *adj*
پذیرایی کردن entertain *v*	پرچ کردن clench, rivet *v*
پذیرش acceptance *n*	پرچم flag *n*
پذیرفتن accept, admit *v*	پرحرف talkative *adj*
پذیرفتنی admissible *adj*	پرحرفی کردن scold *v*
پر feather *n*	پرخاش scolding *n*

پرخاشگری n aggression

پرخطر adj hazardous

پرخور n glutton

پرداخت n payment

پرداخت کردن v pay off

پرداختن v defray

پردازش کردن v process

پرده n curtain, drape, screen

پرده گوش n eardrum

پررو adj cheeky

پرزحمت adj demanding

پرزدار n pile

پرزی adj fuzzy

پرس n press

پرستار n nurse

پرستار بچه n babysitter

پرستش n worship

پرستشگاه n temple

پرستیدن v adore

پرسش کردن v inquire, debrief

پرسش نامه n questionnaire

پرسه زدن v prowl

پرسیدن v question

پرش n jump, leap

پرش از روی مانع n hurdle

پرطاقت adj hardy

پرطنین adj resounding

پرمخاطره adj perilous

پرنده n bird

پرنده نر n cock

پرهیز کردن v abstain

پرهیزگار adj pious

پرهیزگاری n virtue

پرواز n fly, flight

پرواز کن v fly

پروانه n licence

پروانه دادن v charter

پروانه ساخت adj patent

پروانه ساخت n patent

پروانه موتور n flier

پروتئین n protein

پروراندن v nurse

پرورش بده v breed

پرورش دادن v bring up, foster

پرورشگاه n orphanage

پروژه n project

پروستات n prostate

پرونده n dossier, case

پری n fairy

پری دریایی n mermaid

پریدن v skip, hop

پریدن در آب v bail out

پریز n outlet

پریشان adj distraught

پریشان کردن v confound

پزشک n physician

پزشکی n medicine

پزشکی زنان n gynecology

پ

پژمرده کردن v wither	پشمی woolen adj
پس انداز n savings	پشه n mosquito
پس دادن v give back	پشیمان adj remorseful
پس زدن شعله v backfire	پشیمان شدن v relent
پس زدن ضربه v hit back	پشیمانی n repentance
پس گرفتن v recapture	پف دار adj puffy
پس مانده‌ها n leftovers	پک n puff
پست dishonorable adj	پل n bridge
پست کردن v demean	پل روی دره n viaduct
پست هوایی n airmail	پلاکارد n placard
پستاندار n mammal	پلک n eyelid
پستچی n mailman	پلنگ n leopard
پستخانه n post office	پله stair, step n
پستی n meanness	پله برقی n escalator
پسر boy, son n	پله در n doorstep
پسر بچه n page	پله کان n staircase
پسر عمه n nephew	پله ها n stairs
پسند کردن v admire	پلوتونیم n plutonium
پسندیده admirable adj	پلید foul adj
پشت behind pre	پلیس cop, police n
پشت نویس کرد v endorse	پماد n ointment
پشت نویسی n endorsement	پمپ کردن v pump
پشتکار داشتن v persevere	پنالتی n penalty
پشته ridge n	پناه n refuge
پشتیبان n backup	پناه گرفتن v shelter
پشتیبانی کردن v support, back	پناهگاه covert adj
پشم n wool	پناهگاه n shelter
پشم جانوران n fleece	پناهگاه زیرزمینی n bunker
پشمالو furry adj	پناهندگی n asylum

پناهنده refugee n	پودر powder n
پنبه cotton n	پوره puree n
پنج five adj	پوزش apology n
پنج شنبه Thursday n	پوزه muzzle n
پنج ضلعی pentagon n	پوزه بندزدن muzzle v
پنجاه fifty adj	پوست peel, skin n
پنجاه-پنجاه fifty-fifty adv	پوست انداختن peel v
پنجره window n	پوست درخت bark n
پنجم fifth adj	پوست سر scalp n
پنجه paw, toe, claw n	پوست کندن bark v
پنجری puncture n	پوستر poster n
پنداشتن deem v	پوسته shell n
پنکه fan n	پوستی skinny adj
پنگوئن penguin n	پوسیدن rot n
پنهان کردن conceal v	پوسیده rotten adj
پنهانکاری coverup n	پوسیده کن wear v
پنهانی clandestine adj	پوشاک clothing n
پنهانی secrecy n	پوشاندن clothe v
پنهانی secretly adv	پوشش coat, cover n
پنومونی pneumonia n	پوشه folder n
پنی penny n	پول money n
پنی سیلین penicillin n	پول تهیه کردن finance v
پنیر cheese n	پول دوست miser n
پهن plain adj	پوند pound n
پهن کردن flatten v	پونز thumbtack n
پهن کن spread v	پویا dynamic adj
پهن نشستن sprawl v	پی بردن find out v
پهنا width n	پیاده رو pavement n
پوچ absurd adj	پیاده روی hike n

پ

پیاده کردن v disembark	پیش preceding adj
پیاده نظام n infantry	پیش افتادن v outrun
پیاز n onion	پیش افتادن از v surpass
پیام n message	پیش آمدن v come up
پیامبر n prophet	پیش بند n apron
پیانو n piano	پیش بینی کردن v anticipate
پیچ n bolt, screw	پیش بینی n prediction
پیچ کردن v bolt, screw	پیش بینی کردن v dope
پیچ گوشتی n screwdriver	پیش بینی کن v forecast
پیچاندن v twist	پیش بینی نشده adj unexpected
پیچیدگی n complexity	پیش خود خندیدن v chuckle
پیچیدن v wrap	پیش زمینه n foreground
پیچیده adj intricate	پیش قسط n down payment
پیچیده کردن v complicate	پیش نمایش n preview
پیدا کردن v detect	پیش نویس n draft
پیر دختر n spinster	پیش نویس کردن v draft
پیراهن n shirt	پیشانی n forehead
پیراهن خواب n nightgown	پیشتاز n vanguard
پیرکس n casserole	پیشخدمت n waiter
پیرو n follower	پیشخدمت زن n waitress
پیروز adj triumphant	پیشخوان n counter
پیروز شو v win	پیشرس adj precocious
پیروزی n triumph	پیشرفت n progress
پیروی کردن v follow	پیشرفت کردن v progress
پیروی کردن از v abide by	پیشرفته n advance
پیری n old age	پیشرو adj leading
پیری adj senile	پیشروی n headway
پیس ساختن v prefabricate	پیشکش کردن v offer
پیش pre ahead	پیشگام n pioneer

ت

تئاتر theater n

تا until, upon pre

تا till adv

تا اندازه ای somewhat adv

تا حدی rather adv

تا کردن fold v

تا کنون hitherto adv

تائید approval n

تائید کردن corroborate v

تاب swing, twist n

تاب آوردن withstand v

تاب بده swing v

تاب خوردن sway v

تاب دادن warp v

تابستان summer n

تابش radiation n

تابعیت citizenship n

تابه حال ever adv

تابوت coffin n

تابیدن glow v

تاثرانگیز dramatic adj

تاثیر effectiveness n

تاج crown n

تاج گذاری کردن crown v

تاج گل wreath n

تاجگذاری coronation n

تاخت و تاز کردن overrun v

پیشگفتار preface n

پیشگویی prophecy n

پیشگویی کردن foretell v

پیشگیر preventive adj

پیشگیری prevention n

پیشنهاد offer, proposal n

پیشنهاد قیمت بده bid v

پیشنهاد قیمت دادن quote v

پیشنهاد کردن propose v

پیشنهادقیمت bid n

پیشه occupation, n

پیشوند prefix n

پیشی گرفتن از outshine v

پیشین prior adj

پیشینیان antecedents n

پیک courier n

پیله pleat n

پیلی دار pleated adj

پیمان pact n

پیمان بستن contract v

پینه بسته callous adj

پیوست appendix n

پیوست کردن attach v

پیوستگی integration n

پیوستن affix v

پیوسته continuous adj

پیوند link, bond n

پیوند زدن graft v

تاخیر کردن v delay	**تاکسی** n cab
تار n fiber	**تاکید** n emphasis
تار عنکبوت n web	**تالار** n auditorium
تارت n tart	**تالار نشیمن** n lobby
تاریخ n history, date	**تالار ورودی** n hallway
تاریخ گذاشتن v date	**تامل کردن** v hesitate
تاریخ نویس n historian	**تامین کننده** n supplier
تاریک n blackout	**تاوان دادن** v compensate
تاریک adj dark	**تاول** n blister
تاریک روشن n twilight	**تایپ کردن** v type
تاریک کردن v overshadow; darken	**تایپ کردن** n type
تاریکی n darkness	**تایید** n confirmation
تازگی n freshness	**تایید کردن** v confirm
تازه adj fresh	**تأئید کردن** v verify
تازه داماد adj newlywed	**تأخیر** n delay
تازه کردن v freshen	**تأسف** n regret
تازه وارد n newcomer	**تب** n fever
تازیانه زدن v whip	**تب دار** adj feverish
تازیدن v gallop	**تبار** n ancestry
تاس n dice	**تبخیر شدن** v vaporize
تاس کباب n stew	**تبخیر کردن** v evaporate
تاسف آور adj regrettable	**تبدیل** n conversion
تاسف خوردن v lament	**تبدیل کردن** v commute
تاسیس n form	**تبر** n ax, hatchet
تاسیس کردن v establish, base	**تبرئه** n acquittal
تاک n vine	**تبرئه کردن** v acquit
تاکتیک n tactics	**تبریک** n congratulations
تاکتیکی adj tactical	**تبریک گفتن** v congratulate
تاکستان n vineyard	**تبریکات** n greetings

تجربه	experience *n*
تجرد	celibacy *n*
تجزیه	dissolution *n*
تجزیه شدن	decompose *v*
تجزیه کردن	break down *v*
تجسم کردن	visualize *v*
تجلیل کردن	glorify *v*
تجمل	luxury *n*
تجهیزات	equipment *n*
تجویز کردن	prescribe *v*
تحریف کردن	falsify *v*
تحریک	incitement *n*
تحریک کردن	provoke, arouse *v*
تحریم	prohibition *n*
تحریم کردن	ban *v*
تحسین	praise *n*
تحسین آمیز	complimentary *adj*
تحسین کردن	applaud *v*
تحصیل کردن	earn *v*
تحصیل نکرده	uneducated *adj*
تحقیر	disdain, contempt *n*
تحقیر کردن	humiliate *v*
تحقیر نمودن	belittle *v*
تحقیرآمیز	demeaning *adj*
تحقیق	investigation *n*
تحقیق کردن	research *v*
تحلیل	analysis *n*
تحلیل بردن	undermine *v*
تحلیل کردن	analyze *v*

تبعید	banishment *n*
تبعید کردن	deport *v*
تبعیدی	exile *n*
تبعیض	discrimination *n*
تبعیض قائل شدن	discriminate *v*
تبلیغ	advertising *n*
تبلیغات	publicity *n*
تپاله	dung *n*
تپانچه	pistol *n*
تپش	throb *n*
تپش کن	beat *v*
تپل	chubby *adj*
تپه	hill *n*
تپه ماهور	hilly *adj*
تپیدن	pulsate, throb *v*
تجارت	trade *n*
تجاوز به عنف	rape *n*
تجاوز جنسی کردن	rape *v*
تجاوز کردن	exceed *v*
تجدید	renewal *n*
تجدید انتخاب کردن	reelect *v*
تجدید چاپ	reprint *n*
تجدید حیات	rebirth *n*
تجدید خاطره کردن	brush up *v*
تجدید دیدار	reunion *n*
تجدید فراش کردن	remarry *v*
تجدید کردن	renew *v*
تجدید نظر کردن	reconsider *v*
تجدیدنظر	revision *n*

tolerance n تحمل	discharge n تخلیه
bearable adj تحمل پذیر	egg n تخم
endure v تحمل کردن	ovary n تخمدان
bear v تحمل کن	conjecture n تخمین
burden n تحمیل	estimate v تخمین زدن
impose, burden v تحمیل کردن	fancy adj تخیلی
lobby v تحمیل گری کردن	continuity n تداوم
delivery n تحویل	expedient adj تدبیر
deliver v تحویل دادن	devise v تدبیر کردن
take over v تحویل گرفتن	gradual adj تدریجی
couch, throne n تخت	funeral n تدفین
bed n تختخواب	anoint v تدهین کردن
hammock n تختخواب سفری	admonition n تذکر
board n تخته	level n تراز
springboard n تخته پرش	tragedy n تراژدی
blackboard n تخته سیاه	facet n تراش
vandalism n تخریب	chip n تراشه
destroy v تخریب کردن	splinter n تراشه چوب
specialty n تخصص	scrape v تراشیدن
specialize v تخصص یافتن	tractor n تراکتور
major in v تخصص یافتن در	congestion n تراکم
technical adj تخصصی	tram n تراموا
allotment n تخصیص	streetcar n تراموای شهری
ration, allot v تخصیص دادن	exude, leak v تراوش کردن
discount n تخفیف	radish n تربچه
discount v تخفیف دادن	upbringing n تربیت
extenuating adj تخفیف دهنده	rear, raise, educate v تربیت کردن
lessen v تخفیف یافتن	arrangement n ترتیب
violate v تخلف کردن از	ordain v ترتیب دادن

ترقی دادن v boost

ترقی کردن v boom

ترقی n boost

ترقی دادن v escalate

ترقی قیمت n appreciation

ترک n defection, fracture

ترک خوردن v crack

ترک کردن v abandon

ترک کن v quit, leave

ترکانیدن v crack

ترکش n shrapnel

ترکیب n synthesis

ترکیب شده adj composed

ترکیب کردن v blend

ترکیدن v splash

ترکیدنتایر n blowout

ترکیه n Turkey

ترمز n brake

ترمز کردن v brake

ترور n assassination

تروریست n assassin

تروریسم n terrorism

ترومبوز n thrombosis

تریاک n opium

تریبون n lectern

تزئین n ornament

تزار n czar

تزریق n injection

تزریق کردن v inject

ترتیب زمانی n chronology

ترجمه کردن v interpret

ترجیح یافتن v prefer

ترحم n pity

ترحم انگیز adj pitiful

ترخیص کردن v release

ترد adj crunchy

ترد کردن گوشت v marinate

تردست n juggler

تردید n hesitation

تردید کردن v doubt

ترس n fright, fear

ترس آور adj frightening

ترسان adj afraid

ترساندن v horrify

ترسانیدن v dismay

ترسناک adj scary

ترسو adv cowardly

ترسو adj timid

ترسیدن v dread

ترسیم n drawing

ترش adj sour

ترش شدن v ferment

ترش کردگی n heartburn

ترشح کردن v sprinkle

ترغیب کردن v urge

ترفیع n promotion

ترفیع دادن v promote

ترقه n firecracker

تزیینی decorative adj	تشویق applause n
تسبیح rosary n	تشویق کردن encourage v
تستر toaster n	تصادف collision n
تسریع کردن quicken v	تصادف کردن collide v
تسکین relief n	تصادفی accidental adj
تسکین دادن sedate v	تصحیح correction n
تسلسل sequence n	تصحیح کردن correct v
تسلط داشتن dominate v	تصدیق کردن certify v
تسلی appeasement n	تصرف seizure n
تسلیت condolences n	تصفیه purge n
تسلیحات armaments n	تصفیه کردن filter, refine v
تسلیم surrender n	تصلیب crucifixion n
تسلیم شدن surrender v	تصمیم decision n
تسمه strap n	تصمیم گرفتن determine v
تسمه قایق gripe n	تصمیم گیرنده deciding adj
تسویه settlement n	تصور conception n
تسویه کردن compromise v	تصور کردن imagine v
تشتک pan n	تصور غلط illusion n
تشخیص diagnosis n	تصویب ratification n
تشخیص دادن diagnose v	تصویب کردن ratify v
تشدید aggravation n	تصویر image n
تشریفات ceremony n	تضاد contrast n
تشک mattress n	تضمین indemnity n
تشکر thanks n	تضمین کردن warrant v
تشکر کردن thank v	تطابق باقانون legality n
تشکیل دادن organize, constitute v	تطبیق accord n
تشنج convulsion n	تطمیع کردن buy off v
تشنه thirsty adj	تظاهر pose n
تشنه بودن thirst v	تعادل balance n

ت

تعارفی complimentary adj	تعویض کردن substitute v
تعالیم gospel n	تعیین determination n
تعاونی cooperative adj	تعیین کردن assess v
تعجب wonder n	تعیین کننده fateful adj
تعداد تلفات جنگی toll n	تغ تغ کردن rattle v
تعدد frequency n	تغذیه nutrition n
تعدی کردن trespass v	تغذیه کردن graze v
تعدیل پذیر adjustable adj	تغذیه کن feed v
تعرفه tariff n	تغییر change, alteration n
تعریف definition n	تغییر جهت دادن turn over v
تعصب prejudice n	تغییر دادن alter, modify v
تعطیل holiday n	تغییر درجهت بهبود upturn n
تعطیل کردن vacate v	تغییر رنگ دادن color v
تعطیلات vacation n	تغییر شکل distortion n
تعطیلات آخر هفته weekend n	تغییر شکل دادن transform v
تعظیم bow n	تغییر قیافه دادن disguise v
تعظیم کردن bow v	تغییر کردن revolve v
تعقیب chase n	تغییر مسیر diversion n
تعقیب سراسری manhunt n	تغییر ناپذیر immutable adj
تعقیب قانونی کردن sue v	تف کن spit v
تعقیب کردن chase, tail v	تفاوت disparity n
تعلق داشتن belong v	تفاوت ظریف nuance n
تعلیق suspension n	تفریح fun n
تعلیم دادن enlighten v	تفریح کردن recreate v
تعمد کردن deliberate v	تفریق subtraction n
تعمید دادن baptize v	تفسیر annotation, interpretation n
تعمیر کردن mend, repair v	تفسیر کردن rationalize v
تعهد bond, commitment n	تفسیر نوشتن comment v
تعهد کردن guarantee v	تفکر meditation n

تفکر کردن v contemplate	تقویت کننده n amplifier
تفکیک کردن v detach	تقویتها n reinforcements
تفنگ n rifle	تقویم n calendar
تفنگ دستی n handgun	تقویم نجومی n almanac
تفنگ سیگاری n smoking gun	تک adj single
تفنگ شکاری n shotgun	تک حزبی adj totalitarian
تفوق n primacy	تک گویی n monologue
تقارن n symmetry	تک همسری n monogamy
تقاضا n demand, plea	تک و تنها adj lonesome
تقاضا کردن v demand	تکامل n evolution
تقاطع n crossroads	تکان n shock, jolt
تقدس n holiness	تکان بده v shake
تقدیر n destiny, fate	تکان دادن v shock, jolt
تقدیس n consecration	تکان دهنده adj shattering
تقدیس کردن v consecrate, bless	تکان سریع دادن v jerk
تقریباً adv almost	تکان ناگهانی n bump
تقریبی adj approximate	تکانشی adj impulsive
تقسیم کردن v divide	تکبر n arrogance
تقسیم نشدنی adj indivisible	تکثیر کردن v reproduce
تقصیر n culpability	تکخال n ace
تقطیر شدن v distill	تکرار n recurrence
تقلا n exertion	تکرار شدن v recur
تقلب کردن v sharpen	تکرار کردن v reiterate
تقلبی adj fake	تکراری adj redundant
تقلید n imitation	تکریم کردن v venerate
تقلید در آوردن v mime	تکلیف n homework
تقلید کردن v imitate	تکمیل n completion
تقلیل دادن v cut back	تکمیل کردن v augment
تقویت کردن v reinforce, amplify	تکه n chunk, piece

ت

تکه پاره ها wreckage n	تماشا spectacle n
تکهتکه piecemeal adv	تماشاچی bystander n
تکیه repose n	تماشایی picturesque adj
تکیه کردن recline v	تمام all, entire adj
تگرگ hail n	تمام lot adv
تلاش exertion n	تمام کردن end, finish v
تلاش کردن endeavor v	تمامیت integrity n
تلاش کن strive v	تمایز distinction n
تلافی reprisal n	تمایل willingness n
تلافی کردن retaliate, avenge v	تمثیل allegory n
تلافی کردن ضربه strike back v	تمدد اعصاب کردن relax v
تلپ flop n	تمدن civilization n
تلخی bitter adj	تمرد insurgency n
تلخی bitterness n	تمرکز focus, concentration n
تلسکوپ telescope n	تمرکز کردن بر focus on v
تلفات زیاد وارد کردن decimate v	تمرین practice n
تلفن phone, telephone n	تمرین کردن practise v
تلفن زدن phone v	تمساح crocodile n
تلفیق conjunction n	تمسخر ridicule n
تلقین کردن insinuate v	تمسخر کردن deride v
تلگرام telegram n	تمشک جنگلی raspberry n
تلمبه pump n	تمشک سیاه blackberry n
تلنبار lumber n	تمکین کردن deign v
تله trap n	تملق adulation n
تلو تلو خوردن stagger v	تمیز clean, neat adj
تلویزیون television n	تمیز کردن clean v
تماس touching adj	تمیز کننده cleaner n
تماس call, contact n	تمیزی cleanliness n
تماس گرفتن contact v	تن ton, tuna n

تناقض contradiction n	تنه torso, trunk n
تنبل lazy adj	تنها only, alone adv
تنبلی laziness n	تنها solitary adj
تنبیه punishment n	تنهاتر loner n
تنبیه کردن penalize v	تنهایی loneliness n
تند rapid adj	تنور tenor n
تند کردن accelerate v	تنوع variety n
تندباد gust n	تنیس tennis n
تندر thunder n	ته بلیت stub n
تندنویسی shorthand n	ته مانده remnant n
تنزل رتبه دادن demote v	تهاجم invasion n
تنزل قیمت دادن devalue v	تهاجم کردن invade v
تنزل کردن degrade v	تهاجمی aggressive adj
تنزل کنید degenerate adj	تهدید menace, threat n
تنش tension n	تهدید کردن blackmail, bulldoze v
تنش زا stressful adj	تهوع nausea n
تنظیم setup n	تهویه ventilation n
تنظیم adjustment n	تهویه کردن ventilate v
تنظیم کردن regulate v	تهی void adj
تنظیم کردن موتور tune up v	تهی کردن deplete v
تنظیم کننده adapter n	تهیدست indigent adj
تنفر hatred n	تهیه provision n
تنفر داشتن abhor v	تهیه کردن procure v
تنفر داشتن از detest v	تو گذاشتن take in v
تنفرآور revolting adj	توارث descent n
تنفس breathing n	توازن poise n
تنفس کردن inhale v	تواضع humility n
تنگ cramped adj	توافق consensus n
تنگه strait n	توافق داشتن adhere v

توصیه کردن v recommend	توالت n rest room
توضیح n clarification	توانا adj able
توضیح دادن v explain	توانایی n ability
توطئه n conspiracy, intrigue	توانایی ذهنی n mentality
توطئه چیدن v conspire	توبه n penance
توطئه گر n conspirator	توبیخ n rebuke
توفان n hurricane	توپ n cannon, ball
توفان تندری n thunderstorm	توپ زدن v bluff
توفانی adj stormy	توپخانه n artillery
توقف n stop	توپی n hub
توقیف n attachment	توت فرنگی n strawberry
توقیف کردن v confiscate, arrest	توتون n tobacco
تولد n birth	توجه n attention
توله n cub	توجه کردن v attend
توله سگ n puppy	توجیه کردن v justify
تولید n produce, production	توده n stack, bulk
تولید کردن v produce	توده کردن v heap
تولید مثل n reproduction	تور n tour
تولید مثل کردن v clone	توربین n turbine
تونل n tunnel	تورم n swelling
تونیک n tunic	توزیع n distribution
توهین n affront	توزیع کردن v dispense
توهین آمیز adj derogatory	توسعه n development
توهین کردن v affront	توسعه دادن v develop
توهین کردن به v insult	توسل n recourse
تیپ n brigade	توصیف n description
تیر n stake, arrow	توصیف کردن v portray
تیر تراش n graze	توصیفی adj descriptive
تیر چراغ n lamppost	توصیه n suggestion

ث

ثبت کردن v log, record
ثبت نام n enrollment
ثبت نام کردن v enroll
ثروت n affluence
ثروتمند adj wealthy

ج

جا دادن v board
جا گذاشتن v leave out
جابجا شدن v move
جابجا کردن v displace
جاخالی دادن v dodge
جادار adj roomy
جادکمه n buttonhole
جاده n road
جادوگر n sorcerer
جادوگری n witchcraft
جاذب adj absorbent
جاذبه n appeal
جار و جنجال n racket
جارچی n herald
جارو n broom
جارو کن v sweep
جاری adj current
جاری بودن v flow

تیرانداز n sniper
تیرانداز ماهر n marksman
تیرعمودی adj upright
تیرکش n loophole
تیرگی n obscurity
تیره adj dim, gloomy
تیره کردن v dim; blur
تیره و تار شده adj blurred
تیروئید n thyroid
تیز adj sharp
تیز n piercing
تیز کردن v sharpen
تیزرو adj acute
تیزکن n sharpener
تیغ n razor
تیغه n boom, blade
تیم n team
تیمار n groom

ث

ثابت adj steady, constant
ثابت شده adj proven
ثانوی adj secondary
ثبات n recorder
ثبت n record, log; registration

جاری کن v cast	جایگاه تماشاچیان n grandstand
informer n جاسوس	جایگاه قاضی n tribunal
espionage n جاسوسی	جایگزین adj alternate
جاسوسی کردن v spy	جایگزین n alternative
bookcase n جاکتابی	جایگزین کردن v replace
جاکشی کردن v pander	جایگزینی n replacement, switch
key ring n جاکلیدی	جبر n algebra
interesting adj جالب	جبران n reparation
جالب توجه adj notable	جبران کردن v make up for, atone
جام شراب n chalice	جبران ناپذیر adj irreparable
جامع adj catholic	جبهه n front
جامعه n society	جد n ancestor
جامعه خزدار n fur	جدا adv asunder
جامه n apparel	جدا adj separate
جانبی adj lateral	جدا از هم adv apart
substitute n جانشین	جدا شدن v drift apart
جانشین کردن v swap	جدا شدنی adj detachable
جانورشناسی n zoology	جدا شده adj estranged
جانوری adj bestial	جدا کردن v separate, amputate
جاه طلب adj ambitious	جدا نشدنی adj inseparable
جاه طلبی n ambition	جداشدن v dissent
جای پا n footprint	جدال n controversy
جای پارک n parking	جدال کردن v dispute
جای خالی n vacancy	جدایی n segregation
جای دیگری adv elsewhere	جدها n grandparents
جای ویژه n booth	جدول زمانی n timetable
جایزه n bonus, prize	جدی adj serious
جایزه بزرگ n jackpot	جدیت n seriousness
جایگاه n dock	جدید adj modern

جدیدترین up-to-date *adj*	جسارت boldness *n*
جذاب attractive *adj*	جستجو search, quest *n*
جذام leprosy *n*	جستجو کردن search *v*
جذب assimilation *n*	جستجو کن seek *v*
جذب کردن absorb, attract *v*	جستن jump *v*
جذبه attraction *n*	جسد corpse *n*
جذبه جادویی charisma *n*	جسم شنار drifter *n*
جرات courage *n*	جسور bold, daring *adj*
جرات دادن hearten *v*	جشن festivity *n*
جراح surgeon *n*	جشن گرفتن celebrate *v*
جراحی surgical *adv*	جشنی festive *adj*
جرح wound *n*	جعبه box, casket *n*
جرعه gulp, sip *n*	جعفری parsley *n*
جرقه spark *n*	جعل forgery *n*
جرقه زدن spark off *v*	جعل کردن forge, counterfeit *v*
جرم crime; mass *n*	جعل هویت کردن masquerade *v*
جریان circulation *n*	جعلی counterfeit *adj*
جریان آب stream *n*	جغد owl *n*
جریب acre *n*	جغرافیا geography *n*
جریمه penalty *n*	جفت couple, mate *n*
جریمه کردن fine, sanction *v*	جگر liver *n*
جزء ingredient *n*	جگوار jaguar *n*
جزء به جزء نوشتن itemize *v*	جلا gloss *n*
جزئی detail *n*	جلد binding *adj*
جزئی partial *adj*	جلسه conference *n*
جزر و مد tide *n*	جلگه plain *n*
جزمی dogmatic *adj*	جلو front *n*
جزوه pamphlet *n*	جلو front *adj*
جزیره island *n*	جلو کشیدن pull ahead *v*

جلوگیری کردن prevent v	جنسیت sexuality n
جلوه دادن set off v	جنگ fight, war n
جلویی forward adv	جنگ شادی revue n
جلیقه vest n	جنگ کن fight v
جمجمه skull n	جنگ گاو نر bull fight n
جمع addition n	جنگل forest n
جمع total adj	جنگنده fighter n
جمع اوری کردن get in v	جنگنده گاو نر bull fighter n
جمع آوری collection n	جنوب south n
جمع آوری کردن collect v	جنوب شرقی southeast n
جمع شدن congregate v	جنوبغرب southwest n
جمع کردن pile up, agglomerate v	جنوبی southern adj
جمعه Friday n	جنوبی southerner n
جمعی mass n	جنین fetus n
جمعیت population n	جهاد crusade n
جمعیت دوست gregarious adj	جهان universe n
جمله sentence n	جهانگرد explorer n
جمله شرطی conditional adj	جهانگردی tourism n
جمهوری republic n	جهانی universal adj
جن گیر exorcist n	جهت orientation n
جنایت felony n	جهت یابی navigation n
جنایت کار felon n	جهش اقتصادی boom n
جنایت کارروانی psychopath n	جهش کردن take off v
جنایی criminal adj	جهنم hell n
جنباندن wag v	جهیزیه dowry n
جنبه aspect n	جو atmosphere n
جنبه فنی technicality n	جواب answer n
جنجالی fussy adj	جواب دادن counter v
جنس gender n	جواب رد refuse n

lad, youth *n* جوان	چ
young *adj* جوان	
bud *n* جوانه	
sprout *v* جوانه زدن	چابک *adj* brisk
gem, jewel *n* جواهر	چاپ *n* edition, print
jeweler *n* جواهرساز	چاپ ریز *n* small print
chicken *n* جوجه	چاپ کردن *v* print
porcupine *n* جوجه تیغی	چاپگر *n* printer
stocking *n* جوراب	چاپلوسی کردن *v* flatter
pantyhose *n* جوراب شلواری	چادر *n* tent
barometer *n* جوسنج	چارچوب *n* framework
pimple *n* جوش	چاشنی *n* condiment
solder, weld *v* جوش دادن	چاق *adj* corpulent
boil *v* جوشاندن	چاک بده *v* slit
welder *n* جوشکار	چاک دادن *v* strip
rodent *n* جونده	چالاب *n* pothole
ink *n* جوهر	چاله *n* ditch
atmospheric *adj* جوی	چانه *n* chin
stream *n* جویبار	چانه زدن *v* haggle, bargain
munch, chew *v* جویدن	چانه زدن *n* bargaining
pocket *n* جیب	چای *n* tea
pickpocket *n* جیب بر	چتر *n* parachute, umbrella
cricket *n* جیرجیرک	چترباز *n* paratrooper
squeaky *adj* جیرجیری	چرا *adv* why
scream *n* جیغ	چراغ *n* lamp
scream *v* جیغ کشیدن	چراغ خیابان *n* streetlight
mercury *n* جیوه	چراغ قوه *n* torch
	چراغ نورافکن *n* spotlight
	چراگاه *n* pasture
	چرب *adj* greasy

چربی n fat	چشم پوشیدن v relinquish
چرت n nap	چشمک n wink
چرت زدن v doze	چشمک زدن v twinkle, blink
چرخ n wheel	چشمگیر adj striking
چرخ دستی n trolley	چشمه n span
چرخاندن v whirl	چشمه آب معدنی n spa
چرخاننده n crank	چشیدن v sip
چرخش n rotation, twist	چطور adv how
چرخش توپ n stuff	چغندر n beet
چرخه n cycle	چفت n bolt, latch
چرخیدن v rotate, turn	چک n check
چرک n grime, pus	چک پرداخت n paycheck
چرک کردن v fester	چکاندن v instil
چرک گوش n earwax	چکانیدن v trickle
چرم n leather	چکش n hammer
چرند n nonsense	چکمه n boot
چروک n crease	چکه n drip
چروک شدن v crease	چکیدن v drip
چریدن v browse	چگونگی n predicament
چریک n guerrilla	چلچراغ n chandelier
چریکی n partisan	چله تابستان n midsummer
چسب n glue, paste	چلیک کوچک n keg
چسباندن v paste, glue	چماق n club, bat
چسبناک adj sticky	چماق زدن v club
چسبنده adj adhesive	چمدان n luggage
چشم n eye	چمن n grass, lawn
چشم انداز n outlook	چمنزار n prairie
چشم بستن v blindfold	چموش adj unbroken
چشم بند n blindfold	چنان adj such

چنانچه as *adv*	چیز تقلبی ساختن adulterate *v*
چنانچه as *c*	چیزی any *adj*
چند زنه polygamist *adj*	چیزی something *pro*
چند همسری polygamy *n*	چین crease *n*
چندگانه multiple *adj*	چین خوردگی wrinkle *n*
چندین several *adj*	
چنگ grasp, clutch *n*	
چنگ زدن claw *v*	
چنگال fork, pitchfork *n*	ح
چنگه cramp *n*	
چهار four *adj*	حادثه incident *n*
چهارپایه stool *n*	حاشیه margin, verge *n*
چهارده fourteen *adj*	حاشیه ای marginal *adj*
چهارشنبه Wednesday *n*	حاشیه دار کردن border on *v*
چهارم fourth *adj*	حاصل outcome *n*
چهل forty *adj*	حاصل جمعیکجا lump sum *n*
چوب wood *n*	حاضر present *adj*
چوب بست stage *n*	حافظه memory *n*
چوب پنبه cork *n*	حاکم ruler *n*
چوب جنگلی hardwood *n*	حاکمیت dominion *n*
چوب زیربغل crutch *n*	حالا now *adv*
چوب نیمسوز cinder *n*	حالت mood *n*
چوبه دار gallows *n*	حامل bearer *n*
چوبی wooden *adj*	حاملگی pregnancy *n*
چوپان shepherd *n*	حامله بودن expect *v*
چون inasmuch as *c*	حامی supporter *n*
چیدن pluck, trim *v*	حباب bubble *n*
چیدن clipping *n*	حبس کردن detain, jail *v*
چیز thing *n*	

حتی even *adj*	حروف ریز fine print *n*
حتی اگر even if *c*	حریص greedy *adj*
حتی بیشتر even more *c*	حریصانه خوردن gobble *v*
حجاب برداشتن unveil *v*	حریف contender *n*
حجب timidity *n*	حریف شدن cope *v*
حجم volume, bulk *n*	حریم limit *n*
حجیم bulky *adj*	حزب party *n*
حد limit *n*	حزن انگیز tragic *adj*
حداقل minimum *n*	حس sense *n*
حداکثر maximum *adj*	حس کردن sense *v*
حدس speculation, guess *n*	حس کننده detector *n*
حدس زدن guess *v*	حساب arithmetic *n*
حدود scope *n*	حساب کردن calculate *v*
حذر کردن beware *v*	حسابدار accountant *n*
حذف omission *n*	حسادت jealousy, envy *n*
حذف کردن delete, omit *v*	حساس susceptible *adj*
حراج کردن auction *v*	حساسیت friction *n*
حرارت ardor *n*	حسد بردن envy *v*
حرامزاده bastard *n*	حسرت گذشته nostalgia *n*
حرص avarice *n*	حسن تفاهم rapport *n*
حرف letter *n*	حسن نیت goodwill *n*
حرف اضافه preposition *n*	حسود envious *adj*
حرفه profession *n*	حشره insect *n*
حرفه ای professional *adj*	حشیش hashish *n*
حرکت motion, movement *n*	حصار fence *n*
حرکت آهسته slow motion *n*	حضور attendance *n*
حرکت کردن depart *v*	حضور داشتن attend *v*
حرمت reverence *n*	حضور یافتن show up *v*
حروف ایتالیک italics *adj*	حفاری کردن unearth *v*

ح

safeguard n حفاظ	snail n حلزون
conservation n حفاظت	gorge n حلق
armor n حفاظت شده	ring n حلقه
boring adj حفر	curly adj حلقه حلقه
cavity, hollow n حفره	noose n حلقه طناب
conserve n حفظ	curl v حلقه کردن
prerogative n حق	garland n حلقه گل
blackmail n حق السکوت	folly n حماقت
option n حق انتخاب	bath n حمام
copyright n حق تالیف	backing n حمایت
priority n حق تقدم	uphold, defend v حمایت کردن
dues n حق عضویت	freight n حمل
salary n حقوق	carry v حمل کردن
truth, fact n حقیقت	transport v حمل و نقل کردن
carve v حک کردن	assault, raid n حمله
engraving n حکاکی	offensive adj حمله
anecdote n حکایت	onslaught n حمله بی امان
rule, decree n حکم	lash out v حمله زبانی کردن
ban n حکم توقیف	attack; set about v حمله کردن
pronounce v حکم دادن	larynx n حنجره
decree v حکم کردن	eve n حوا
doom n حکم مجازات	apostle n حواری
arbitration n حکمیت	apostolic adj حواریون
sovereign adj حکومت	distraction n حواس پرتی
govern v حکومت کردن	money order n حواله
soluble adj حل شدنی	vicinity n حول و حوش
resolve v حل کردن	towel n حوله
insoluble adj حل نشدنی	bathrobe n حوله حمام
lawful adj حلال	outskirts n حومه

ح

حیاتی *adj* vital	خارجی *adj* external
حیاط *n* courtyard	خارجی *n* foreigner
حیاط خلوت *n* patio	خارجی *adv* overseas
حیاط مزرعه *n* farmyard	خاردار *adj* thorny
حیرت انگیز *adj* amazing	خارق العاده *adj* fantastic
حیرت آور *adj* marvelous	خاریدن *v* itch
حیطه *n* range	خاص *adj* specific
حیله *n* ruse	خاطرات *n* memoirs
حیله زدن *v* trick	خاک *n* soil
حیله گر *adj* wily	خاک رس *n* clay
حیوان *n* beast	خاکریز *n* bulwark
حیوانیت *n* bestiality	خاکستر *n* ash
	خاکستر کردن *v* cremate
	خاکستردان *n* urn
	خاکستری *adj* gray
	خاکستری گانه *adj* grayish
	خاکی شده *adj* soiled
خ	خال گوشتی *n* mole
	خالدار *adj* freckled
	خالص *n* net
خائن *adj* disloyal	خالص *adj* pure
خائن *n* traitor	خالص کردن *v* purify
خاتمه یافتن *v* wrap up	خاله *n* aunt
خاخام *n* rabbi	خالی کردن آب *v* drain
خادم کلیسا *n* deacon	خالی *adj* blank, empty
خادم میخانه *n* barmaid	خالی از تظاهر *adj* unassuming
خار *n* thorn	خالی کردن *v* evacuate
خارج *adv* away, out	خام *adj* raw, crude
خارج ازکشور *adv* abroad	خامه ای *adj* creamy
خارج شدن *v* step out	
خارج کردن *v* emit	

خاموش extinct adj	خرابکاری sabotage n
خاموش off adv	خرابکاری کردن sabotage v
خاموش کردن turn off v	خرابگری کردن vandalize v
خانگی domestic adj	خرابی malfunction n
خانم madam n	خراش scratch, graze n
خانمخانه housewife n	خراش دادن prick v
خانه home, house n	خراشیدن scrub v
خانه مجلل mansion n	خرافه superstition n
خانواده family n	خرامیدن stalk v
خاییدن gnaw v	خربزه melon n
خبر غیرمترقبه bombshell n	خرچنگ lobster n
خبرنامه newsletter n	خرد شدن crumble, crash v
خبرنگار correspondent n	خردکردن batter v
ختنه circumcision n	خردکننده crushing adj
ختنه کردن circumcise v	خردل mustard n
خجالت دادن embarrass v	خردمند wise adj
خجلت mortification n	خرده fragment n
خداحافظ bye e	خرده چوب chip n
خداحافظی farewell n	خرده کاری chore n
خداوند God n	خرده نان crumb n
خدایی divine adj	خرس bear n
خدمت service n	خرس آبی beaver n
خدمت کردن service v	خرف کردن deaden v
خدمتکار barman, servant n	خرگوش hare, rabbit n
خدمه crew n	خرما date n
خر chop n	خرناس کشیدن snore v
خر و پف snore n	خروج از سیستم log off v
خراب decay n	خروج جمعی exodus n
خراب کردن wreck, botch v	خروجی output n

rooster *n* خروس	extremities *n* خشونت
purchase, shopping *n* خرید	privacy *n* خصوصی
buyer *n* خریدار	private *adj* خصوصی
purchase *v* خریداری کردن	alignment *n* خط
shop *v* خریدن	equator *n* خط استوا
treasurer *n* خزانه دار	trunk *n* خط اصلی
reptile *n* خزنده	railroad *n* خط راه آهن
moss *n* خزه	sideburns *n* خط ریش
crawl, creep *v* خزیدن	cross out, scratch *v* خط زدن
wheeze *v* خس خ کردن	coastline *n* خط ساحلی
havoc *n* خسارت	course, track *n* خط سیر
exhaustion *n* خستگی	pipeline *n* خط لوله
tireless *adj* خستگی ناپذیر	policy *n* خط مشی
tired, weary *adj* خسته	oblique *adj* خط مورب
exhaust *v* خسته کردن	miss *n* خطا
wind *v* خسته کن	err *v* خطا کردن
exhausting *adj* خسته کننده	foolproof *adj* خطاناپذیر
worn-out *adj* خسته و کوفته	danger, peril *n* خطر
dried, dry *adj* خشک	risk *v* خطر کردن
dry, parch *v* خشک کردن	unsafe, risky *adj* خطرناک
wipe *v* خشک کردن	scale *n* خطکش
drought *n* خشکسالی	trick *n* خطوط
dryclean *v* خشکشوئی کردن	outline *n* خطوط اصلی
stiffness *n* خشکی	burdensome *adj* خطیر
wrath, rage *n* خشم	bat *n* خفاش
angry *adj* خشمگین	disgrace *v* خفت آوردن بر
aggravate, anger *v* خشمگین کردن	asphyxiation *n* خفگی
fierce, harsh *adj* خشن	stuffy *adj* خفه
satisfy *v* خشنود کردن	choke, stifle, asphyxiate *v* خفه کردن

خ

stifling *adj* خفه کننده	pulp *n* خمیره
nut *n* خل	neutral *adj* خنثی
emptiness *n* خلاء	neutralize *v* خنثی کردن
relieve *v* خلاص کردن	undo *v* خنثی کردن فعالیت
brief, short *adj* خلاصه	dagger *n* خنجر
summary *n* خلاصه	stab *v* خنجر شدن
roundup *n* خلاصه اخبار	laugh *v* خندان بودن
summarize, brief *v* خلاصه کردن	laugh, laughter *n* خنده
briefs *n* خلاصه ها	amusing *adj* خنده دار
misdemeanor *n* خلاف	cool *adj* خنک
creative *adj* خلاق	cool *v* خنک کردن
toothpick *n* خلال دندان	cooling *adj* خنک کننده
pilot, flier *n* خلبان	coolness *n* خنکی
trance *n* خلسه	acclimatize *v* خو دادن
disarmament *n* خلع سلاح	addicted *adj* خو گرفته
disarm *v* خلع سلاح کردن	sleep *n* خواب
temper *n* خلق	drowsy *adj* خواب آور
create *v* خلق شدن	dream *v* خواب ببین
deserted *adj* خلوت	hypnosis *n* خواب مصنوعی
purity, candor *n* خلوص	dormitory *n* خوابگاه
gulf *n* خلیج	lowly *adj* خوار
cove *n* خلیج کوچک	despise *v* خوار شمردن
hunched *adj* خم شده	groceries *n* خواربار
bend, lean *v* خم شو	would-be *adj* خواستار
incline *v* خم کردن	court *n* خواستگاری
yawn *n* خمیازه	want *v* خواستن
yawn *v* خمیازه کشیدن	legible *adj* خوانا
curve *v* خمیدن	reading *n* خواندن
dough *n* خمیر	reader, singer *n* خواننده

خ

خواهان plaintiff n	خورشیدی solar adj
خواهر sister n	خوش cheerful adj
خواهر زن sister-in-law n	خوش آمد گفتن welcome v
خواهش کردن beg, ask v	خوش آمدگوئی welcome n
خوب fine, good adj	خوش آیند appealing adj
خوب fine, well adv	خوش آیند نبودن displease v
خوبی goodness n	خوش بخت lucky adj
خود oneself pre	خوش بنیه sturdy adj
خود شیرینی کردن ingratiate v	خوش بین optimistic adj
خودآگاه self-conscious adj	خوش بینی optimism n
خودبخود spontaneous adj	خوش خلق amiable adj
خودبخودی spontaneity n	خوش شانس fortunate adj
خودت yourself pro	خوش مشرب genial adj
خودخواه selfish adj	خوش منظر scenic adj
خودخواهی selfishness n	خوش نما good-looking adj
خودستایی کردن boast v	خوشایند pleasant adj
خودش herself pro	خوشبو fragrant adj
خودشان themselves pro	خوشحال happy adj
خودکار automatic adj	خوشحال کننده gratifying adj
خودکشی suicide n	خوشحالی happiness n
خودم myself pro	خوشمزه delicious adj
خودمان ourselves pro	خوشنود کردن agree v
خودمختاری autonomy n	خوشه cluster n
خودنما ostentatious adj	خوشی pleasure n
خودنمائی کردن show off v	خوف انگیز eerie adj
خور creek n	خوک pig n
خوراک nourishment n	خون blood n
خوراکی edible adj	خون مردگی bruise n
خورشید sun n	خونابه serum n

خ

خیلی many *adj*

خیلی much, very *adv*

خیلی بد stinking *adj*

خیلی سیاه pitch-black *adj*

خیلی کم few *adj*

خیلی کم n little bit

د

دائم ceaselessly *adv*

دائم permanent *adj*

دائمی standing *n*

داخل aboard *adv*

داخل inside *pre*

داخل interior *adj*

داخل شدن در go in *v*

داخل وریدی intravenous *adj*

داخلی indoor *adv*

داخلی inner *adj*

داد کشیدن roar *v*

دادخواست claim *v*

دادخواست claim *n*

دادخواهی litigation *n*

دادرسی trial *n*

دادگاه courthouse *n*

داده ها data *n*

دادیار prosecutor *n*

خونریزی bleeding *n*

خونریزی کن bleed *v*

خونسرد composed *adj*

خونی gory *adj*

خونین bloody *adj*

خویشاوند akin *adj*

خویشاوند relative *n*

خویشاوندان سببی in-laws *n*

خویشاوندی kinship *n*

خیابان street *n*

خیابان اصلی avenue *n*

خیار cucumber *n*

خیاط tailor *n*

خیاط زنانه seamstress *n*

خیاطی sewing *n*

خیال باطل کردن daydream *v*

خیال پردازی fantasy *n*

خیانت betrayal *n*

خیانت کردن double-cross *v*

خیرخواه benevolent *adj*

خیرخواهی benevolence *n*

خیره شدن stare *v*

خیره کردن dazzle *v*

خیره کننده breathtaking *adj*

خیره نگاه کردن gaze *v*

خیس soggy, wet *adj*

خیس خوردن soak up *v*

خیس شدن در soak in *v*

خیساندن soak *v*

دارا بودن contain v	دانش آموز pupil n
دارائی ها assets n	دانش فنی know-how n
دارابی grapefruit n	دانشجو student n
دارای گرایش oriented adj	دانشکده college n
دارایی property n	دانشگاه university n
داربست scaffolding n	دانشمند scientist n
دارت dart n	دانشنامه encyclopedia n
دارچین cinnamon n	دانمارک Denmak n
دارو medication n	دانه bean, grain, seed n
داروخانه drugstore n	دانه برف snowflake n
داروساز pharmacist n	دانه سبز green bean n
داروسازی pharmacy n	داور referee n
داروی تقویت tonic n	داوری کردن arbitrate v
دارویی medicinal adj	داوطلب volunteer n
داس sickle n	داوطلب بودن stand for v
داستان fiction, story n	دایر live adj
داستان نویس novelist n	دایره circle n
داشته باش have v	دایناسور dinosaur n
داغ torrid, hot adj	دخالت interference n
داغدار bereaved adj	دخالت کردن interfere v
دالان lobby n	دختر daughter, girl n
دام pitfall n	دختر خواهر niece n
داماد bridegroom n	دخمه محل قبور catacomb n
دامپزشک veterinarian n	در at pre
دامن کوتاه miniskirt n	در آغاز initially adv
دامن لباس skirt n	در آنوقت then adv
دامنه flank n	در برداشتن include v
دامنه تپه hillside n	در پایان lastly adv
دانش knowledge n	در تردید بودن hover v

در خود فرو رفته withdrawn adj	درجه degree n
در درجه اول primarily adv	درجه ترشی acidity n
در دسترس available adj	درجه حرارت temperature n
در شگفت شدن wonder v	درجه گرفتن graduate v
در ضمن meantime adv	درحال آمدن incoming adj
در طول along pre	درحال جنبش vibrant adj
در طی during pre	درحال رفتن outgoing adj
در عرض across pre	درحال مرگ dying adj
در عمق in depth adv	درحالی که whereas c
در عوض instead adv	درخت tree n
در مقابل versus pre	درخت زبان گنجشک ash n
در مواجه با facing pre	درخت کاج pine n
در میان آمدن intervene v	درخت مو grapevine n
در هم آمیختن scramble v	درخت نارون elm n
در هم شکستن crash n	درخشان brilliant adj
در واقع indeed adv	درخشش glare n
دراز کردن lengthen v	درخشیدن glitter v
درآغوش کشیدن caress v	درخواست request, appeal n
درآغوش گرفتن embrace v	درخواست کردن plead, solicit v
درآمد income n	درخواست کردن از implore v
درب door n	درخواست نامه application n
درباره about adv	درخور worthy adj
درباره concerning pre	درخور توجه noteworthy adj
دربازکن قوطی can opener n	درد ache, pain, suffering n
دربان janitor n	درد شدید pang n
دربطری ریختن bottle v	دردناک painful adj
درپوش plug n	درز seam n
درج insertion n	درس lesson n
درج کردن insert v	درس بده teach v

د

درست okay adv	دروازه بان goalkeeper n
درست right adj	درودگر carpenter n
درست کردن manufacture v	دروغ falsehood n
درست نفهمیدن misunderstand v	دروغ untrue adj
درشت کردن magnify v	دروغ گفتن lie v
درشکه carriage n	دروغگو liar adj
درصد percent adv	درون in pre
درصد percentage n	درون inside adj
درک understanding n	درون گرا introvert adj
درک کردن realize, seize v	درونی inward adj
درکنار alongside pre	دریا sea n
درکونی زدن spank v	دریاچه lake n
درگیری implication n	دریازده seasick adj
درمان remedy n	دریاسالار admiral n
درمان کردن remedy v	دریافت receipt n
درمانگاه clinic n	دریافت کردن receive v
درمدت within pre	دریایی marine adj
درمیان amid pre	دریچه gate, valve n
درمیان گذاشتن enclose v	دریچه قلک تلفن drop n
درنا crane n	دریغ داشتن spare v
درنگ کردن linger v	دزد burglar, thief n
دره valley n	دزد دریایی pirate n
دره باریک وتنگ canyon n	دزد مسلح gunman n
دره عمیق و باریک ravine n	دزدی theft n
درهم پیچیدن intertwine v	دزدی از مغازه shoplifting n
درهم شکستن vanquish v	دزدی دریایی piracy n
درهم و برهمی mix-up n	دزدی کردن rip off v
درو کردن harvest v	دزدیدن embezzle v
دروازه (در فوتبال) goal n	دزدیدن هواپیما hijack n

د

fortress *n* **دژ**	glove *n* **دستکش**
December *n* **دسامبر**	notation *n* **دستگاه علائم**
hand, limb *n* **دست**	arrest *n* **دستگیر**
hoax *n* **دست انداختن**	apprehend, capture *v* **دستگیر کردن**
rail *n* **دست انداز**	knob *n* **دستگیره**
bump *n* **دست انداز جاده**	handkerchief *n* **دستمال**
pet *n* **دست آموز**	napkin *n* **دستمال سفره**
overestimate *v* **دست بالا گرفتن**	wage *n* **دستمزد**
singlehanded *adj* **دست تنها**	bundle, batch *n* **دسته**
handshake *n* **دست دادن**	classify *v* **دسته بندی کردن**
outrage *n* **دست درازی**	checkbook *n* **دسته چک**
encroach *v* **دست درازی کردن**	swarm *n* **دسته زیاد**
handle *v* **دست زدن به**	cluster, bundle *v* **دسته کردن**
desist *v* **دست کشیدن**	precept *n* **دستور**
minimize *v* **دست کم گرفتن**	dictate *v* **دستور دادن**
intact *adj* **دست نخورده**	grammar *n* **دستور زبان**
handwritting *n* **دست نوشته**	recipe *n* **دستور عمل**
manuscript *n* **دست نویس**	code *n* **دستورالعمل**
cumbersome *adj* **دست و پا گیر**	agenda *n* **دستورکار**
achieve, attain *v* **دست یافتن**	access *n* **دستیابی**
attainable *adj* **دست یافتنی**	aide *n* **دستیار**
ploy *n* **دستاویز**	dessert *n* **دسر**
handcuffs *n* **دستبند**	discharge *n* **دشارژ**
script *n* **دستخط**	rye *n* **دشت**
adrift *adv* **دستخوش حوادث**	enemy, foe *n* **دشمن**
disposal *n* **دسترس**	hostile *adj* **دشمن**
reach *n* **دسترسی**	antagonize *v* **دشمن کردن**
handmade *adj* **دستساز**	hostility *n* **دشمنی**
basin *n* **دستشوئی**	problematic *adj* **دشوار**

د

pray v دعا کردن	dollar n دلار
prayer n دعا گوینده	imply v دلالت کردن
benediction n دعای خیر	implicate v دلالت کردن بر
brawl, feud, quarrel n دعوا	suggestive adj دلالت کننده
lawsuit n دعوای حقوقی	gallant adj دلاور
quarrelsome adj دعوایی	admirer n دلباخته
invitation n دعوت	sweetheart n دلبر
invite v دعوت کردن	please v دلپذیر کردن
defense n دفاع	depress v دلتنگ کردن
advocate, appeal v دفاع کردن	harrowing adj دلخراش
office n دفتر	annoy v دلخور کردن
branch office n دفتر انشعابی	consolation n دلداری
ledger n دفتر حسابداری	console v دلداری دادن
directory n دفتر راهنما	glamorous adj دلربا
journal n دفتر روزنامه	discourage, dishearten v دلسرد کردن
diary n دفتر یادداشت	discouraging adj دلسردکننده
clerical adj دفتری	disappointment n دلسردی
repulse n دفع	caring adj دلسوز
repulse v دفع کردن	tenderness n دلسوزی
bury v دفن کردن	deplore v دلسوزی کردن
accuracy n دقت	delight v دلشاد کردن
precise, exact adj دقیق	premonition n دلشوره
minute n دقیقه	dolphin n دلفین
doctor n دکتر	clown n دلقک
mast n دکل	daunting adj دلهره آور
button n دکمه	reason n دلیل
décor n دکور	reason v دلیل آوردن
transformation n دگرگونی	blast n دم
obsession n دل مشغولی	brew v دم کردن

د

دماپا thermostat *n*	دو چندان کردن redouble *v*
دماغه cape *n*	دو ماهانه bimonthly *adj*
دماغه کشتی prow *n*	دو نسخه کردن duplicate *v*
دمپایی slipper *n*	دوئل duel *n*
دمدمی moody *adj*	دوا زدن drug *v*
دموکراتیک democratic *adj*	دوازده twelve *adj*
دموکراسی democracy *n*	دوازدهمی twelfth *adj*
دنبال کردن track *v*	دوام stability *n*
دنباله stern *adj*	دوام داشتن last *v*
دنج cozy *adj*	دوبار twice *adv*
دندان tooth *n*	دوباره پر کردن refill *v*
دندان درد toothache *n*	دوباره تجربه کردن relive *v*
دندان مصنوعی dentures *n*	دوباره جوان کردن rejuvenate *v*
دندان نیش fang *n*	دوباره ساختن rebuild *v*
دندانپزشک dentist *n*	دوباره شارژ کردن recharge *v*
دندانه کردن dent *v*	دوباره ظاهر شدن reappear *v*
دندانها teeth *n*	دوبرابر کردن double *v*
دنده rib *n*	دوپینگ dope *n*
دنده، drive *n*	دوجانبه reciprocal *adj*
ده ten *adj*	دوجین dozen *n*
دهان mouth *n*	دوچرخه bicycle *n*
دهانه muzzle *n*	دوچرخه سوار cyclist *n*
دهانه آتشفشان crater *n*	دوختن sew *v*
دهمین tenth *n*	دود fumes *n*
دهنه span *n*	دودزده smoked *adj*
دهه decade *n*	دودستگی schism *n*
دو two *adj*	دودکش chimney *n*
دو برابر double *adj*	دودل بودن vacillate *v*
دو تا couple *n*	دور afar, far *adv*

دور remote adj	**دوشس** duchess n
دور از انصاف unfair adj	**دوشنبه** Monday n
دور از دسترس inaccessible adj	**دوشیزه** maiden n
دور انداختن throw away v	**دوطرفه** mutually adv
دور ریختن scrap v	**دوقلو** twin n
دور کردن fend off v	**دوک** duke n
دوراهی dilemma n	**دوگانه** dual adj
دورآگاهی telepathy n	**دولت** government n
دوربین camera n	**دولت ستیز** anarchist n
دوربیندوچشمی binoculars n	**دوم** second n
دورتر farther adv	**دومی** latter adj
دورنما prospect n	**دونده** runner n
دوره epoch, period n	**دونیم کردن** halve v
دوره سه ماهه trimester n	**دیپلم** diploma n
دوری کردن از avoid v	**دیپلماتیک** diplomatic adj
دوز doze n	**دیپلماسی** diplomacy n
دوزبانه bilingual adj	**دید** visibility n
دوزنی bigamy n	**دیدار** visit n
دوزیست amphibious adj	**دیدار مکرر کردن** haunt v
دوست friend n	**دیدکلی** overview n
دوست پسر boyfriend n	**دیدگاه** standpoint n
دوست داشتن love, like v	**دیدن** watch, notice v
دوست داشتنی likable adj	**دیدن کردن از** visit v
دوست دختر girlfriend n	**دیدنی** visual adj
دوست صمیمی crony n	**دیده ور** scout n
دوست نداشتن dislike v	**دیر** late adv
دوستانه amicable adj	**دیر** monastery n
دوستی friendship n	**دیروز** yesterday adv
دوش shower n	**دیسک** disk n

د

دیکتاتور n dictator
دیگ بخار n boiler
دیگچه n pot
دیگر adj other
دیگری adj another
دیلم n crowbar
دین n religion
دین شناس n theologian
دین شناسی n theology
دینامیت n dynamite
دینی adj religious
دیوار n wall
دیوان سالار n bureaucrat
دیوان سالاری n bureaucracy
دیوانگی n craziness
دیوانه adj insane, mad
دیوانه شدن v rave
دیوانه کردن v madden
دیوانه وار adv madly

ذ

ذاتی adj intrinsic
ذخیره n stockpile
ذخیره کردن v save, store
ذرت n corn

ذرت بوداده n popcorn
ذره n bit, particle
ذکر n mention
ذهن n mind
ذهنی adj mental
ذوب n fusion
ذینفع n beneficiary

ر

رئالیسم n realism
رئیس n boss, chief
رئیس دانشگاه n chancellor
رئیسی adj bossy
رابطه n relationship
رابطه نامشروع n misconduct
راجع به pre regarding
راحت adj comfortable
راحت کردن v ease
راحتی بخش n comforter
رادار n radar
رادیاتور n radiator
رادیویی n radio
راز n secret
رازگشایی n revelation
راس n apex

راست right *adv*	راه راه striped *adj*
راست right *n*	راه رفتن walk *v*
راست right *adj*	راه فرعی detour *n*
راستروده rectum *n*	راهب monastic *adj*
راستگو truthful *adj*	راهب monk *n*
راضی شدن به settle for *v*	راهب صومعه friar *n*
راضی کردن content *v*	راهببزرگ abbot *n*
راغب willing *adj*	راهبرد strategy *n*
راکت racket *n*	راهبه nun *n*
راکد stagnant *adj*	راهرو corridor *n*
راکد کردن stagnate *v*	راهروی زیرزمینی subway *n*
راکون raccoon *n*	راهزن bandit *n*
رام کردن daunt, tame *v*	راهنما key, manual, clue, guide *n*
ران thigh *n*	راهنما manual *adj*
راندن dislodge *v*	راهنمایی کردن guide *v*
رانده شده outcast *adj*	رای verdict *n*
راننده driver *n*	رای دادن vote *v*
راننده کامیون trucker *n*	رای مخالف دادن veto *v*
راه lane, way *n*	رایانه computer *n*
راه افتادن move out *v*	رایج prevalent *adj*
راه انداختن initiate *v*	رایگان free *adj*
راه اندازی trigger *n*	رأی vote *n*
راه اندازی کردن set up *v*	رأی دادن voting *n*
راه بند blockade *n*	ربع quarter *n*
راه پیمایی کردن march *v*	ربعها quarters *n*
راه حل solution *n*	ربودن seize, grab *v*
راه خروج way out *n*	رتبه بخشان ordination *n*
راه دخول way in *n*	رتبه بندی کردن rank *v*
راه دزدی hijack *v*	رتیل tarantula *n*

revert v رجوع کردن	formalize v رسمی کردن
uterus, womb n رحم	formal adj رسمی
blessing n رحمت	formality n رسمیت
occur v رخ دادن	notorious adj رسوا
cubicle n رخت کن	scandalize v رسوا کردن
ocurrence n رخداد	scandal n رسوایی
breakthrough n رخنه	slip n رسید
vestige, rejection n رد	sale slip n رسید فروش
reject, refute v رد کردن	look into v رسیدگی کردن
cloak n ردا	reach, arrive v رسیدن
class n رده	come across v رسیدن به
sort out v رده بندی کردن	ripe adj رسیده
trace v ردیابی کردن	thread, string n رشته
queue, row n ردیف	growth n رشد
align v ردیف کردن	flourish v رشد کردن
set v ردیف کن	grow v رشد کن
wicked adj رذل	bribe n رشوه
combatant n رزمنده	bribe v رشوه دادن
combat n رزمی	bribery n رشوه دهی
parade n رژه	observatory n رصدخانه
regime, diet n رژیم	consent, satisfaction n رضایت
thesis n رساله	consent v رضایت دادن
conductor n رسانا	satisfactory adj رضایتبخش
convey v رساندن	humidity, moisture n رطوبت
medium adj رسانه	observe v رعایت کردن
redemption n رستگاری	thunderbolt n رعد و برق
restaurant n رستوران	zest n رغبت
custom n رسم	fellowship n رفاقت
plot, sketch v رسم کردن	welfare, conduct n رفاه

رفتار behavior n	رنجیدن resent v
رفتار کردن treat, conduct v	رنگ color, dye n
رفتارکردن behave v	رنگ ارغوانی purple adj
رفع کردن eliminate v	رنگ پریدگی paleness n
رفع کردن مانع brush aside v	رنگ پریده ghastly adj
رفو کردن darn v	رنگ رفته faded adj
رفیع lofty adj	رنگ کردن color, dye v
رفیق buddy n	رنگ و رو complexion n
رقابت competition n	رنگارنگ colorful adj
رقابت کردن compete, challenge v	رنگین کمان rainbow n
رقابتی competitive adj	رها کردن extricate v
رقص dance n	رهایی یافتن get off v
رقصیدن dance v	رهبر leader n
رقم digit, figure n	رهبری leadership n
رقیب rival n	رهبری کردن spearhead v
رقیق شونده attenuating adj	رهن mortgage n
رقیق کردن dilute, attenuate v	رهن دادن pawn v
رک outspoken adj	رهنمود guidelines n
رک و راست candid adj	رهیافت approach n
رکود stagnation n	رو به بالا upwards adv
رگ به رگ کردن sprain v	رو به شمال north n
رگبار downpour n	رواقی stoic adj
رم stampede n	روان پزشک psychiatrist n
رمان novel n	روان پزشکی psychiatry n
رمز code, password n	روان شناسی psychology n
رمزی شده scrambled adj	روانداز bedding n
رنج بردن suffer v	روانرنجور neurotic adj
رنج بردن از suffer from v	روبالشی pillowcase n
رنجش resentment n	روباه fox n

ر

confront, envisage v **روبرو شدن**	illuminate, brrighten v **روشن کردن**
bedspread n **روتختی**	light v **روشن کن**
spirit, soul n **روح**	refurbish v **روشن و تازه کردن**
clergyman n **روحانی**	open-minded adj **روشنفکر**
spiritual adj **روحانی**	brightness n **روشنی**
priestess n **روحانی زن**	grease n **روغن**
clergy n **روحانیون**	varnish n **روغن جلا**
cheer up v **روحیه دادن**	lard n **روغن خوک**
river n **رودخانه**	lubricate, grease v **روغن زدن**
bowels, guts n **روده**	lubrication n **روغن کاری**
colon n **روده بزرگ**	upholstery n **روکش**
scooter n **روروک بچه ها**	recap v **روکش زدن**
day n **روز**	rheumatism n **روماتیسم**
birthday n **روز تولد**	tablecloth n **رومیزی**
daily adv **روزانه**	copy n **رونوشت**
weekday adj **روزکار**	transcribe v **رونویسی کردن**
newspaper n **روزنامه**	on pre **روی**
journalist n **روزنامه نگار**	stand up v **روی پا ایستادن**
village n **روستا**	happen v **روی دادن**
peasant n **روستایی**	overboard adv **روی کشتی**
rural adj **روستایی**	overlap v **روی هم افتادن**
scarf n **روسری**	huddle v **روی هم ریختن**
Russian adj **روسی**	showdown n **رویارویی نهایی**
Russia n **روسیه**	embryo n **رویان**
method, way n **روش**	dream n **رویایی**
bright, vivid adj **روشن**	episode n **رویداد**
light n **روشن**	chronicle n **رویدادشمار**
kindle v **روشن شدن**	circumstancial adj **رویدادی**
broadminded adj **روشن فکر**	upper adj **رویه**

ر

ز

رویه n crust	زادگاه n hometown
رویهم افتادگی n lap	زاده n descendant
رویهمرفته adj altogether	زادهشده adj born
ریاضت دادن v mortify	زاری کردن v moan
ریا n hypocrisy	زاغه نشین n gutter
ریاست جمهوری n presidency	زالو n leech
ریاست کردن بر v preside	زانو n knee
ریاضی n math	زانو بزن v kneel
ریاکار adj hypocrite	زانو خم کردن v genuflect
ریتم n rhythm	زاویه n angle
ریختن v pour	زبان n language
ریخته گری n foundry	زبری n harshness
ریخته و پاشیده n litter	زجر n hassle
ریز adj tiny	زجر دادن v torment
ریز باریدن v drizzle	زجر کشی کردن v lynch
ریز ریز کردن v chop, mince	زحمت دادن v bother
ریزموج n microwave	زحمت کشیدن v toil
ریزنقش adj petite	زخم n ulcer
ریسمان n cord	زخم چاقو n stab
ریش n beard	زخم زدن v hack
ریشخند n mockery	زخمی کردن v wound
ریشدار adj bearded	زد و خورد n scuffle
ریشه adj radical	زدن n beating
ریشه n root	زده شده adj beaten
ریشه دار adj ingrained	زراعتی adj agricultural
ریشه کن کردن v uproot	زرافه n giraffe
ریگ n pebble	زرد adj yellow
ریه n lung	
رییس n president	

زردآلو apricot n	زن ها women n
زردک parsnip n	زنا adultery n
زرده yolk n	زناشویی marital adj
زرنگ shrewd adj	زناشویی matrimony n
زشت disgraceful adj	زنبور wasp n
زشت کردن deform v	زنبور عسل bee n
زشتی ugliness n	زنجبیلی ginger n
زغال چوب charcoal n	زنجیر curb; chain n
زغال سنگ coal n	زنجیر کردن chain v
زگیل wart n	زندان prison, jail n
زمان time n	زندان کردن imprison v
زمان دادن time v	زندانبان jailer n
زمانبندی کردن schedule v	زندانی prisoner n
زمانیکه while c	زندانی کردن incarcerate v
زمخت crude, coarse adj	زندگی life n
زمرد emerald n	زندگی کردن live v
زمزمه murmur n	زندگینامه biography n
زمزمه کردن murmur v	زنده alive, live adj
زمستان winter n	زنده شدن revive v
زمین terrain, land n	زنده کردن resuscitate v
زمین بازی playground n	زنگ buzzer, bell n
زمین شخم زده furrow n	زنگ در doorbell n
زمین شناسی geology n	زنگ زدن corrode, rust v
زمین لرزه earthquake n	زنگ زده rust n
زمینی ground, field n	زنگ زده rusty adj
زمینی terrestrial adj	زه border n
زن woman n	زهر venom n
زن بیوه divorcee n	زهکشی drainage n
زن سبزه brunette adj	زودرس premature adj

ز

squeamish *adj* زودرنج	sharp *adj* زیرک
compulsion *n* زور	underpass *n* زیرگذر
mighty *adj* زورمند	footnote *n* زیرنویس
howl *n* زوزه	biological *adj* زیست شناختی
large *adj* زیاد	biology *n* زیست شناسی
overrate *v* زیاد اهمیت دادن	subsist *v* زیست کردن
extravagance *n* زیاده روی	exist *v* زیستن
pilgrimage *n* زیارت	saddle *n* زین
shrine *n* زیارتگاه	
loss *n* زیان	
detrimental *adj* زیان بخش	
damage *v* زیان زدن	
injurious *adj* زیانمند	ژ
fair, beautiful *adj* زیبا	
nicely *adv* زیبا	
beautify *v* زیبا کردن	Japan *n* ژاپن
beauty *n* زیبایی	Japanese *adj* ژاپنی
zipper *n* زیپ	sweater *n* ژاکت
olive *n* زیتون	frost *n* ژاله
below, under *pre* زیر	bacon, ham *n* ژامبون
duck *v* زیر آب رفتن	January *n* ژانویه
submerge *v* زیر آب کردن	jersey *n* ژرسه
armpit *n* زیر بغل	abysmal *adj* ژرف
underlie *v* زیر چیزی قرار دادن	gimmick *n* ژست
mumble *v* زیر لب سخن گفتن	gene *n* ژن
because *c* زیرا	June *n* ژوئن
inferior *adj* زیردست	July *n* ژوئیه
basement *n* زیرزمین	
underground *adj* زیرزمین	

س

سابق n predecessor
سابقاً adj used to
سابقه n precedent
ساچمه n ball
ساحر n magician
ساحل n beach, coast
ساحلی adj coastal
ساختار n structure, fabric
ساختگی adj dummy
ساختمان n building
ساختن v construct
ساختن n construction
سادگی n simplicity
ساده adj simple
ساده کردن v simplify
ساده لوح adj naive
ساردین n sardine
سارق n robber
سازگار adj consistent; compatible
سازگار n match
سازگاری n compatibility
سازمان n organization
سازنده n builder
سازنده adj constructive
سازوکار n mechanism
ساس n bug
ساطور n chopper

ساعت n clock, hour
ساعت زنگدار n alarm clock
ساعت ساز n watchmaker
ساقدوش n best man
ساقه دار کردن v stem
ساکت n gag, hush
ساکت adj silent
ساکت بودن v shut up
ساکت کردن v conciliate, appease
ساکن n inhabitant
ساکن شدن v inhabit
ساکن شدن در v colonize
سال n year
سال کبیسه n leap year
سالاد n salad
سالانه adj annual
سالگرد n anniversary
سالم adj healthy
سالن n saloon
سالن رقص n ballroom
سالن شهر n city hall
سالن ورزش n gymnasium
سانتی متر n centimeter
ساندویچ n sandwich
سانسور n censorship
سایبان n awning, shade
سایت n site
سایش n wear
سایه n shadow

shady _adj_ سایه دار	ستمدیده _adj_ downtrodden
pulverize _v_ ساییدن	لیeutenant _n_ ستوان lieutenant
cause, account _n_ سبب	column _n_ ستون
cause _v_ سبب شدن	spine _n_ ستون فقرات
basket _n_ سبد	backbone _n_ ستون مهره ها
waste basket _n_ سبد باطله	altercation _n_ ستیزه
green _adj_ سبز	belligerent _adj_ ستیزه جو
overtake _v_ سبقت گرفتن بر	contend _v_ ستیزه کردن
lightweight _n_ سبک	magic _n_ سحر
alleviate _v_ سبک کردن	wizard _n_ سحرآمیز
grotesque _adj_ سبک گروتسک	magical _adj_ سحرآمیز
mustache _n_ سبیل	generosity _n_ سخاوت
gratitude _n_ سپاس	bitterly _adv_ سخت
grateful _adj_ سپاسگزار	stringent, rigid _adj_ سخت
legion _n_ سپاه	hardware _n_ سخت افزار
September _n_ سپتامبر	toughen _v_ سخت کردن
shield _n_ سپر	industrious _adj_ سخت کوش
scapegoat _n_ سپربلا	rigor _n_ سخت گیری
entrust _v_ سپردن	militant _adj_ سختگیر
lapse, expire _v_ سپری شدن	hardship _n_ سختی
dawn _n_ سپیده دم	speech, lecture _n_ سخنرانی
headquarters _n_ ستاد	speaker _n_ سخنگو
asterisk, star _n_ ستاره	dam, barrier _n_ سد
comet _n_ ستاره دنباله دار	blockade _v_ سدراه کردن
tribute _n_ ستایش	head _n_ سر
praise _v_ ستایش کردن	glide _v_ سر خوردن
bathe _v_ ستحمام کردن	stop by _v_ سر زدن
sterile _adj_ سترون	noise _n_ سر و صدا
oppress _v_ ستم کردن	mirage _n_ سراب

س

سرازیر شدن plummet v	سرخ فام lurid adj
سرازیر شو spill v	سرخ کردن fry, toast, broil v
سرازیری downhill adv	سرخ کرده fried adj
سراسر overall adv	سرخک measles n
سراسیمه frantic adj	سرخوردگی disillusion n
سراسیمه بودن flutter v	سرخورده disenchanted adj
سراسیمه کردن stun v	سرخوشی euphoria n
سراشیبی ramp n	سرخی صورت blush n
سرامیک ceramic n	سرد chill n
سرانجام eventually adv	سرد chilly, cold adj
سرانگشت fingertip n	سرد کردن chill v
سرایت مرض plague n	سردخانه mortuary n
سرایدار caretaker n	سردرد headache n
سرآستین cuff n	سردسته ringleader n
سرآشپز chef n	سردستی sketchy adj
سرب lead n	سردی coldness n
سرب گرفته leaded adj	سرریز شدن boil over v
سرباز soldier n	سرزده آمدن intrude v
سرباز قدیمی veteran n	سرزمین محصور enclave n
سربه راه docile adj	سرزندگی vitality n
سربه راهی docility n	سرزنش blame n
سرپرست guardian n	سرزنش کردن chide, blame v
سرپرستی custody n	سرسخت implacable adj
سرپرستی کردن supervise v	سرسره chute n
سرپوش lid n	سرشار شدن overflow v
سرتپه hilltop n	سرشماری census n
سرتکان دادن nod v	سرشناس ترین foremost adj
سرجوخه corporal adj	سرطان cancer n
سرحد threshold n	سرطان خون leukemja n

س

سرطانی cancerous adj	سرمه ای navy blue adj
سرعت speed n	سرنگ syringe n
سرعت بده speed v	سرنوشتساز decisive adj
سرفصل topic n	سرنیزه bayonet n
سرفه cough n	سرهنگ colonel n
سرفه کردن cough v	سرو cypress n
سرقت robbery n	سرود chant, anthem n
سرقت ادبی crib n	سرود کریسمس carol n
سرکارگر foreman n	سرود مذهبی hymn n
سرکش disobedient adj	سرودن compose v
سرکشی کردن oversee v	سریع fast, swift adj
سرکه vinegar n	سریع الانتقال agile adj
سرکوبی repression n	سریع حرکت کردن zap v
سرگردان stranded adj	سزاوار بودن deserve v
سرگردان wanderer n	سزاوار تنبیه punishable adj
سرگردان بودن wander v	سس sauce n
سرگردان شدن strangle v	سس گوشت gravy n
سرگردانی quandery n	سست flimsy adj
سرگرم busy adj	سست کردن weaken v
سرگرم کردن amuse v	سطح surface n
سرگرمی pastime n	سطل pail, bucket n
سرگیجه dizziness n	سطل آشغال trash can n
سرما chill n	سعی effort n
سرمازدگی frostbite n	سفارت embassy n
سرمازده frostbitten adj	سفارش order n
سرمایه داری capitalism n	سفاک bloodthirsty adj
سرمایه گذار investor n	سفال tile n
سرمایه گذاری investment n	سفت کردن tighten v
سرمست jubilant adj	سفته draft n

س

سفتی n firmness

سفر n trip, journey

سفر پرماجرا n odyssey

سفر تفریحی n outing

سفر دریایی n voyage

سفسطه n fallacy

سفید adj white

سفید کردن v galvanize

سفید کننده n bleach

سفیدرو adj blond

سفیده تخم مرغ n egg white

سفیدی n candor

سفیر n ambassador

سقط n miscarriage

سقط جنین n abortion

سقط کردن v abort

سقف n ceiling, roof

سقوط کردن v come down

سقوط ناگهانی n precipice

سک زدن v prod

سکان n rudder

سکان کشتی n helm

سکته قلبی adj coronary

سکسکه n hiccup

سکنی بگزین v dwell

سکه n coin

سکو n platform

سکوت n quietness

سکوت کردن v hush up

سگ n dog

سگ تازی n greyhound

سگ شکاری n hound

سگ قطبی adj husky

سل n tuberculosis

سلاح n weapon

سلام e hello

سلام کردن v hail

سلامت n health

سلامت عقل n sanity

سلسله n dynasty

سلسله مراتب n hierarchy

سلطنت n monarchy

سلطنت کردن v reign

سلطنتی adj royal

سلطه n domination

سلطه پذیر adj submissive

سلطه جو adj domineering

سلف سرویس n cafeteria

سلمانی n hairdresser

سم n toxin, poison

سماجت n persistence

سماجت کردن v persist

سمج adj persistent

سمفونی n symphony

سمور آبی n otter

سمی adj poisonous

سن n age

سنا n senate

senator n سناتور	سهام دار n shareholder
sandpaper n سنباده	سهم n share
tradition n سنت	سهمیه n ration
orthodox adj سنتی	سهولت n convenience
squirrel n سنجاب	سوء اداره کردن v malpractice
ponder v سنجیدن	سوء استفاده n abuse
voucher n سند	سوء تغذیه n malnutrition
deed n سند مالکیت	سوء هاضمه n indigestion
anvil n سندان	سوئد n Sweden
stone, rock n سنگ	سوئدی adj Sweedish
limestone n سنگ آهک	سوئیس adj Swiss
granite n سنگ خارا	سوئیس n Switzerland
tombstone n سنگ قبر	سوا کردن v segregate
slate n سنگ لوح	سوار شو v ride
marble n سنگ مرمر	سوار کردن v embark
ore n سنگ معدن	سواره نظام n cavalry
epitaph n سنگ نبشته مزار	سوال n question
heartless adj سنگدل	سوال برانگیز adj questionable
entrenched adj سنگربندی شده	سوپ n broth, soup
stone v سنگسار کردن	سوت n whistle
rocky adj سنگی	سوت زدن v whistle
heavy adj سنگین	سوخت n fuel
gravitate v سنگین کردن	سوخت گیری کردن v fuel
heaviness n سنگینی	سوختگی سطحی n burn
three adj سه	سود n benefit, profit
triple adj سه برابر	سود بردن v profit, benefit
tripod n سه پایه	سودا n soda
Tuesday n سه شنبه	سوداگری کردن v speculate
quarterly adj سه ماه یکبار	سودآور adj profitable

س

سودسهام *n* dividend	سیانور *n* cyanide
سودمند *adj* beneficial	سیاه *adj* black
سودمند بودن *v* avail	سیاه چال *n* dungeon
سودمندی *n* usefulness	سیاه گوش *n* lynx
سوراخ *n* hole, slot	سیاهرگ *n* vein
سوراخ بینی *n* nostril	سیب *n* apple
سوراخ شدگی *n* perforation	سیب زمینی *n* potato
سوراخ کردن *v* drill, pierce, bore	سیخ *n* spur
سورتمه *n* sleigh	سیر *n* garlic
سوزان *adj* ablaze	سیر *adj* replete
سوزاندن *v* scorch	سیرک *n* circus
سوزش *n* sting	سیری ناپذیر *adj* insatiable
سوزن *n* needle, pin	سیزده *adj* thirteen
سوسک *n* cockroach	سیستم *n* system
سوسو *n* glimmer	سیفیلیس *n* syphilis
سوسول *adj* sissy	سیگار *n* cigarette
سوسیالیست *adj* socialist	سیگار برگ *n* cigar
سوسیالیسم *n* socialism	سیگار کشیدن *v* smoke
سوسیس *n* sausage	سیل *n* deluge
سوق دادن *v* propel	سیل زده کردن *v* inundate
سوگواری کردن *v* mourn	سیلاب *n* torrent
سوگواری *n* mourning	سیلی *n* slap
سوم *adj* third	سیلی زدن *v* slap
سی *adj* thirty	سیم *n* wire
سیار *adj* mobile	سیما *n* countenance
سیارک *n* asteroid	سیمان *n* cement
سیاره *n* planet	سینما *n* cinema
سیاست *n* politics	سینه *n* bosom, breast
سیاستمدار *n* politician	سینه بند *n* bra

س

سینی tray n

ش

شاخ horn n
شاخ به شاخ head-on adv
شاخص index n
شاخک tentacle n
شاخه bough n
شاد elated, joyful adj
شادی joy n
شادی کردن rejoice v
شارژ کردن charge v
شاعر poet n
شاغل practising adj
شام dinner, supper n
شام خوردن dine v
شامل inclusive adv
شامل بودن consist, entail v
شانزده sixteen adj
شانس odds n
شانه shoulder n
شانه کردن heckle v
شاه بلوط chestnut n
شاه میگو prawn n
شاهانه sumptuous adj

شاهد witness, testament n
شاهد عینی eyewitness n
شاهزاده prince n
شاهزاده خانم princess n
شاهکار masterpiece n
شاهین hawk n
شاید may-be, perhaps adv
شایستگی decency n
شایسته decent adj
شایسته بودن merit v
شایع widespread adj
شایع شدن prevail v
شایعه rumor n
شب night n
شب پره moth n
شب گذشته last night adv
شبانه nocturnal adj
شبانه دزدیدن burglarize v
شباهت resemblance n
شباهت داشتن resemble v
شبح apparition n
شبح وار spooky adj
شبکه network n
شبنم dew n
شبه ghost n
شبه جزیره peninsula n
شبیه alike adj
شبیه سازی کردن simulate v
شپش louse n

شپش ها lice *n*	شرط بندی stake *n*
شپشو lousy *adj*	شرط لازم prerequisite *n*
شتاب haste *n*	شرطبندی bet *n*
شتاب دهنده accelerator *n*	شرطبندی کن bet *v*
شتاب کردن hurry *v*	شرعی کردن canonize *v*
شتاباندن hasten *v*	شرق east *n*
شتر camel *n*	شرقی eastern *adj*
شترمرغ ostrich *n*	شرقی تر easterner *n*
شجاع courageous *adj*	شرکت company *n*
شجاعانه bravely *adv*	شرکت در جرم complicity *n*
شجاعت bravery *n*	شرکت کردن subscribe *v*
شخص person *n*	شرکت کننده contributor *n*
شخص احمق goof *n*	شرکت وابسته subsidiary *adj*
شخصی personal *adj*	شرم shame *n*
شخصیت personality *n*	شرم آور shameful *adj*
شخصیت دادن personify *v*	شرمنده ashamed *adj*
شخم زدن plow *v*	شرمنده شدن blush *v*
شدت intensity *n*	شرور evil *adj*
شدید severe, excruciating *adj*	شرور thug *n*
شر rowdy *adj*	شروع beginning *n*
شراب wine *n*	شروع شو begin *v*
شراب سیب cider *n*	شروع کردن launch, commence *v*
شرارت evil *n*	شروع کردن به burst into *v*
شرافت نفس self-respect *n*	شری sherry *n*
شراکت partnership *n*	شریان artery *n*
شربت cordial *adj*	شریف scrupulous *adj*
شرح دادن describe *v*	شریک partner *n*
شرشره cascade *n*	شریک جرم accomplice *n*
شرط clause *n*	شریک شدن participate *v*

شست thumb n	شکافته کن v split
شستشو laundry n	شکاک skeptic adj
شستشو دادن v rinse	شکایت complaint n
شستن wash v	شکایت کردن v complain
شش six adj	شکر sugar n
ششم sixth adj	شکست failure, defeat n
شصت sixty adj	شکست خوردن v outdo, defeat
شطرنج chess n	شکست ناپذیر unbeatable adj
شعار slogan n	شکستگی break n
شعاع radius, ray n	شکستن break down v
شعبه branch n	شکستن کشتی shipwreck n
شعر poem, poetry n	شکستنی fragile adj
شعر شبانی pastoral adj	شکسته broken adj
شعله flame n	شکل shape, format, form n
شعله دار flamboyant adj	شکل دادن shape v
شعله ور alight adv	شکل گیری formation n
شغال jackal n	شکلات chocolate n
شفا دادن v heal	شکم stomach n
شفابخش healer n	شکنجه torture n
شفاعت intercession n	شکنجه دادن v torture
شفاف transparent adj	شکننده brittle adj
شقایق poppy n	شکوفه کردن v bloom
شک doubt n	شکوه splendor n
شکار hunting n	شکوهمند awesome adj
شکار کردن v hunt	شگفت انگیز stupendous adj
شکار کن v shoot	شگفتآور fabulous adj
شکارچی hunter n	شگفتی amazement n
شکاف chasm, gap, fracture n	شگون omen n
شکاف دادن v slash	شل loose adj

ش

شل کردن loosen v	شن gravel n
شلاق lash, whip n	شن کش rake n
شلاق خوردن lash v	شنا swimming n
شلاق زدن flog v	شنا کردن skim v
شلخته shoddy adj	شنا کن swim v
شلوار trousers n	شناختن identify v
شلوار راحتی slacks n	شناخته‌شده conspicuous adj
شلوارجین jeans n	شناگر swimmer n
شلوغ bustling adj	شناور afloat adv
شلیک gunfire n	شناور شدن float v
شلیک کردن run up v	شنبه Saturday n
شلیک کن shoot v	شنل cape n
شما you pro	شنوندگان audience n
شمار count n	شنونده listener n
شمارش معکوس countdown n	شنیدن listen v
شماره number n	شهاب meteor n
شماره گرفتن dial v	شهادت testimony n
شماره گیری dial n	شهادت دادن attest v
شمالشرق northeast n	شهادت دروغ perjury n
شمالی northern adj	شهر city, town n
شمپانزه chimpanzee n	شهرت reputation n
شمردن count v	شهردار mayor n
شمش ingot n	شهرداری town hall n
شمشیر sword n	شهروند citizen n
شمشیر بازی fencing n	شهری civic, urban adj
شمشیر ماهی swordfish n	شهریه tuition n
شمع plug, candle n	شهوانی prurient adj
شمع موتور spark plug n	شهوت داشتن lust v
شمعدان candlestick n	شهوت ران lewd adj

ش

شهود intuition n	شیره کشیدن sap v
شهوی lustful adj	شیره گیاهی sap n
شهوی lust n	شیری milky adj
شهید martyr n	شیرین sweet adj
شوالیه knight n	شیرین کردن sweeten v
شوخ witty adj	شیرینها sweets n
شوخی humor, joke n	شیرینی sweetness n
شوخی کردن joke v	شیشه glass n
شور passion n	شیطان devil n
شور salty adj	شیطانی diabolical adj
شور و شوق gusto n	شیطنت mischief n
شورا council n	شیفت کاری shift n
شورانگیز rousing adj	شیفته fond adj
شورای کلیسایی synod n	شیک posh adj
شورت shorts n	شیلنگ hose n
شورش uprising n	شیمی chemistry n
شورش کردن riot v	شیمی دان chemist n
شوره سر dandruff n	شیوع outbreak n
شوریده crazy adj	شیوع یافتن break out v
شوم ominous adj	شیون کردن wail v
شوهر husband n	شیوه fashion n
شیاد swindler n	شیوه زندگی lifestyle n
شیار groove n	
شیب fall, slope n	
شیپور trumpet n	
شیدا maniac adj	
شیر faucet, tap n	
شیرجه رفتن nosedive, dive v	
شیرخوارگاه nursery n	

ش

ص

صاحب owner n
صاحب قوه تمیز judicious adj
صاحبخانه landlord n
صادر کردن export v
صادق honest adj
صاف flat, smooth adj
صافی strainer n
صالح competent adj
صامت consonant n
صامت دندانی dental adj
صبح morning n
صبحانه breakfast n
صبر patience n
صحبت خودمانی gap n
صحبت کردن talk v
صحبت کن speak v
صحت authenticity n
صحنه scene n
صحیح correct adj
صحیح و سالم unharmed adj
صخره cliff n
صد hundred adj
صدا sound, voice n
صدا خفه کن muffler n
صدا کردن click, call v
صداقت sincerity n
صدای تلفن dial tone n

صدای زنگ bell n
صددرصد مطمئن cocky adj
صدف خوراکی oyster n
صدف دار shellfish n
صدقه alms n
صدم hundredth adj
صدمه زدن harm v
صدمین سالگرد centenary n
صدور issue, emission n
صراحت frankness n
صرع epilepsy n
صرف expenditure n
صرف کردن conjugate v
صرف کن spend v
صرفاً merely, solely adv
صرفنظر کردن withdraw v
صرفنظر کردن از waive v
صرفه جو thrifty adj
صرفه جویی کردن economize v
صریح unequivocal adj
صعود climbing n
صعود کردن climb, ascend v
صف پلیس cordon n
صف مقدم forefront n
صفت adjective n
صفحه page n
صفحه آرایی lay-out n
صفحه کلید keyboard n
صفحه نمایش display n

ص

ض

guarantor n ضامن	zero n صفر
waste v ضایع کردن	bile n صفرا
recording n ضبط	peace n صلح
record v ضبط کردن	crucifix n صلیب
thickness n ضخامت	gum n صمغ
thick adj ضخیم	homely adj صمیمانه
thicken v ضخیم کردن	intimate adj صمیمی
rust-proof adj ضد زنگ	intimacy n صمیمیت
disinfect v ضد عفونی کردن	sandal n صندل
waterproof adj ضدآب	chair, seat n صندلی
deodorant n ضدبو	wheelchair n صندلی چرخ دار
silhouette n ضدنور	mailbox n صندوق پست
oppose v ضدیت کردن	cashier n صندوقدار
multiplication n ضرب	craft n صنعت
multiply v ضرب کردن	artisan n صنعتگر
beat n ضربان	guild n صنف
heartbeat n ضربان قلب	acoustic adj صوتی
blow n ضربت	face n صورت
inflict v ضربت زدن	poll n صورت رأی
shock, hit n ضربه	constellation n صورت فلکی
traumatic adj ضربه ای	facet n صورت کوچک
stroke n ضربه با کنترل	feminine adj صورت مونث
strike v ضربه بزن	bill n صورتحساب
whip v ضربه زدن	pink adj صورتی
coup n ضربه کاری	convent n صومعه
sock n ضربه مشت	mesh n صید
concussion n ضربه مغزی	singular adj صیغه مفرد
	polish n صیقل
	polish v صیقل دادن

ص
ض

ضرر detriment n	طبخ کردن v bake
ضروری essential adj	طبق according to pre
ضریب coefficient n	طبقه category n
ضعف weakness n	طبقه پایین downstairs adv
ضعف کردن v faint	طبقه دوم upstairs adv
ضعیف faint, weak adj	طبقه هم کف ground floor n
ضعیف poorly adv	طبل drum n
ضعیف و ترسو wimp adj	طبلک reel n
ضغیف feeble adj	طبیعت nature n
ضلع frontage n	طبیعت وحشی wildlife n
ضمانت warranty n	طبیعی کردن v normalize
ضمانت کردن v vouch for	طراحی design n
ضمنی implicit adj	طرح design, plan, project n
ضمیر pronoun n	طرح ریختن plan v
ضمیمه attached adj	طرح ریزی کردن v outline
ضمیمه attachment n	طرح کردن v project
ضوابط terms n	طرز manner n
ضیافت banquet n	طرز لباس costume n
	طرف side n
	طرفدار henchman n
	طرفداری کردن v opt for
	طعمه bait n

ط

	طعمه کردن v victimize
	طعنه sarcasm n
	طغیان rebel n
	طفره آمیز evasive adj
طاس bald adj	طفره زدن v stall
طالع بین astrologer n	طلا gold n
طالع بینی astrology n	طلاق divorce n
طاوس peacock n	
طایفه clan n	

ظ

طلاق دادن v	divorce
طلای سفید n	platinum
طلایی adj	golden
طلب کردن v	invoke
طلبکار n	creditor
طلسم n	charm
طلوع آفتاب n	sunrise
طمع n	greed
طناب n	lash, rope
طنز n	irony, satire
طنزآمیز adj	ironic
طنین n	tone; echo
طوطی n	parrot
طوطی دم دراز n	parakeet
طوفان n	storm
طوفانی adj	windy
طوق n	fringe
طول n	length
طول جغرافیایی n	longitude
طول دادن v	protract
طولانی adj	protracted
طولانی کردن v	prolong
طوماری n	scroll
طیور n	poultry

ظالم adj	ruthless
ظاهر n	semblance
ظاهر شدن v	turn up
ظاهر شو v	spring
ظاهراً adv	allegedly
ظاهرشدن v	appear
ظاهری n	cosmetic
ظرافت n	tact
ظرف n	container
ظرفیت n	capacity
ظروف بلوری n	glassware
ظروف چینی n	porcelain
ظروف سفالی n	crockery
ظریف adj	tenuous
ظریف طبع adj	aesthetic
ظلم n	atrocity
ظهر n	noon
ظهور مجدد مسیح n	Advent
ظهور ناگهانی n	outburst

ط
ظ

ع

عابر passer-by n

عابر پیاده pedestrian n

عاج ivory n

عاجز lame adj

عادت habit n

عادت دادن accustom v

عادلانه justly adv

عادلانه fair adj

عادی common, usual adj

عاری از devoid adj

عازم bound adj

عازم باشید bound for adj

عازم شرق eastbound adj

عاشق lover n

عاطفه emotion n

عاطفی emotional adj

عاق کردن disown, disinherit v

عاقل sane, sober adj

عالی wonderful adj

عامل factor n

عاملها parameters n

عامه مردم grassroots adj

عایق بندی insulation n

عبارت phrase n

عبور transit n

عبور سریع fleet n

عبور و مرور passage n

عبوس grim adj

عجله hustle n

عجله کردن rush v

عجول hasty adj

عجولانه hastily adv

عجیب odd adj

عجیب oddity n

عجیب و غریب bizarre adj

عدالت justice n

عدس lentil n

عدل bale n

عدم lack n

عدم اتحاد disunity n

عدم استعمال disuse n

عدم امکان impossibility n

عدم بلوغ immaturity n

عدم توازن imbalance n

عدم رضایت disapproval n

عدم صلاحیت incompetence n

عذاب ordeal n

عذاب دادن agonize v

عذاب وجدان qualm n

عذر خواهی کردن apologize v

عربی Arabic adj

عرشه deck n

عرصه arena n

عرض breadth n

عرفی custom-made adj

عرق sweat n	عفت chastity n
عرق کردن sweat v	عفو absolution, clemency n
عرق نیشکر rum n	عفو کردن forgive v
عروس bride n	عفیف chaste adj
عروسک doll n	عقاب eagle n
عروسی bridal adj	عقب back adv
عروسی wedding n	عقب back n
عریض کردن widen v	عقب افتادن fall behind v
عزیز dear adj	عقب انداختن defer, hinder v
عزیمت departure n	عقب زدن retreat v
عسل honey n	عقب کشیدن move back v
عشق love n	عقب مانده retarded adj
عشقبازی courtship n	عقب نشستن bow out v
عصا stick n	عقب نشینی کردن fall back v
عصاره juice n	عقب نشینی retirement n
عصاره گرفتن press v	عقبی rear adj
عصب nerve n	عقبی rear n
عصبانی furious adj	عقد conclusion n
عصبانی کردن enrage v	عقرب scorpion n
عصبانیت anger, fury n	عقل wisdom n
عصبی jumpy, tense adj	عقلی rational adj
عصر evening n	عقیده belief n
عضو member n	عکاس photographer n
عضویت membership n	عکاسی photography n
عطر cologne, perfume n	عکس photo n
عطسه sneeze n	عکسبرداری کردن photograph v
عطسه کردن sneeze v	علاقمند fond adj
عظمت majesty n	علاقه fondness n
عظیم tremendous adj	علاقه مند interested adj

ع

sign, brand, mark *n* علامت	operate *v* عمل کردن
trademark *n* علامت تجارتی	pragmatist *adj* عمل گرا
mark *v* علامت گذاشتن	feasible *adj* عملی
besides *pre* علاوه بر	uncle *n* عمو
furthermore *adv* علاوه بر این	cousin *n* عموزاده
herb *n* علف	popular *adj* عمومی
mow *v* علف چیدن	generalize *v* عمومیت دادن
hay *n* علف خشک	deep *adj* عمیق
meadow *n* علفزار	providence *n* عنایت خداوند
science *n* علم	element *n* عنصر
occult *adj* علم غیبی	spider *n* عنکبوت
scientific *adj* علمی	title *n* عنوان
publicly *adv* علناً	subtitle *n* عنوان فرعی
humanities *n* علوم انسانی	state *v* عنوان کردن
against *pre* علیه	vow *v* عهد کردن
premeditation *n* عمد	unfaithful *adj* عهدشکن
purposely *adv* عمداً	undertake *v* عهده دار شدن
mostly *adv* عمدتاً	charge *v* عهده دار کردن
leading *adj* عمده	toll *n* عوارض راهداری
wholesale *n* عمده فروشی	proceeds *n* عواید
deliberate *adj* عمدی	change *v* عوض کردن
knowingly *adv* عمدی	bark *n* عوعو
lifetime *adj* عمر	carat *n* عیار
depth *n* عمق	defect, fault *n* عیب
fathom out *v* عمق پیمایی کردن	pick *v* عیب جوئی کردن
castaway *n* عمق یابی	nitpicking *adj* عیب جویی
action, task *n* عمل	nag *v* عیب جویی کردن
act *v* عمل	Easter *n* عید پاک
leverage *n* عمل اهرم	eyeglasses *n* عینک

ع

غرش rumble n

غرض malice n

غرغر کردن growl v

غرغره کردن gargle v

غرفه pavilion n

غرق شده swamped adj

غرق کردن drown v

غرق کردن در engulf v

غروب dusk n

غروب آفتاب sunset n

غرور pride n

غریبه stranger n

غریدن rumble v

غریزه instinct n

غزلها lyrics n

غژغژ creak n

غسل تعمید baptism n

غشا membrane n

غصب کردن usurp v

غصه grief n

غضب آلود irate adj

غفلت negligence, neglet n

غلبه کردن overcome v

غلت خوردن roll v

غلط erroneous adj

غلط چاپی misprint n

غلطک drum n

غلغلک tickle n

غلغلک دادن tickle v

عینک ایمنی goggles n

عینک آفتابی sunglasses n

عینک ساز optician n

غ

غار cave, den n

غارت کردن loot, ravage v

غارتگری sack v

غارتگری sack n

غاز goose n

غازها geese n

غایب absent adj

غبارآلود haze n

غده gland n

غذا food, meal n

غذا دادن foster, nourish v

غذاخوری canteen n

غذای دریایی seafood n

غذایغلات oatmeal n

غرامت پرداختن recompense v

غرب west n

غربال riddle n

غربت زده homesick adj

غربزنید crab n

غربی western adj

lump n غلنبه	unfriendly adj غیردوستانه
cereal n غله	impersonal adj غیرشخصی
dense adj غلیظ	unnecessary adj غیرضروری
sadness n غم	unjust adj غیرعادلانه
distressing adj غم انگیز	abnormal adj غیرعادی
sad, dismal adj غمگین	impractical adj غیرعملی
sadden v غمگین کردن	unavoidable adj غیرقابل اجتناب
loot n غنائم	useless adj غیرقابل استفاده
booty n غنائم جنگی	unreliable adj غیرقابل اعتماد
rich adj غنی	undeniable adj غیرقابل انکار
enrich v غنی کردن	indisputable adj غیرقابل بحث
spoils n غنیمت	unbearable adj غیرقابل تحمل
diver n غواص	unmistakable adj غیرقابل تردید
diving n غواصی	unthinkable adj غیرقابل تصور
duck v غوض کردن	irreversible adj غیرقابل تغییر
plunge v غوطه ور ساختن	inexplicable adj غیرقابل توضیح
immersion n غوطه وری	inadmissible adj غیرقابل قبول
uproar n غوغا	indecisive adj غیرقاطع
giant n غول	unlawful adj غیرقانونی
gigantic adj غول پیکر	surprise n غیرمترقبه
absence n غیبت	unforeseen adj غیرمترقبه
informal adj غیر رسمی	indirect adj غیرمستقیم
needless adj غیر ضروری	illogical adj غیرمنطقی
queer adj غیر عادی	zealous adj غیور
unpopular adj غیر مشهور	
unreal, unrealistic adj غیر واقعی	
immoral adj غیراخلاقی	
exotic adj غیربومی	
amateur adj غیرحرفه ای	

غ

ف

فاتح	conqueror *n*
فاجعه	disaster *n*
فاجعه آمیز	disastrous *adj*
فاحشه خانه	brothel *n*
فارغ التحصیلی	graduation *n*
فاسد	corrupt, tainted *adj*
فاسد شدن	degenerate *v*
فاسد شدنی	perishable *adj*
فاسد کردن	rot *v*
فاش کردن	disclose *v*
فاصله	interval *n*
فاصله دار	distant *adj*
فاضلاب	sewer *n*
فاقد انسجام	incoherent *adj*
فاقد عقل	irrational *adj*
فاکتور	invoice *n*
فانوس	lantern *n*
فانوس دریایی	beacon *n*
فایق آمدن بر	get over *v*
فایل	file *n*
فتح	conquest *n*
فتح کردن	conquer *v*
فتق	hernia *n*
فتنه جویانه	intriguing *adj*
فتوکپی	photocopy *n*
فجیع	heinous *adj*
فحش دادن	cuss *v*

فداکاری	sacrifice *n*
فدرال	federal *adj*
فراخواندن	recall *v*
فراخوانی	call *n*
فرار کردن	escape *v*
فراری	fugitive *n*
فراصوت	ultrasound *n*
فراغت	leisure *n*
فراگرفتن	engulf *v*
فراموش کردن	forget *v*
فراموش نشدنی	unforgettable *adj*
فراموشی	oblivion *n*
فرانسه	France *n*
فرانسوی	French *adj*
فرانما	schedule *n*
فراهم آوردن	get together *v*
فراهم کردن	supply *v*
فراوان	abundant *adj*
فراوان بودن	abound *v*
فراوانی	abundance *n*
فرآیند	process *n*
فربه	obese *adj*
فربه کردن	fatten *v*
فرتوت	decrepit *adj*
فرخنده	auspicious *adj*
فرد (مذکر)	guy *n*
فردا	tomorrow *adv*
فرزند	offspring *n*
فرستاده	envoy *n*

ف

sender n فرستنده	plunge v فرو رفتن
rug, carpet n فرش	collapse v فرو ریختن
angel n فرشته	humble adj فروتن
angelic adj فرشته وار	modesty n فروتنی
tapestry n فرشینه	condescend v فروتنی کردن
chance n فرصت	sold-out adj فروخته شده
assumption n فرض	pent-up adj فروخورده
presume v فرض کردن	descent, landing n فرود
hypothesis n فرضیه	airport n فرودگاه
parting n فرق	airfield n فرودگاه نظامی
differ v فرق داشتن	sunken adj فرورفته
cult, sect n فرقه	sale n فروش
wheelbarrow n فرقون	sellout n فروش کامل
handle n فرمان	supermarket n فروشگاه بزرگ
command v فرمان دادن	salesman n فروشنده
obedience n فرمانبرداری	ebb v فروکش کردن
governor n فرماندار	neglect v فروگذار کردن
commander n فرمانده	stifle, quell v فرونشاندن
lord n فرمانروا	roar, shout n فریاد
despot n فرمانروای مستبد	shriek v فریاد دلخراش زدن
rule v فرمانروایی کردن	cry, yell v فریاد زدن
formula n فرمول	shout v فریاد کشیدن
custard n فرنی	clamor v فریادکشیدن
charismatic adj فرهمند	swindle n فریب
culture n فرهنگ	cheat, fool v فریب دادن
vocabulary n فرهنگ لغات	sly adj فریب کار
cultural adj فرهنگی	cheater n فریبکار
sink v فرو بردن	deceitful adj فریبکار
immerse v فرو بردن	deception n فریبکاری

ف

فریبنده deceptive adj	فقدان رواداری intolerance n
فریزر freezer n	فقر poverty n
فریفتن entice, lure v	فقیر impoverished, destitute adj
فساد corruption n	فک cheek n
فسخ کردن revoke v	فکر thought n
فسفر phosphorus n	فکر کن think v
فسیل fossil n	فلات plateau n
فشار press, pressure n	فلاش flashlight n
فشار pressing adj	فلج paralysis n
فشار آوردن screw v	فلج کردن paralyze v
فشار دادن push, press v	فلز metal n
فشردگی density n	فلزکار smith n
فشردن pressure v	فلزی metallic adj
فشرده compact adj	فلسفه philosophy n
فشرده کردن compact v	فلفل pepper n
فشنگ cartridge n	فلفل زنگ bell pepper n
فصاحت eloquence n	فلوت flute n
فصل season n	فن technique n
فصلی seasonal adj	فن آوری technology n
فصیحانه fluently adv	فناپذیری mortality n
فضا space n	فناناپذیر immortal adj
فضانورد astronaut n	فنجان cup n
فضای هوایی airspace n	فندق hazelnut n
فضول nosy adj	فندک lighter n
فضولی کردن meddle v	فنر spring n
فعال energetic adj	فنلاند Finland n
فعال سازی activation n	فنلاندی Finnish adj
فعالیت activity n	فهرست list, menu n
فعل verb n	فهرست کردن list v

ف

فهمیدن grasp, savor v

فواره fountain n

فوت demise n

فوت کردن die v

فوتبال football n

فوران eruption n

فوران کن blow out v

فوری early adv

فوری urgent adj

فوریت urgency n

فوریه February n

فوق العاده grossly adv

فوق العاده سرد ice-cold adj

فولاد steel n

فی البداهه impromptu adv

فیزیک physics n

فیزیکی physically adv

فیش حقوق payslip n

فیصله دادن evict v

فیل elephant n

فیل دریایی walrus n

فیلسوف philosopher n

فیلم movie n

فیلم نامه scenario n

فیوز fuse n

ق

قاب frame n

قاب بند تزیینی medallion n

قاب کردن frame v

قابل اجرا applicable adj

قابل اشتعال flammable adj

قابل اعتماد reliable adj

قابل انجام affordable adj

قابل بحث debatable adj

قابل پذیرش acceptable adj

قابل پرداخت payable adj

قابل تحسین praiseworthy adj

قابل تحمیل tolerable adj

قابل تغییر reversible adj

قابل توجه substantial adj

قابل حمل portable adj

قابل دسترسی approachable adj

قابل رویت visible adj

قابل ستایش adorable adj

قابل سکونت habitable adj

قابل شرب drinkable adj

قابل شستشو washable adj

قابل شنیدن audible adj

قابل علاج curable adj

قابل فهم understandable adj

قابل قبول alright adv

قابل قبول eligible adj

قابل قسمت divisible adj

قانقاریا gangrene n	قابل مقایسه comparable adj
قانون law, statute n	قابلیت capability n
قانون اساسی constitution n	قابلیت دسترسی availability n
قانون شکنی breach n	قابلیت قبول credibility n
قانون گذار lawmaker n	قاتل killer n
قانون گذاری legislation n	قاچ کردن plug v
قانون وضع کردن legislate v	قاچاق contraband n
قانونی legal adj	قاچاق کردن traffic v
قانونی کردن legalize v	قاچاقچی smuggler n
قایق boat n	قادر بودن can v
قایق بادبانی sailboat n	قادر ساختن enable v
قایق باری barge n	قارچ fungus n
قایق باریک canoe n	قاره continent n
قایقرانی sail n	قارهای continental adj
قبای کشیشان cassock n	قاش کردن slice v
قبضه کردن preempt v	قاشق spoon n
قبلاً before adv	قاشق وچنگال cutlery n
قبلاً before pre	قاصد messenger n
قبلی previous adj	قاضی judge n
قبول کردن adopt v	قاطر mule n
قبول نکردن refuse v	قاطع conclusive adj
قبولی approbation n	قاطع بودن predominate v
قبیله tribe n	قاعدگی menstruation n
قتل murder n	قافیه rhyme n
قتل عام massacre n	قالب mold n
قتل غیرعمد manslaughter n	قالب گرفتن mold v
قتلگاه death trap n	قالب یخ ice cube n
قحطی famine n	قالبی moldy adj
قدرت authority n	قانع کننده persuasive adj

ق

imagination *n* قدرت تخیل	redden *v* قرمز کردن
virility *n* قدرت جنسی	century *n* قرن
almighty *adj* قدرتمند	clarinet *n* قره نی
appreciate *v* قدردانی کردن	medieval *adj* قرون وسطی
appreciation *n* قدردانی	corresponding *adj* قرینه
acknowledge *v* قدردانی کردن	oath *n* قسم
pace, step *n* قدم	swear *v* قسم بخور
march *n* قدم رو	portion, part *n* قسمت
stroll *v* قدم زدن	dole out *v* قسمت کردن
antiquity *n* قدمت	pretty *adj* قشنگ
ancient *adj* قدیمی	butcher *n* قصاب
lay *v* قرار بده	butchery *n* قصابی
lie *v* قرار بگیر	intention *n* قصد
park *v* قرار دادن	intend *v* قصد داشتن
arrange *v* قرار گذاشتن	drive at *v* قصد کردن
appointment *n* قرار ملاقات	tale *n* قصه
charter, contract *n* قرارداد	judgment *n* قضاوت
victim *n* قربانی	pole *n* قطب
pill, tablet *n* قرص	compass *n* قطب نما
loaf *n* قرص نان	polar *adj* قطبی
loan *n* قرض	diameter *n* قطر
lend *v* قرض بده	tar *n* قطران
loan *v* قرض دادن	globule, drop *n* قطره
Lent *n* قرض داده شده	diagonal *adj* قطری
borrow *v* قرض کردن	amputation *n* قطع
ballot, raffle *n* قرعه کشی	break off *v* قطع کردن
pheasant *n* قرقاول	hang up *v* قطع کردن گوشی
reel, spool *n* قرقره	excerpt *n* قطعه
red *adj* قرمز	mainland *n* قطعه اصلی

ق

قطعه یدکی	spare part n	قهرمانی	heroism n
قطعی	irrevocable adj	قهوه	coffee n
قفس	cage n	قهوه ای	brown adj
قفسه	shelf, cabinet n	قو	swan n
قفسه ها	shelves n	قوچ	ram n
قفل	padlock, lock n	قورباغه	frog n
قفل ساز	locksmith n	قورت دادن	swallow, gulp v
قفل کردن	lock, bar v	قوری	teapot n
قلاب	buckle, hook n	قوز	hunch n
قلب	heart n	قوز کردن	crouch v
قلب شناسی	cardiology n	قوزک	ankle n
قلبی	cardiac adj	قوس	arc n
قلدر	bully adj	قوطی	canister n
قلع	tin n	قوطی حلبی	can n
قلعه	castle, fort n	قول	pledge n
قلک	piggy bank n	قولنج	colic n
قلم	item, pen n	قوم وخویش	folks n
قلم زدن	engrave v	قوی	strong, potent adj
قلم مو	paintbrush n	قوی کردن	strengthen v
قلمرو	territory n	قوی نر	cob n
قلمرو اسقف	diocese n	قوی هیکل	burly adj
قلنبه	hump n	قیافه گرفتن	pose v
قله	summit n	قیام	revolt n
قلوه سنگ	rubble n	قیام کردن	revolt v
قمار کردن	gamble v	قیچی	scissors n
قناری	canary n	قید	adverb n
قناعت	frugality n	قیم	mandatory adj
قهرمان	champion n	قیمت	cost, price n
قهرمانانه	heroic adj	قیمت بدار	cost v

ق

ک

كابل *n* cable, cord

كابوس *n* mare

كابوى *n* cowboy

كابين *n* cabin

كابين خلبان *n* cockpit

كابينه *n* cabinet

كاپيتان *n* captain

كاتالوگ *n* catalog

كاخ *n* palace

كار *n* job, labor, work

كار عظيم *n* feat

كار كردن *v* work

كار گذاشتن *v* install

كار هنرى *n* artwork

كارائى *n* performance

كاراته *n* karate

كارآئى *n* efficiency

كارآفرين *n* entrepreneur

كارآگاه *n* detective

كارآمد *adj* efficient

كارآموز *n* apprentice

كاربرد *n* application

كاربوراتور *n* carburetor

كارت *n* card

كارت پستال *n* postcard

كارخانه *n* factory

كارد *n* knife

كاردان فنى *n* technician

كاردفترى *n* paperwork

كارشناس *adj* expert

كار عقب افتاده *n* backlog

كارفرما *n* employer

كاركرد *n* operation

كاركن *adj* workable

كاركنان *n* personnel

كارگاه *n* workshop

كارگر *n* worker

كارگر معدن *n* miner

كارگشا *n* pawnbroker

كارمند *n* employee

كارهاى مقدماتى *n* groundwork

كاروان *n* caravan

كاروبار *n* affair

كاريكاتور *n* caricature

كازينو *n* casino

كاست *n* caste

كاسه *n* bowl

كاشتن *v* implant

كاشى *n* tile

كاغذ *n* paper

كاغذ پوستى *n* parchment

كافئين *n* caffeine

كافر *n* heathen

كافى *adj* sufficient

كاكائو *n* cocoa

كاكايى *n* seagull

کاکل crest *n*	کباب کردن roast *v*
کالا stock, goods *n*	کبک partridge *n*
کالبد frame *n*	کبوتر pigeon *n*
کالبدشناسی anatomy *n*	کبود livid *adj*
کالبدگشایی autopsy *n*	کپسول capsule *n*
کالری calorie *n*	کپک mildew *n*
کالیبر caliber *n*	کپک زده mouldy *adj*
کالیبره کردن calibrate *v*	کپه heap *n*
کام palate *n*	کپه آشغال landfill *n*
کامل perfect, full *adj*	کپی کردن copy *v*
کامل شدن ripen *v*	کپی کننده copier *n*
کاملاً fully, quite *adv*	کت jacket *n*
کامیون جرثقیل دار tow truck *n*	کتاب book *n*
کامیاب شدن prosper *v*	کتاب درسی textbook *n*
کامیون truck *n*	کتاب راهنما guidebook *n*
کاناپه sofa *n*	کتاب شناسی bibliography *n*
کانال canal, channel *n*	کتاب فروش bookseller *n*
کاندید کردن nominate *v*	کتاب فروشی bookstore *n*
کانگورو kangaroo *n*	کتاب مبانی handbook *n*
کانی mineral *n*	کتاب مقدس bible *n*
کاه straw *n*	کتابچه booklet *n*
کاهش decrease *n*	کتابچه راهنما workbook *n*
کاهش دادن reduce *v*	کتابخانه library *n*
کاهش نرخ devaluation *n*	کتابدار bookkeeper, librarian *n*
کاهو lettuce *n*	کتابداری bookkeeping *n*
کاوش کردن explore *v*	کتان linen *n*
کاویدن excavate *v*	کتری kettle *n*
کباب roast *n*	کتک spanking *n*
کباب پز broiler *n*	کتک زدن mug, smack *v*

ک

dirt, filth *n* كثافت	tie *n* كروات
dirty, crappy *adj* كثيف	bracket *n* كروشه
crook *n* كج	deafness *n* كرى
crooked *adj* كج	Christmas *n* كريسمس
distort *v* كج كردن	cricket *n* كريكت
where *adv* كجا	recession *n* كسادى
zip code *n* كد پستى	deductible *adj* كسرپذير
what, which *adj* كدام	deficit *n* كسرى
dull *adj* كدر	tedious *adj* كسلكننده
pumpkin *n* كدو تنبل	someone *pro* كسى
deaf *adj* كر	elastic *adj* كش
deafen *v* كر كردن	snitch, pilfer *v* كش رفتن
reluctantly *adv* كراهاً	groin *n* كشاله ران
necktie *n* كراوات	farmer *n* كشاورز
fare *n* كرايه	agriculture *n* كشاورزى
hire *v* كرايه كردن	cultivation *n* كشت
canvas *n* كرباس	cultivate *v* كشت كردن
numb *adj* كرخ	slaughter *n* كشتار
numbness *n* كرخى	slaughter *v* كشتار كردن
celery *n* كرفس	kill, zap *v* كشتن
vulture *n* كركس	gun down *v* كشتن با تفنگ
rhinoceros *n* كرگدن	wrestling *n* كشتى
worm *n* كرم	wrestle *v* كشتى گرفتن
caterpillar *n* كرم حشره	wrestler *n* كشتى گير
sunblock *n* كرم ضدآفتاب	ark *n* كشتى نوح
strain *v* كرنش كردن	stretch *n* كشش
butter *n* كره	stretch *v* كشش
colt *n* كره اسب	discovery *n* كشف
globe *n* كره زمين	figure out *v* كشف كردن

ك

kneecap *n* کشکک زانو	raven *n* کلاغ سیاه
raisin *n* کشمش	metropolis *n* کلان شهر
virulent *adj* کشنده	hat, cap *n* کلاه
country *n* کشور	helmet *n* کلاه ایمنی
strain *n* کشیدگی	fraud *n* کلاه برداری
haul, pull *v* کشیدن	beret *n* کلاه بره
drag *v* کشیده شدن	wig *n* کلاه گیس
chaplain *n* کشیش	defraud *v* کلاهبرداری کردن
rector *n* کشیش منطقه	hood *n* کلاهک
floor *n* کف	cottage, hut *n* کلبه
palm *n* کف دست	chalet *n* کلبه کوهستانی
clap *v* کف زدن	cholesterol *n* کلسترول
abstinence *n* کف نفس	raft *n* کلک
expiation *n* کفاره	cabbage *n* کلم
expiate *v* کفاره دادن	word *n* کلمه
competence *n* کفایت	verbatim *adv* کلمه به کلمه
serve *v* کفایت کردن	totality *n* کلیت
hyena *n* کفتار	switch, key *n* کلید
blasphemy *n* کفر	church *n* کلیسا
profane *adj* کفر آمیز	cathedral *n* کلیسای جامع
blaspheme *v* کفرگویی کردن	kidney *n* کلیه
shoe *n* کفش	deficient *adj* کم
hip *n* کفل	debunk *v* کم ارزش کردن
shroud *n* کفن	insignificant *adj* کم اهمیت
flea *n* کک	inefficient *adj* کم بازده
class *n* کلاس	depreciate *v* کم بها کردن
classroom *n* کلاس درس	anemic *adj* کم خون
classy *adj* کلاسی	anemia *n* کم خونی
classic *adj* کلاسیک	bashful *adj* کم رو

ک

کمیته committee n	کم شدن diminish v
کمیسیون commission n	کم عمر shortlived adj
کمین raid n	کم عمق shallow adj
کمین کردن ambush v	کم کردن subtract v
کنار aside adv	کم کم little by little adv
کنار از aside from adv	کم هوشی mediocrity n
کنار دریا seaside adj	کمال perfection n
کنار کشیدن recede v	کمال مطلوب ideal adj
کنار گذاشتن put aside, bypass v	کمانچه fiddle n
کنارگذر bypass n	کمبود shortage n
کناره rim n	کمتر fewer, lesser adj
کناره گیری کردن secede v	کمتر از beneath pre
کنار هگیری abdication n	کمتری less adj
کنایه insinuation n	کمترین least adj
کنایه دار sarcastic adj	کمد closet n
کنترل control n	کمدی comedy n
کنترل پذیر manageable adj	کمدین comedian n
کنترل کردن control v	کمر waist n
کنتس countess n	کمرو shy adj
کنجکاو curious adj	کمرویی shyness n
کنجکاوی curiosity n	کمک aid, help n
کند sluggish adj	کمک خرج دادن subsidize v
کند کردن slow down v	کمک کردن help, aid v
کنده log, stub n	کمک کننده contributor n
کندو beehive n	کمونیست communist adj
کنس stingy adj	کمونیسم communism n
کنسرت concert n	کمیاب scarce adj
کنسرو شده canned adj	کمیابی scarcity n
کنسول consul n	کمیت quantity n

ک

کنسولگری n consulate	کوسن n cushion
کنگره n congress	کوسه n shark
کنیاک n brandy	کوشش n attempt
کنیسه n synagogue	کوفته قلقلی n meatball
که او pro whom	کوک n tune
که آن pro who	کوکائین n cocaine
که در نتیجه آن c whereupon	کوکتل n cocktail
کهکشان n galaxy	کوله پشتی n backpack
کهنه adj shabby	کولی n gypsy
کهنه بچه n diaper	کومه کردن v stack
کوبیدن v pound, knock	کوه n mountain
کوپن n coupon	کوه یخ n iceberg
کوتاه adj short	کوهستانی adj mountainous
کوتاه کردن v shorten	کی adv when
کوتاهی n brevity	کیپ adj hermetic
کوته فکر adj parochial	کیست n cyst
کوتوله n dwarf	کیسه n sack
کوچک adj petty, small	کیسه صفرا n gall bladder
کوچکتر adj minor	کیش n creed
کوچه n alley	کیف n bag
کود n manure	کیف بغلی n wallet
کودک n infant	کیف پول n purse
کودکی n infancy	کیف دستی n briefcase
کودن adj moron	کیف زنانه n handbag
کور adj blind	کیف زنی n mugging
کورکورانه adv blindly	کیفیت n quality
کورنت n cornet	کیک n bun, cake
کوره n furnace	کیلوگرم n kilogram
کوری n blindness	کیلومتر n kilometer

ک

کیلومتر شمار odometer n	گپ زدن v chat
کیلووات kilowatt n	گچ chalk n
کینه rancor n	گچ زدن v plaster
کیهانی cosmic adj	گدا beggar n
	گداختن v thaw
	گذاردن v invest
	گذرا fleeting adj

گ

گاراژ garage n	گذراندن spending n
گاری wagon n	گذرگاه ferry n
گاز bite n	گذرگاه عابرپیاده crosswalk n
گاز بگیر v bite	گذرنامه passport n
گاز زدن v nibble	گذشتن v elapse
گاز گرفتن v nip	گذشته last, past adj
گازانبر pincers n	گراز hog, wild boar n
گالن gallon n	گراز نر boar n
گام walk n	گرافیک graphic adj
گام بردار v stride	گرامی داشتن v cherish
گام زدن v pace	گران expensive adj
گامبهگام step-by-step adv	گرانبها precious adj
گانگستر gangster n	گرانش gravity n
گاهگاهی occasionally adv	گرایش tendency, trend n
گاو cow n	گربه cat n
گاو نر bull n	گرد round adj
گاومیش buffalo n	گرد آمدن v convene
گاونر ox n	گرد آوری کردن v gather
گاوهای نر oxen n	گرد و خاک dust n
	گرداب whirlpool n
	گردان battalion n
	گرداندن v wield

گرد‌آوردن v compile	گروگان n hostage
گرد‌آوری کننده n collector	گروه n group, throng
گرد‌باد n cyclone	گروه موسیقی n band
گردش n promenade	گروهبان n sergeant
گردش کردن v roam	گریان n crying
گردن n neck	گریان adj tearful
گردن زدن v decapitate, behead	گریختن v desert
گردنبند n necklace	گریز n evasion
گرده n pollen	گریز زدن از v evade
گردو n walnut	گریز کردن v sidestep
گرسنگی n hunger	گریزپا adj elusive
گرسنگی کشیدن v starve	گرینلند n Greenland
گرسنه adj hungry	گریه n cry
گرفتار کردن v entangle	گزارش n recital, report
گرفتگی n blockage	گزارش دادن v report
گرفتن n capture	گزارشگر n reporter
گرگ n wolf	گزاف adj exorbitant
گرم n gram	گزنده adj stinging
گرم adj warm	گستاخ adj arrogant
گرم کردن v warm up	گستاخی n rudeness
گرما n heat	گسترده adj wide
گرمازدگی n heatstroke	گسترش n expansion
گرماسنج n thermometer	گسترش یافتن v deploy
گرمایش n heating	گسستن v rupture
گرمک n cantaloupe	گسیختن v interrupt
گرمی n warmth	گشت n patrol
گره n tangle, tie, knot	گشت زدن v cruise
گره زدن v tie	گشتن به دنبال v look for
گرو گذاشتن v pledge	گشودن دکمه v unbutton

گشوده outstretched adj	گمراه کننده misleading adj
گفتگو dialogue n	گمنام anonymous adj
گفتگو کردن negotiate v	گمنام ماندن anonymity n
گفتن saying n	گناه guilt, sin n
گل flower n	گناه کار sinner n
گل دادن blossom v	گناهکار sinful adj
گل سرخ rose n	گنبد dome n
گل کلم cauliflower n	گنج treasure n
گل لاله tulip n	گندزدایی کردن sterilize v
گلابی pear n	گندم wheat n
گلادیاتور gladiator n	گندم سیاه crap n
گلبرگ petal n	گندیده putrid adj
گلبول corpuscle n	گهواره cradle n
گلخانه nursery n	گوارشی digestive adj
گلدان vase n	گواهی certificate n
گلدوزی embroidery n	گوجه فرنگی tomato n
گلدوزی کردن embroider v	گود کردن deepen v
گلگون rosy adj	گودال سرپوشیده pitfall n
گله cattle n	گودال عمیق plunge n
گله کردن grumble v	گودی dent n
گلو throat n	گور grave adj
گلوکز glucose n	گور grave n
گلوگاه bottleneck n	گوراسب zebra n
گلوله bullet, shot n	گورستان cemetery n
گلی muddy adj	گوریل gorilla n
گم شده missing adj	گوزن deer n
گم کن lose v	گوزن شمالی reindeer n
گمراه misguided adj	گوزن نر buck n
گمراه کردن mislead, baffle v	گوسفند sheep n

گوش n ear

گوش به زنگ adj watchful

گوش خراش adj deafening

گوش درد n earache

گوشت n flesh, meat

گوشت آهو n venison

گوشت چرخ کرده n mincemeat

گوشت خوک n pork

گوشت راسته n sirloin

گوشت کباب کن n grill

گوشت کباب کن v grill

گوشت گاو n beef

گوشت گوساله n veal

گوشتی adj succulent

گوشه n corner

گوشه جامه n hem

گوشهگیر n recluse

گوشواره n earring

گوشی n headphones

گوشی ها n earphones

گوگرد n sulphur

گول زدن v dupe, swindle

گوناگون n diversity

گوناگون adj varied, various, diverse

گونه ها n species

گوه n wedge

گوینده n announcer

گیاه n vegetation

گیاه چندساله adj perennial

گیاه خزنده n trailer

گیاه شناسی n botany

گیتار n guitar

گیج adj dazed, dizzy

گیج کردن v confuse, bewilder

گیج کننده adj confusing

گیجی n muddle

گیچ کردن v mystify

گیر کردن v bog down

گیرنده n addressee

گیره n clamp

گیره کاغذ n paperclip

گیس n braid

گیشه n box office

گیلاس n cherry

گیوتن n guillotine

ل

لاادری n agnostic

لات n hooligan

لازم adj necessary

لاس زدن v flirt

لاستیک n rubber

لاشه n carcass

لاغر adj slim, thin

لاغر کردن atrophy v	لحظه instant n
لاف زدن brag v	لخت naked adj
لاک پشت turtle n	لخت کردن skin v
لاک زدن varnish v	لذت enjoyment n
لال dumb, mute adj	لذت بخش blissful adj
لامپ bulb n	لذت بردن enjoy v
لانه سگ kennel n	لرزان shaky adj
لایق capable adj	لرزش shiver, tremor n
لایق دانستن esteem v	لرزیدن vibrate, quake v
لایه layer n	لطف grace, favor n
لایی padding n	لعنت damnation n
لب lip n	لعنت کردن damn v
لباس clothes n	لغزش lapse n
لباس بلند gown n	لغزنده slippery adj
لباس بلند و گشاد robe n	لغزیدن slip v
لباس پوشیدن dress v	لغو repeal n
لباس خواب pajamas n	لغو حکم اعدام reprieve n
لباس زیر underwear n	لغو کردن repeal, annul v
لباس زیرزنانه lingerie n	لفاف wrapping n
لباس کندن undress v	لفاف دار shrouded adj
لباسی dress n	لفظ به لفظ literally adv
لبخند smile, beam n	لقمه morsel n
لبخند زدن smile v	لک لک stork n
لبریز شدن run over v	لکنت پیدا کردن stammer v
لبنیات کشاورزی dairy farm n	لکنت داشتن stutter v
لبه brim, brink n	لکه blot, stain, freckle n
لجاجت obstinacy n	لکه دار کردن blot, stain v
لجوج obstinate adj	لکه صورت freckle n
لحاف quilt n	لگد زدن kick v

لگد زدن n kickback	لوله کشی n plumbing
لگن n tub, basin	لولو n pearl
لم n lounge	لیتر n liter
لم دادن v lean on	لیز بخور v slide
لمس n touch	لیز خوردن n slip
لمس کردن v touch	لیزر n laser
لنز n lense	لیسانسیه n bachelor
لنگ n limp	لیست حقوق n payroll
لنگ adj lame	لیسیدن v lick
لنگ بودن v wobble	لیکور n liqueur
لنگ کردن v cripple	لیگ n league
لنگر n berth, anchor	لیموترش n lemon, lime
لنگر انداختن v moor	لیموناد n lemonade
لنگرگاه n harbor	لیوان دسته دار n mug
لنگیدن v limp	
له کردن v mangle	
لهجه n accent, dialect	
لهستان n Poland	
لهستانی adj Polish	
لو دادن v betray	
لوازم n gear	
لوبیا سبز n kidney bean	ما pro we
لوزالمعده n pancreas	مابین pre between
لوزه n tonsil	مات adj opaque
لوکس adj de luxe	ماجرا n adventure
لولا n butt	مادر n mother
لولا زدن v hinge	مادر همسر n mother-in-law
لوله n pipe	مادربزرگ n grandmother
لوله کش n plumber	مادری adj maternal
	مادری n substance, matter

م

ماده پاک کننده n detergent	مال او pro hers, his, yours
ماده شیر n lioness	مال او adj his, your
ماده شیمیایی adj chemical	مال خودم adj own
ماده ضدعفونی n disinfectant	مال ما adj our
ماده غذایی n foodstuff	مال ما pro ours
ماده گرایی n materialism	مال من pro mine
مادهمحرک n stimulant	مال من adj my
مادهمخدر n narcotic	مالاریا n malaria
مادی adj worldly	مالک بودن v own
مار n snake, serpent	مالکیت n ownership
مارپیچ n maze	مالکیت مشترک n condo
مارپیچی adj winding	مالی adj financial
مارچوبه n asparagus	مالیات n tax
مارس n March	مالیخولیا n melancholy
مارشال n marshal	مالیدن v rub
مارکسیست adj marxist	ماما n midwife
مارمولک n lizard	مامان n mummy
ماز n labyrinth	مامان بزرگ n granny
مازاد n excess, surplus	ماموت n mammoth
ماساژ n massage	مامور n officer
ماساژ دادن v massage	مامور adj official
ماساژور n masseur	مامور آتش نشانی n fireman
ماسک n mask	مامور پلیس n policeman
ماسه n sand	مامور کردن v appoint
ماسه بادی n quicksand	ماموریت n mission
ماشین n machine	ماندن v stay
ماشین حساب n calculator	ماندن n stay
ماشین دوخت n stapler	مانده n remains
ماشینی کردن v mechanize	مانع n obstacle

hold back *v* مانع شدن	combat *v* مبارزه کردن
like *pre* مانند	bailiff *n* مباشر
maneuver *n* مانوور	beginner *n* مبتدی
month, moon *n* ماه	disguise *n* مبدل
honeymoon *n* ماه عسل	armchair *n* مبل
monthly *adv* ماهانه	hike *v* مبلغ را بالا بردن
crack *n* ماهر	missionary *n* مبلّغ مذهبی
skillful *adj* ماهر	cistern *n* مبنع آب
master *v* ماهر شدن	ambiguous *adj* مبهم
satellite *n* ماهواره	amaze *v* مبهوت کردن
fish *n* ماهی	sorrowful *adj* متاسف
salmon *n* ماهی آزاد	married *adj* متاهل
saucepan *n* ماهی تابه	aggressor *n* متجاوز
cod *n* ماهی روغن	rapist *n* متجاوز جنسی
trout *n* ماهی قزل آلا	ally *n* متحد
anchovy *n* ماهی کولی	allied *adj* متحد
muscle *n* ماهیچه	unify, ally *v* متحد کردن
calf *n* ماهیچه ساق پا	mobilize *v* متحرک کردن
fisherman *n* ماهیگیر	incur *v* متحمل شدن
squid *n* ماهیمرکب	astonish *v* متحیر کردن
fluid, liquid *n* مایع	mind-boggling *adj* متحیر کننده
slanted *adj* مایل	porous *adj* متخلخل
disappoint, let down *v* مایوس کردن	meter *n* متر
argument *n* مباحثه	synonym *n* مترادف
interchange *n* مبادله	aggregate, amass *v* متراکم کردن
exchange *v* مبادله کردن	interpreter *n* مترجم
genteel *adj* مبادی آداب	derelict *adj* متروک
warrior *n* مبارز	metric *adj* متری
campaign *n* مبارزه	waver *v* متزلزل شدن

م

thankful *adj* متشکر	fit *n* متناسب بودن
curator *n* متصدی	frequent *adj* متناوب
receptionist *n* متصدی پذیرش	alternate *v* متناوب کردن
auctioneer *n* متصدی مزایده	cater to *v* متنعم کردن
apply *v* متصل کردن	disgust *n* متنفر
discordant *adj* متضاد	varied *adj* متنوع
balance *v* متعادل کردن	diversify *v* متنوع کردن
standardize *v* متعارف کردن	drill *n* مته
surprise *v* متعجب کردن	defendant *n* متهم
numerous *adj* متعدد	accuse, denounce *v* متهم کردن
fanatic *adj* متعصب	collateral *adj* متوازی
committed *adj* متعهد	modest *adj* متواضع
different *adj* متفاوت	humbly *adv* متواضعانه
thoughtful *adj* متفکر	consecutive *adj* متوالی
applicant *n* متقاضی	mindful *adj* متوجه
cross *adj* متقاطع	point *v* متوجه کردن
cross *n* متقاطع	swollen *adj* متورم
ensure, convince *v* متقاعد کردن	inflate *v* متورم شدن
persuasion *n* متقاعدسازی	lay off *v* متوقف ساختن
con man *n* متقلب	stop *v* متوقف کردن
haughty *adj* متکبر	be born *v* متولد شدن
motel *n* متل	example *n* مثال
disintegrate *v* متلاشی شدن	bladder *n* مثانه
splinter *v* متلاشی شدن	affirmative *adj* مثبت
distinctive *adj* متمایز	proverb *n* مثل
civilize *v* متمدن کردن	ladylike *adj* مثل یک خانم
concentrate *v* متمرکز کردن	triangle *n* مثلث
text *n* متن	lawful, legitimate *adj* مجاز
body *n* متن پیام	may *v* مجاز کن

م

مجازی fictitious adj	مچاله کردن crush v
مجالست companionship n	محاسبه calculation n
مجاهد crusader n	محاسبه کردن compute v
مجاور adjacent, next door adj	محاصره siege n
مجبور کردن compel, constrain v	محاصره کردن siege v
مجدداً پر کردن replenish v	محاصره کن besiege v
مجدداً پرداختن refund v	محافظت escort, guard n
مجذوب engrossed adj	محافظت کردن protect, care v
مجذوب کردن fascinate v	محافظه کار conservative adj
مجرا duct, trench n	محبت affection n
مجرد single, unmarried adj	محبوب beloved adj
مجرد single n	محبوس کردن confine v
مجروح casualty n	محتاط cautious adj
مجزا کردن isolate v	محتمل likely adv
مجسم کردن embody v	محتوا content adj
مجسمه statue n	محتویات contents n
مجسمه ساز sculptor n	محدود کردن limit, restrict v
مجسمه سازی sculpture n	محدودیت constraint, limitation n
مجلس parliament n	محراب altar n
مجلل luxurious adj	محرک stimulus n
مجله magazine n	محرم confidant n
مجمع assembly n	محرمانه confidential adj
مجموعه complex adj	محروم deprived adj
مجموعه series, set n	محروم کردن exclude v
مجنون paranoid adj	محرومیت deprivation n
مجهز outfit n	محسوس palpable adj
مجهز کردن furnish v	محصول crop, harvest n
مچ wrist, cuff n	محصول عمده staple n
مچاله twisted adj	محصول فرعی by-product n

م

محفظه chamber *n*	مختل کردن *v* disturb
محفوظ secure *adj*	مخرب destructive *adj*
محقق scholar *n*	مخرج کسر denominator *n*
محکم firm, tough *adj*	مخروط cone *n*
محکم firm *n*	مخزن reservoir *n*
محکم کردن *v* consolidate, clinch	مخصوص special *adj*
محکم نگهداشتن *v* secure	مخصوصاً particularly *adv*
محکوم doomed *adj*	مخفی undercover *adj*
محکوم کردن *v* condemn	مخفی کردن *v* camouflage
محکومیت condemnation *n*	مخفی کن hide *v*
محل location *n*	مخفی گاه hideaway *n*
محل اقامت dwelling *n*	مخلوط blend, mixture *n*
محل خروج exit *n*	مخلوط assorted *adj*
محل ذخیره store *n*	مخلوط کردن *v* mix
محل ذخیره سازی storage *n*	مخلوط کن blender, mixer *n*
محله parish *n*	مخمر ferment, yeast *n*
محله فقیرنشین slum *n*	مخمل velvet *n*
محلول lotion *n*	مخملی flock *n*
محلول خیسانده infusion *n*	مخوف grisly *adj*
محلی local, national *adj*	مد fashionable *adj*
محموله shipment *n*	مد vogue *n*
محو کردن *v* wipe out	مداخله intervention *n*
محور axis, axle *n*	مداد pencil *n*
محیط surroundings *n*	مداد پاک کن eraser *n*
مخالف adverse *adj*	مداد شمعی crayon *n*
مخالفت opposition *n*	مدار orbit, circuit *n*
مخالفت نکردن *v* indulge	مدافع defender *n*
مختصر terse *adj*	مدال medal *n*
مختصر کردن *v* abbreviate	مدت duration *n*

م

مدرسه school *n*	مرتب tidy *adj*
مدرسه مذهبی seminary *n*	مرتب کردن straighten out *v*
مدرک evidence *n*	مرتباً regularly *adv*
مدل model, replica *n*	مرتد heretic *adj*
مدل برهنه nude *adj*	مرتکب شدن perpetrate *v*
مدنی civil *adj*	مرجع antecedent *n*
مدیر director *n*	مرحله stage, phase *n*
مدیر داخلی dean *n*	مرحوم deceased *adj*
مدیریت management *n*	مرخص کردن dismiss, license *v*
مذاکره bargain *n*	مرد male, man *n*
مذکر masculine *adj*	مرد خانواده patriarch *n*
مراجعه کردن recourse *v*	مرداب lagoon *n*
مراسم تعمید christening *n*	مردانگی manliness *n*
مراسم شامگاه retreat *n*	مردانه manly *adj*
مرافعه کردن litigate *v*	مردد hesitant *adj*
مراقب بودن look after, mind *v*	مردم people *n*
مراقبت care *n*	مردن pass away *v*
مراقبت کردن look out *v*	مرده dead *adj*
مرام ideology *n*	مردها men *n*
مربا jam *n*	مردود ساختن put away *v*
مربای پرتقال marmalade *n*	مرز border, boundary *n*
مربع square *adj*	مرز borderline *adj*
مربع square *n*	مرسوم conventional *adj*
مربوط relevant *adj*	مرصع inlaid *adj*
مربوط بودن concern *v*	مرطوب humid *adj*
مربوط ساختن affiliate, associate *v*	مرطوب کردن dampen *v*
مربوطه respective *adj*	مرغ hen *n*
مربی coach, trainer *n*	مرغ ماهی خوار pelican *n*
مربیگری coaching *n*	مرغ نوروزی gull *n*

مرفين morphine n	مسئله problem n
مرکب compound n	مسئول responsible adj
مرکز center n	مسئولیت responsibility n
مرکز خرید mall n	مسابقه contest, race n
مرکز شهر downtown n	مسابقه دادن race v
مرکزی central adj	مسافت distance n
مرگ death n	مسافت پیموده mileage n
مرموز mysterious adj	مسافت نما milestone n
مرور review n	مسافر westbound adv
مرور کردن browse v	مسافر transient adj
مرورگر browser n	مسافر traveler n
مری esophagus n	مسافر کشتی voyager n
مریخ Mars n	مسافرت crossing n
مرید disciple n	مسافرت کردن travel v
مریض کردن sicken v	مسافرت مفتی hitchhike n
مزاحم bothersome adj	مسافرخانه inn n
مزاحم nuisance n	مسامحه کار negligent adj
مزاحم شدن molest v	مست loaded adj
مزاحمت intrusion n	مستأجر tenant n
مزایده auction n	مستأصل desperate adj
مزخرف bum n	مستبد despotic adj
مزرعه ranch n	مستحکم کردن fortify v
مزمن chronic adj	مسترد کردن reimburse v
مزه flavor, taste n	مستطیل oblong adj
مزه دادن taste v	مستطیل rectangle n
مزه کردن taste v	مستعد prone adj
مزیت advantage n	مستعمره colony n
مژه eyelash n	مستعمره سازی colonization n
مس copper n	مستقل independent adj

مستقیم direct adj	مشاهده کردن view v
مستند documentary n	مشاور adviser n
مستندسازی documentation n	مشاور حقوقی lawyer n
مستهلک شدن cushion v	مشت fist, punch n
مسجد mosque n	مشت زدن punch v
مسدود کردن obstruct, block v	مشت زن boxer n
مسرف wasteful adj	مشت زنی boxing n
مسری infectious adj	مشتاق avid, eager adj
مسطح کردن level v	مشترکاً jointly adv
مسکن painkiller n	مشتری customer, patron n
مسکونی inhabitable adj	مشتریان clientele n
مسلح armed adj	مشتعل fiery adj
مسلح کردن arm v	مشتق derivative adj
مسلسل machine gun n	مشخص کردن define, denote v
مسلط بودن بر overlook v	مشخصه feature n
مسلط شدن بر come over v	مشروب booze n
مسلمان Muslim adj	مشروب الکلی liquor n
مسموم کردن poison v	مشروب خور drinker n
مسمومیت poisoning n	مشروب فروشی bar n
مسن elderly adj	مشعل flare n
مسواک زدن brush v	مشغول engaged adj
مسیح Messiah n	مشغول کردن employ v
مسیحی christian adj	مشغولانه busily adv
مسیحیت Christianity n	مشق نظامی drill n
مسیر path, route n	مشکل difficult adj
مسیر گلوله trajectory n	مشکل difficulty n
مشابه similar adj	مشکل پسند choosy adj
مشارکت participation n	مشکل کردن harden v
مشاهده observation n	مشکوک dubious adj

م

مشهور famous adj	مطرح شدن come up v
مشهور کردن popularize v	مطرح کردن pose v
مشورت advice n	مطلع prologue n
مشورت کردن confer v	مطلق absolute adj
مشوق incentive n	مطلوب favorable adj
مشیت will n	مطیع obedient adj
مصاحبه interview n	مطیع کردن subdue v
مصادره confiscation n	مظلومیت oppression n
مصب estuary n	مظنون suspect n
مصرف consumption n	معادلهٔ tantamount to adj
مصرف بیش از حد overdose n	معادله equation n
مصرف کردن consume v	معاش livelihood n
مصرف کننده consumer n	معاشر companion n
مصلحت expediency n	معاف exempt adj
مصمم resolute adj	معافیت exemption n
مصوت vowel n	معالجه treatment n
مصوت مرکب diphthong n	معامله dealings n
مصونیت immunity n	معامله به مثل retaliation n
مصونیت دار کردن immunize v	معاهده treaty n
مصیبت calamity n	معاوضه swap n
مضحک comical adj	معاوضه کردن trade v
مضر harmful adj	معاون vice n
مضطرب کردن upset v	معاینه check up n
مطابق با قانون law-abiding adj	معاینه کردن look over v
مطابق کردن adjust v	معبد oracle n
مطابقت کردن match v	معتاد کننده addictive adj
مطالبه کردن call on v	معتبر valid adj
مطالعه کردن study v	معتبر ساختن validate v
مطبوع delicate adj	معتکف hermit n

معجزه	miracle n	معیوب	blemish n
معجزه آسا	miraculous adj	معیوب	faulty adj
معجون	concoction n	معیوب کردن	mutilate v
معده ای	gastric adj	مغازه	store, shop n
معذور داشتن	excuse v	مغذی	nutritious adj
معرفی	introduction n	مغرور	conceited adj
معرفی کردن	introduce v	مغز	brain n
معزول کردن	depose v	مغز استخوان	marrow n
معصیت کردن	sin v	مغز متفکر	mastermind n
معقول	reasonable adj	مغزی	cerebral adj
معکوس	reversal n	مغناطیس	magnetism n
معلق کردن	suspend v	مغناطیسی	magnetic adj
معلم	instructor n	مفتخر	proud adj
معلم خصوصی	tutor n	مفصل	lengthy adj
معلمی کردن	coach v	مفصل	joint n
معلول	disabled adj	مفهوم	concept n
معلولیت	disability n	مفید	helpful adj
معلوم کردن	uncover, ascertain v	مقابل	contrary adj
معمار	architect n	مقابل	opposite adv
معماری	architecture n	مقابل	opposite n
معمول	standard n	مقابله کردن	repel v
معمولی	mediocre adj	مقاله	essay n
معمولی	ordinarily adv	مقام پاپ	papacy n
معنی	meaning n	مقام عالی رتبه	dignitary n
معنی دار	significant adj	مقام کشیشی	priesthood n
معهذا	though c	مقاوم	adamant adj
معوق	pending adj	مقاومت	strength n
معوق گذراندن	procrastinate v	مقاومت کردن	resist v
معیار	norm n	مقاومت ناپذیر	irresistible adj

م

comparison *n* مقایسه	مکتوب *n* epistle
comparative *adj* مقایسه ای	مکث کردن *v* halt
compare *v* مقایسه کردن	مکر *adj* cunning
frugal *adj* مقتصد	مکزیکی *adj* Mexican
advisable *adj* مقتضی	مکش *n* admission
amount *n* مقدار	مکعب *n* cube
plenty *n* مقدار زیاد	مکعب *adj* cubic
dosage *n* مقدارخوراک	مکمل *n* complement
some *adj* مقداری	مکنده *adj* sucker
sacred *adj* مقدس	مکیدن *v* suck
saint *n* مقدس	مگر اینکه *pre* barring
precede *v* مقدم بودن	مگر اینکه *c* unless
preliminary *adj* مقدماتی	ملاط *n* mortar
prelude *n* مقدمه	ملاقات *n* meeting
allowance *n* مقرری	ملاقات کردن *v* assemble
target, destination *n* مقصد	ملاقات کن *v* meet
culprit, guilty *n* مقصر	ملاک *n* criterion
syllable *n* مقطع	ملالت *n* tedium
cardboard *n* مقوا	ملایم *adj* lenient
scale *n* مقیاس	ملت *n* nation
scale *v* مقیاس کردن	ملتفت شدن *v* notice
bind *v* مقید کن	ملحد *n* atheist
settle *v* مقیم کردن	ملحق شدن *v* combine
foxy *adj* مکار	ملحق کردن *v* join
place *n* مکان	ملخ *n* locust
sanctuary *n* مکان مقدس	ملزم *adj* obliged
tablet *n* مکان نما	ملزم کدن *v* tie
locate *v* مکان یابی کردن	ملزوم *n* necessity
mechanic *n* مکانیک	ملزومات *n* supplies

estate *n* ملک	digress *v* منحرف شدن
queen *n* ملکه	pervert *v* منحرف کردن
tangible *adj* ملموس	distract *v* منحرف کردن توجه
sailor *n* ملوان	unique *adj* منحصربفرد
nationalize *v* ملی کردن	ebb *v* منحط شدن
nationality *n* ملیت	lodge *v* منزل کردن
laxative *adj* ملین	cloister *n* منزوی
tangent *n* مماس	secluded *adj* منزوی
excellence *n* ممتازی	coherent *adj* منسجم
possible *adj* ممکن	origin *n* منشا
seal off *v* ممنوع الورود کردن	prism *n* منشور
outlaw *v* ممنوع ساختن	clerk *n* منشی
forbid *v* ممنوع کن	dissuade *v* منصرف کردن
I *pro* من	logic *n* منطق
resource *n* منابع	region, zone *n* منطقه
litany *n* مناجات	regional *adj* منطقه ای
quarrel *v* منازعه	logical *adj* منطقی
convenient *adj* مناسب	sight, view *n* منظر
fitness *n* مناسبت	panorama *n* منظره
debate *v* مناظره کردن	systematic *adj* منظم
pulpit *n* منبر	purpose *n* منظور
source *n* منبع	mean *v* منظور بدار
boil down to *v* منتج شدن به	rebuff, snub *n* منع
propagate, broadcast *v* منتشر کردن	curfew *n* منع رفت و آمد
spread *v* منتشر کن	inhibit *v* منع کردن
waiting *n* منتظر	flare-up *v* منفجر شدن
await *v* منتظر بودن	blow up *v* منفجر شو
wait *v* منتظر ماندن	disconnect *v* منفصل کردن
pervert *adj* منحرف	gain *n* منفعت

مهلک fatal, lethal *adj*	منفعت شخصی self-interest *n*
مهم momentous *adj*	منفور laughing stock *n*
مهمات ammunition *n*	منفی negative *adj*
مهمان guest *n*	منقبض کردن retract *v*
مهمان نوازی hospitality *n*	منقضی overdue *adj*
مهماندار زن stewardess *n*	منقطع کردن disrupt *v*
مهمانی party *n*	منقلکباب barbecue *n*
مهمتر بودن از outweigh *v*	منکوب کردن suppress *v*
مهمیز زدن spur *v*	منگنه fringe, nip *n*
مهندس engineer *n*	منگنه زدن staple *v*
مهو شدن die out *v*	مه fog *n*
مواجه encounter *n*	مه آلود mist *n*
مواجهه confrontation *n*	مه آلود foggy, hazy *adj*
مواد material *n*	مهاجر immigrant *n*
مواد سوختنی combustible *n*	مهاجرت immigration *n*
موازی parallel *n*	مهاجرت کردن immigrate *v*
مواظب wary *adj*	مهاجرمقیم settler *n*
مواظب بودن watch out *v*	مهاجرنشین colonial *adj*
موافق نبودن disagree *v*	مهاجم attacker *n*
موافقت کردن comply, assent *v*	مهار leash, rein *n*
موافقتنامه agreement *n*	مهار هواپیما barricade *n*
موبایل cellphone *n*	مهارت skill *n*
موتور engine, motor *n*	مهتابی terrace *n*
موتورسیکلت motorcycle *n*	مهر stamp, seal *n*
موثر effective *adj*	مهر stamp *v*
موج ripple, wave *n*	مهربان affable, gentle *adj*
موج جزر و مدی tidal wave *n*	مهربانی kindness *n*
موج دار wavy *adj*	مهرپست postmark *n*
موج سواری کردن surf *v*	مهره پشت vertebra *n*

م

م

موج هوای گرم heatwave *n*	موعظه کردن preach *v*
موجب conducive *adj*	موفق successful *adj*
موجر lessor *n*	موفق شدن succeed *v*
موجز concise *adj*	موفقیت hit, success *n*
موجه plausible *adj*	موقت temporary *adj*
موجود creature *n*	موقرانه gravely *adv*
موجودی inventory *n*	موقعیت occasion *n*
موچین tweezers *n*	مولد generator *n*
مودار hairy *adj*	مولفه component *n*
مودب courteous *adj*	مولکول molecule *n*
مورچه ant *n*	مومن believer *n*
مورد case, instance *n*	مومیایی کردن embalm *v*
موریانه termite *n*	مونتاژ assembly *n*
موز banana *n*	مونث female *n*
موزاییک mosaic *n*	موی hair *n*
موزه museum *n*	می May *n*
موزیک و رقص waltz *n*	میانبر shortcut *n*
موسس founder *n*	میانجی mediator *n*
موسسه foundation *n*	میانگین average *n*
موسیقی music *n*	میانگین mean *adj*
موسیقی دان musician *n*	میخانه tavern *n*
موسیقی نواختن play *v*	میخانهچی bartender *n*
موش mouse, rat *n*	میخک carnation *n*
موش ها mice *n*	میخمحور linchpin *n*
موشک missile *n*	میدان arena, square *n*
موضع position *n*	میدانمین minefield *n*
موضوع subject, matter *n*	میراث heritage *n*
موعد deadline *n*	میز desk, table *n*
موعظه homily *n*	میز آرایش dresser *n*

م
ن

میز تحریر desk n
میزان کردن tune v
میزبان host n
میکروب germ n
میکروسکپ microscope n
میکروفن microphone n
میگرن migraine n
میگو shrimp n
میل urge n
میل داشتن desire v
میله rod, bar n
میله پرچم flagpole n
میلی گرم milligram n
میلیمتر millimeter n
میلیون million n
میلیونر millionaire n
میمون ape, monkey n
مینا daisy n
مینیاتور miniature n
میهن پرست patriot n
میوه fruit n
میوه ای fruity adj

ن

ناامنی insecurity n
ناامید despair n
ناامید hopeless adj
ناامید کردن frustrate v
ناامیدکننده bleak adj
ناآرامی unrest n
ناآزموده clumsy adj
ناآگاه ignorant adj
نابالغ immature adj
ناباور infertile adj
ناباوری disbelief n
نابجا inept adj
نابخردانه unwise adj
نابخشودنی inexcusable adj
نابرابر unequal adj
نابرابری inequality n
نابغه genius n
نابود ravage n
نابود کردن annihilate v
ناپایدار uncertain adj
ناپدری stepfather n
ناپدید شدن disappear v
ناپدیدشدگی disappearance n
ناپسری stepson n
ناپسند شمردن disapprove v
ناتمام incomplete adj
ناتوان helpless adj

ناتوان کردن v invalidate	نارنگی n tangerine
ناتوانی n inability	نازک adj slim, thin
ناجور adj awkward	ناسازگار adj incompatible
ناچیز adj paltry	ناسالم adj unhealthy
ناچیزی n pettiness	ناسپاس adj ungrateful
ناحساس adj insensitive	ناسپاسی n ingratitude
ناحق adj undeserved	ناسزاوار adj abusive
ناخالص adj gross	ناسودآور adj unprofitable
ناخشنود adj unhappy	ناشر n publisher
ناخن n fingernail	ناشناخته adj unknown
ناخن پا n toenail	ناشناس adj unfamiliar
ناخوانا adj illegible	ناشی از وحشت n panic
ناخواهری n stepsister	ناشی شدن v derive
ناخوش adj indisposed	ناصحیح adj wrong
ناخوشی n sickness	ناظر n butler, onlooker
نادختری n stepdaughter	ناف n belly button
نادر adj infrequent	نافرمان adj defiant
نادرست adj dishonest	نافرمانی n defiance
نادرستی n dishonesty	نافرمانی کردن v disobey
نادقیق adj imprecise	ناقابل ساختن v incapacitate
نادیده گرفتن v disregard	ناقص adj defective
ناراحت adj uncomfortable	ناکافی adj insufficient
ناراحت کردن v perturb	ناگزیر ساختن v necessitate
ناراحت کننده adj annoying	ناگزیر کردن v coerce
ناراحتی n discomfort	ناگهان adv suddenly
نارضایی adj discontent	ناگهانی adj sudden
نارضایی n grievance	ناگوار کردن v embitter
نارگیل n coconut	ناله n groan, moan
نارنجک n grenade	ناله کردن v groan

نالیدن whine v	**ناموزون** dissonant adj
نام name n	**ناموفق** unsuccessful adj
نام خانوادگی surname n	**نامیده شده** so-called adj
نام گذاری کردن christen v	**نان** bread n
نام مستعار nickname n	**نان شیرینی** pastry n
نام نویسی کردن matriculate, enlist v	**نانوا** baker n
نامادری stepmother n	**نانوایی** bakery n
نامتراکم sparse adj	**ناهار** lunch n
نامتعارف uncommon adj	**ناهار ـ صبحانه** brunch n
نامحتمل improbable adj	**ناهمانند** unlike adj
نامحدود unlimited adj	**ناهموار** bumpy adj
نامرئی invisible adj	**ناهمواری** rough adj
نامربوط irrelevant adj	**ناهنجاری** abnormality n
نامرتب messy adj	**ناو جنگی** warship n
نامرغوب substandard adj	**ناو کلیسا** nave n
نامزد fiancé, candidate n	**ناو محافظ** frigate n
نامزد کردن designate v	**ناودان** gutter n
نامزدی candidacy n	**ناوشکن** destroyer n
نامطبوع obnoxious adj	**نای** windpipe n
نامطبوع rank n	**نایب السلطنه** regent n
نامطلوب unfavorable adj	**نبرد** struggle n
نامعقول unreasonable adj	**نبرد کردن** battle v
ناممکن impossible adj	**نترس** intrepid adj
نامناسب unsuitable adj	**نتیج ندادن** miscarry v
نامنظم irregular adj	**نتیجه** result n
نامه letter, mail n	**نتیجه اخلاقی** moral adj
نامه رسان postman n	**نتیجه اخلاقی** moral n
نامهسرمایه capital letter n	**نتیجه گرفتن** derive, conclude v
ناموجه unjustified adj	**نثر** prose n

نجات *n* salvation	نزدیک *adj* close, near
نجات بده از *v* rid of	نزدیک *adv* closely
نجات دادن *v* rescue, save	نزدیک به *pre* close to
نجات دهنده *n* savior	نزدیک بین *adj* nearsighted
نجات غریق *n* lifeguard	نزدیکی *n* proximity
نجاری *n* carpentry	نزول کردن *v* decrease
نجس کردن *v* pollute	نژاد *n* race
نجوا کردن *n* whisper	نژادپرست *adj* racist
نجوا کردن *v* whisper	نژادپرستی *n* racism
نجومی *adj* astronomic	نسبت *n* proportion
نخ *n* string, yarn	نسبت دادن *v* attribute
نخ کردن *v* thread	نسخه *n* prescription
نخست *adj* prime	نسل *n* generation
نخست وزیر *adj* premier	نسل کشی *n* genocide
نخستین *adj* initial	نسیم *n* breeze
نخود *n* pea	نشا کردن *v* transplant
نداشتن *v* lack	نشاسته *n* starch
نرخ *n* rate	نشاسته ای *adj* starchy
نردبان *n* ladder	نشان *n* indication
نردبان آهنی *n* stepladder	نشان بده *v* show
نرده *n* handrail	نشان دادن *v* indicate
نرم *adj* soft, tender	نشان دو نقطه *n* colon
نرم شدن *v* soften	نشان کردن *v* earmark
نرم کردن *v* smooth	نشانه *n* symptom
نرم کننده *n* conditioner	نشانه گرفتن *v* aim
نرمش *n* leniency	نشانی *n* address
نرمی *n* smoothness	نشت *n* leak
نروژ *n* Norway	نشتی *n* leakage
نروژی *adj* Norwegian	نشریه *n* journal

نشست session n	نقد cash; criticism n
نشسته seated adj	نقد ادبی کردن v criticize
نصب installation n	نقرس gout n
نصب کن v lay	نقره اندود silverplated adj
نصحیت کردن v exhort	نقره ای silver n
نصیحت کردن v admonish	نقره آلات silverware n
نظارت surveillance n	نقره کار silversmith n
نظر estimation n	نقش infraction n
نظریه doctrine n	نقش برجسته effigy n
نظم regularity n	نقشه map, chart n
نظیر peer n	نقشه تقریبی sketch n
نعره outcry n	نقص handicap n
نعلبکی saucer n	نقض breach n
نعنا mint n	نقض کردن v quash
نفت oil n	نقطه dot, point n
نفت خام petroleum n	نقل recount n
نفرت انگیز despicable adj	نقل قول quotation n
نفرت داشتن از v hate, loathe	نقل کردن v convey
نفرین کردن v curse	نقل مکان relocation n
نفس breath n	نقل و انتقال دادن v shuttle
نفس کشیدن v breathe	نکته point, tip n
نفس نفس زدن v gasp	نکوهشی critical adj
نفوذ infiltration n	نگارخانه gallery n
نفوذ کردن v infiltrate, bleach	نگارش version n
نفوذناپذیر watertight adj	نگاه look, glance n
نقاب برداشتن v unmask	نگاه آنی glimpse n
نقاش painter n	نگاه داشتن v preserve
نقاشی draw, portrait, painting n	نگاه کردن v look
نقاشی کن v draw	نگاه کردن به v look at

ن

نگاه ها n looks	نمدار کردن v moisten
نگران adj anxious	نمک n salt
نگران کردن v worry	نمودار n chart, diagram
نگران کننده adj alarming	نمونه adj exemplary
نگرانی n worry	نمونه n sample, pattern
نگرش n attitude	ننگ n dishonor
نگه بدار v hold	نُه adj nine
نگهبان n sentry	نه c nor
نگهداری n maintenance	نه adv not
نگهداری کردن v get by	نهاد n institution
نگهداری کن v keep	نهان adj hidden
نگهداشتن v sustain	نهایت adj ultimate
نگونبخت adj wretched	نهایی adj final
نم دار adj damp	نهفته adj underlying
نم نم باران n drizzle	نهم adj ninth
نماد n symbol	نوا n melody
نمادی adj symbolic	نواحی روستایی n countryside
نمازخانه n chapel	نواختن v strike up
نمای کلی n outline	نوار n ribbon, tape
نمایش n play	نوار باریک قرمز n red tape
نمایش دادن v display	نوازش n caress
نمایش کمدی n farce	نوازش کردن v fondle
نمایشگاه n exhibition	نوازنده پیانو n pianist
نمایشی adj scenic	نوازنده ویولن n violinist
نمایندگی کردن v represent	نوامبر n November
نمایندگی n agency	نوآوری n innovation
نماینده n agent	نوبت n turn
نماینده سیاسی n diplomat	نوتوان کردن v rehabilitate
نمایه n profile	نوجوان adj juvenile

ن

نوجوان teenager n	**نومید** despondent adj
نوجوانی adolescence n	**نوه** grandson n
نود ninety adj	**نوین کردن** modernize v
نور افکن floodlight n	**نویسنده** author, writer n
نور دادن gleam v	**نی** bamboo, cane n
نوررسانی lighting n	**نیاز** requirement n
نورگیر سقف skylight n	**نیاز داشتن** require v
نوری optical adj	**نیتروژن** nitrogen n
نوزاد chick, newborn n	**نیرنگ** trick, guile n
نوزده nineteen adj	**نیرو** stress, power n
نوسازی renovation n	**نیرو گرفتن** grip v
نوسان swing n	**نیروبخش** refreshing adj
نوسان دادن vary v	**نیرومند** powerful adj
نوسان داشتن fluctuate v	**نیروی امدادی** auxiliary adj
نوسان کردن swivel v	**نیروی انسانی** manpower n
نوشت افزار stationery n	**نیروی تازه گرفتن** recruit n
نوشتن write down v	**نیروی دریایی** navy n
نوشته inscription n	**نیزه** spear n
نوشته written adj	**نیش** sting n
نوشیدنی drink n	**نیش بزن** bite, sting v
نوع type, sort n	**نیشکر** cane n
نوعجدید brand-new adj	**نیشگون** pinch n
نوعی سیر ramson n	**نیشگون گرفتن** pinch v
نوک beak n	**نیکل** nickel n
نوک پستان nipple n	**نیکوتین** nicotine n
نوک دار pointed adj	**نیم** half adj
نوک زدگی peck n	**نیم** half n
نوک زدن peck v	**نیمسال تحصیلی** semester n
نوکپخش کننده nozzle n	**نیمکت** bench, pew n

نیمکره hemisphere n	**هر یک ساعت** hourly adv
نیمه باز ajar adj	**هراسی** phobia n
نیمه شب midnight n	**هرج و مرج** jungle n
	هرجا wherever c
	هرچه whatever adj
	هرچیز everything pro
ه	**هردو** both adj
	هرز گیاه weed n
	هرزگی obscenity n
هاله روشنائی loom n	**هرزه** obscene adj
هاملت hamlet n	**هرس کردن** prune v
هایفن hyphen n	**هرکس** whoever pro
هتل hotel n	**هرگز** never adv
هجو libel n	**هرم** pyramid n
هجوم influx n	**هروئین** heroin n
هجوم آوردن raid v	**هریک** apiece adv
هجی spelling n	**هزار** thousand adj
هدایت lead n	**هزاره** millennium n
هدایت کردن conduct v	**هزینه** expense n
هدایت کن lead v	**هزینه پست** postage n
هدف target, goal n	**هسته** core, pit n
هدیه gift n	**هسته ای** nuclear adj
هذیانی شدن hallucinate v	**هشت** eight adj
هر each, every adj	**هشت پا** octopus n
هر چیز anything pro	**هشتاد** eighty adj
هر روز everyday adj	**هشتم** eighth adj
هر کس anyone pro	**هشتی** porch n
هر کسی anybody pro	**هشدار** alarm, alert n
هر وقت whenever adv	**هشدار دادن** warn, alert v

هضم digestion *n*	هم میهن compatriot *n*
هضم کردن digest *v*	همان same *adj*
هفت seven *adj*	همانطور likewise *adv*
هفتاد seventy *adj*	همانندی similarity *n*
هفتم seventh *adj*	هماهنگ کردن coordinate *v*
هفته week *n*	هماهنگی coordination *n*
هفته ای یکبار weekly *adv*	همبرگر hamburger *n*
هفده seventeen *adj*	همبستگی solidarity *n*
هق هق sob *n*	همبستگی داشتن correlate *v*
هق هق کردن sob *v*	همتا counterpart *n*
هل shove *n*	همچنین too *adv*
هلاک شدن perish *v*	همدردی sympathy *n*
هلند Holland, Netherlands *n*	همدردی کردن sympathize *v*
هلندی Dutch *adj*	همراهی کردن accompany *v*
هلو peach *n*	همرنگ با جماعت conformist *adj*
هلیکوپتر helicopter *n*	همزمان بودن coincide *v*
هم also *adv*	همساز کردن accommodate *v*
هم either *adj*	همسانی uniformity *n*
هم اکنون currently *adv*	همسایگان Hispanic *adj*
هم آهنگ کردن harmonize *v*	همسایگی neighborhood *n*
هم آهنگ کننده coordinator *n*	همسایه neighbor *n*
هم آهنگی harmony *n*	همسر spouse, wife *n*
هم بند inmate *n*	همسرایان choir *n*
هم زمان simultaneous *adj*	همسرها wives *n*
هم زمان کردن synchronize *v*	همفکری کردن consult *v*
هم سرایان chorus *n*	همکار colleague *n*
هم عصر contemporary *adj*	همکاری contribution *n*
هم کلاسی classmate *n*	همگرا بودن converge *v*
هم مرکز concentric *adj*	همنوایی کردن conform *v*

ه

cloning n همنوع سازی	hormone n هورمون
everybody pro همه	whim n هوس
referendum n همه پرسی	conscious adj هوشیار
holocaust n همه سوزی	conciousness n هوشیاری
buzz n همهمه	formidable adj هولناک
hum v همهمه کردن	identity n هویت
cooperate v همیاری کردن	carrot n هویج
unfailing adj همیشگی	board n هیئت
always adv همیشه	legislature n هیئت مقننه
geometry n هندسه	jury n هیئت منصفه
watermelon n هندوانه	commotion n هیاهو
art n هنر	mesmerize v هیپنوتیزم کردن
actor n هنرپیشه	frenzy, thrill n هیجان
actress n هنرپیشه زن	exciting adj هیجان انگیز
artist n هنرمند	frenzied adj هیجان زده
artistic adj هنری	eighteen adj هیجده
regiment n هنگ	null adj هیچ
still adj هنوز	nothing n هیچ چیز
still adv هنوز	nowhere adv هیچ کجا
yet c هنوز	none pre هیچکدام
air n هوا	no one pro هیچکس
airtight adj هوابندی شده	hydrogen n هیدروژن
airplane n هواپیما	hydraulic adj هیدرولیک
hijacker n هواپیماربا	firewood n هیزم
airline n هواپیمایی	hiss v هیس کردن
fan n هوادار	hysteria n هیستری
vent n هواکش	hysterical adj هیستریایی
aviation n هوانوردی	monster n هیولا
overcast adj هوای ابری	

و

و *c* and

وابستگی *n* dependence

وابسته *adj* dependent

وابسته بودن *v* depend

وابسه به بیماری قند *adj* diabetic

واپس نگری *n* hindsight

واپیچیدن *v* unwrap

وات *n* watt

واجد شرایط شدن *v* qualify

واحد *n* module

واحه *n* oasis

وادار کردن *v* persuade

وارث *n* heir

وارث شدن *v* inherit

وارد شدن *v* enter

وارد کردن *v* import

واردات *n* importation

وارسی *n* check

وارونه *adv* upside-down

وارونه کردن *v* convert

واژگون شدن *v* capsize

واژگون کردن *v* overturn

واژه نامه *n* dictionary

واسطه *n* middleman

واضح *adj* distinct

واضح کردن *v* clarify

واعظ *n* preacher

واقع *adj* located

واقعاً *adv* actually

واقعه *n* affair

واقعی *adj* actual, real

واقعیت *n* reality

واکس *n* wax

واکس کفش *n* shoepolish

واکسن *n* vaccine

واکسن زدن به *v* vaccinate

واکنش *n* backlash

واکنش نشان دادن *v* react

واگذار کردن *v* abdicate, assign

واگذاری *n* assignment

واگن رستوران *n* diner

واگیردار *adj* contagious

والا *adj* sublime

والدین *n* parents

والیبال *n* volleyball

وان *n* bathtub

وانت *n* van

وانمود کردن *v* fake, feign

وانمودسازی *n* pretense

وب *n* web

وبا *n* cholera

وجد *n* ecstasy

وجد *adj* ecstatic

وجدان *n* conscience

وجدانها *n* scruples

وجدآور *adj* exhilarating

وجه remittance *n*	ورود arrival *n*
وجه الضمان bail *n*	ورود مجدد reentry *n*
وجه فرستادن remit *v*	ورودی entrance *n*
وجه وصفی participle *n*	وزارت ministry *n*
وجود essence *n*	وزارتخانه ministry *n*
وجوه funds *n*	وزغ toad *n*
وجین کردن weed *v*	وزن weight *n*
وحدت unity *n*	وزن کردن weigh *v*
وحشت horror *n*	وزیر minister *n*
وحشت زده petrified *adj*	وساطت کردن mediate *v*
وحشت زده کردن terrify *v*	وسایل آسایش amenities *n*
وحشتناک appalling *adj*	وسط middle *n*
وحشی barbarian *n*	وسط زمین و هوا midair *n*
وحشی brutal *adj*	وسعت extent *n*
وحشی شدن brutalize *v*	وسواس hangup *n*
وحشیگری savagery *n*	وسواسی compulsive *adj*
وحشیگری کردن rampage *v*	وسوسه allure *n*
وخامت deterioration *n*	وسوسه انگیز tempting *adj*
وخیم شدن deteriorate *v*	وسیع broad, vast *adj*
ودیعه deposit *n*	وسیله device *n*
وراثت شناختی genetic *adj*	وسیله نقلیه vehicle *n*
ورزش exercise, sport *n*	وصف ناپذیر unspeakable *adj*
ورزشکار sportman *n*	وصل کردن connect *v*
ورزشی athletic *adj*	وصلت دادن match *v*
ورشکست شدن bankrupt *v*	وصله graft, patch *n*
ورشکستگی bankruptcy *n*	وصیت کردن bequeath *v*
ورشکسته bankrupt *adj*	وضع situation *n*
ورطه abyss *n*	وضع اضطراری emergency *n*
ورق leaf *n*	وضع کردن مالیات levy *v*

وضعیت n status	ویران کردن v devastate, demolish
وضوح n clarity	ویرانی n devastation
وطن n homeland	ویرگول n comma
وطن پرست adj patriotic	ویروس n virus
وظیفه n duty	ویژگی n trait
وعظ n sermon	ویفر n wafer
وفادار adj staunch, loyal	ویولن n violin
وفاداری n loyalty	
وفق دادن v reconcile	
وقار n seriousness, elegance	# یا
وقف کردن v devote	
وقفه n interruption	
وقفه adj standstill	یا c or
وقیح adj insolent	یائسگی n menopause
وکالت n proxy	یاد بگیر v learn
وکالت دادن v delegate	یادآور n reminder
وکالت نامه n mandate	یادآوری n recollection
وکیل دادگستری n attorney	یادآوری کردن v remind
ولتاژ n voltage	یادداشت n annotation
ولخرج adj extravagant	یادداشت کردن v note
ولخرجی کردن v squander	یادداشت نوشتن v annotate
ولرم adj lukewarm	یادزدودگی n amnesia
ولگرد n prowler	یادگاری adj monumental
ولگردی کردن v stray	یادگاری n souvenir
وهم n delusion	یادگیرنده n learner
وول خوردن v wiggle	یادگیری n learning
ویتامین n vitamin	یارا بودن v dare
ویران adj dilapidated	یارانه n subsidy
ویران شده adj devastating	

یارد yard n	یک دست batch n
یاری کردن assist v	یک دنده stubborn adj
یازده eleven adj	یک دور lap n
یازدهم eleventh adj	یک دوره مسابقه tournament n
یاس chagrin n	یک روز someday adv
یاس آور disappointing adj	یک شبه overnight adv
یاسمن jasmine n	یک طرفه unilateral adj
یاقوت ruby n	یک مشت handful n
یاقوت کبود saphire n	یکبار once adv
یاور helper n	یکبار once c
یاوه گفتن babble v	یکجا lump n
یبس constipated adj	یکدیگر each other adj
یبوست constipation n	یکسان equal adj
یبوست دادن constipate v	یکسان کردن assimilate v
یتیم orphan n	یکسره nonstop adv
یخ ice n	یکشنبه Sunday n
یخ ببند freeze v	یکنواخت monotonous adj
یخ زده frozen adj	یکنواختی monotony n
یخچال glacier n	یکه خورده shaken adj
یخدان icebox n	یکی کردن merge v
یخگشاد thaw n	یهودی Jew n
ید iodine n	یهودی Jewish adj
یعنی namely adv	یهودیت Judaism n
یقه collar n	یوغ yoke n
یک a, an a	یونان Greece n
یک بار مصرف disposable adj	یونانی Greek adj
یک جوری someway adv	یونیفرم uniform n

Word to Word® Bilingual Dictionary Series

Language - Item Code - Pages ISBN #

Albanian - 500X - 306 pgs
ISBN - 978-0-933146-49-5

Amharic - 820X - 362 pgs
ISBN - 978-0-933146-59-4

Arabic - 650X - 378 pgs
ISBN - 978-0-933146-41-9

Bengali - 700X - 372 pgs
ISBN - 978-0-933146-30-3

Burmese - 705X - 310 pgs
ISBN - 978-0-933146-50-1

Cambodian - 710X - 376 pgs
ISBN - 978-0-933146-40-2

Chinese - 715X - 340 pgs
ISBN - 978-0-933146-22-8

Farsi - 660X - 328 pgs
ISBN - 978-0-933146-33-4

French - 530X - 320 pgs
ISBN - 978-0-933146-36-5

German - 535X - 352 pgs
ISBN - 978-0-933146-93-8

Gujarati - 720X - 334 pgs
ISBN - 978-0-933146-98-3

Haitian-Creole - 545X - 322 pgs
ISBN - 978-0-933146-23-5

Hebrew - 665X - 316 pgs
ISBN - 978-0-933146-58-7

Hindi - 725X - 362 pgs
ISBN - 978-0-933146-31-0

Hmong - 728X - 294 pgs
ISBN - 978-0-933146-31-0

Italian - 555X - 362 pgs
ISBN - 978-0-933146-51-8

Japanese - 730X - 372 pgs
ISBN - 978-0-933146-42-6

Korean - 735X - 374 pgs
ISBN - 978-0-933146-97-6

Lao - 740X - 319 pgs
ISBN - 978-0-933146-54-9

Pashto - 760X - 348 pgs
ISBN - 978-0-933146-34-1

Polish - 575X - 358 pgs
ISBN - 978-0-933146-64-8

Portuguese - 580X - 362 pgs
ISBN - 978-0-933146-94-5

Punjabi - 765X - 358 pgs
ISBN - 978-0-933146-32-7

Romanian - 585X - 354 pgs
ISBN - 978-0-933146-91-4

Russian - 590X - 298 pgs
ISBN - 978-0-933146-92-1

Somali - 830X - 320 pgs
ISBN- 978-0-933146-52-5

Spanish - 600X - 346 pgs
ISBN - 978-0-933146-99-0

Swahili - 835X - 308 pgs
ISBN - 978-0-933146-55-6

Tagalog - 770X - 332 pgs
ISBN - 978-0-933146-37-2

Thai - 780X - 354 pgs
ISBN - 978-0-933146-35-8

Turkish - 615X - 348 pgs
ISBN - 978-0-933146-95-2

Ukrainian - 620X - 337 pgs
ISBN - 978-0-933146-25-9

Urdu - 790X - 322 pgs
ISBN - 978-0-933146-39-6

Vietnamese - 795X - 324 pgs
ISBN - 978-0-933146-96-9

All languages are two-way:
English-Language / Language-English.
More languages in planning and production.

Order Information

To order our Word to Word® Bilingual Dictionaries or any other products from Bilingual Dictionaries, Inc., please contact us at (951) 296-2445 or visit us at **www.BilingualDictionaries.com**. Visit our website to download our current Catalog/Order Form, view our products, and find information regarding Bilingual Dictionaries, Inc.

 **Bilingual Dictionaries, Inc.**

PO Box 1154 • Murrieta, CA 92562 • Tel: (951) 296-2445 • Fax: (951) 461-3092
www.BilingualDictionaries.com

Special Dedication & Thanks

Bilingual Dicitonaries, Inc. would like to thank all the teachers from various districts accross the country for their useful input and great suggestions in creating a Word to Word® standard. We encourage all students and teachers using our bilingual learning materials to give us feedback. Please send your questions or comments via email to support@bilingualdictionaries.com.